PHASES OF ECONOMIC GROWTH, 1850–1973

Kondratieff waves and Kuznets swings

PHASES OF ECONOMIC GROWTH, 1850–1973

Kondratieff waves and Kuznets swings

SOLOMOS SOLOMOU

Fellow of Peterhouse Cambridge, and Lecturer in Economics, University of Cambridge

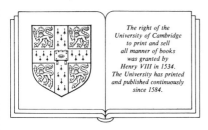

The right of the
University of Cambridge
to print and sell
all manner of books
was granted by
Henry VIII in 1534.
The University has printed
and published continuously
since 1584.

CAMBRIDGE UNIVERSITY PRESS

Cambridge
New York New Rochelle Melbourne Sydney

Published by the Press Syndicate of the University of Cambridge
The Pitt Building, Trumpington Street, Cambridge CB2 1RP
32 East 57th Street, New York, NY 10022, USA
10 Stamford Road, Oakleigh, Melbourne 3166, Australia.

First published 1987

Printed in Great Britain at the University Press, Cambridge

British Library cataloguing in publication data

Solomou, Solomos
Phases of economic growth, 1850–1973:
Kondratieff waves and Kuznets swings.
1. Economic history – 1750–1918
2. Economic history – 1918–
I. Title
339.5′09′034   HC53

Library of Congress cataloguing in publication data

Solomou, Solomos.
Phases of economic growth, 1850–1973.
Bibliography.
Includes index.
1. Long waves (Economics) – Econometric models.
2. Economic development – Econometric models.
I. Title.
HB3729.S65   1987   338.9   86–34324

ISBN 0 521 33457 8

IP

To Wendy Jammy Guise

Contents

Figures

Tables

Preface

The existence of sharp long swings in economic growth since 1950 has shown the inadequacies of models of growth and cycles developed in the 1950s and 1960s. The failure of existing economic paradigms to provide an adequate explanation for the pattern of economic growth since the early 1970s has given rise to a renewed interest in long-term economic growth fluctuations. The Kondratieff wave and the Kuznets swing are two such long cycle ideas.

The Kondratieff wave is a cycle of prices and output with an approximate periodicity of fifty to sixty years. The idea has seen a revival in recent years because the postwar growth phases fall within the expected periodicity of twenty-five to thirty-year 'upswings' and 'downswings'. The Kondratieff wave perspective needs to be studied over a long time period if it is to be regarded as of any relevance to understanding recent economic trends. One question that this book seeks to answer is whether the postwar swings are unique episodes or representative of previous experiences.

The Kuznets swing refers to a variation in economic growth that is longer than the trade cycle but shorter than the Kondratieff wave. The swings observed are variations either in levels or in rates of growth, depending upon the variables being analysed. The actual length of the swings found varies with different authors, but something between fourteen to twenty-two years is representative. Kuznets swings have generally been viewed as a pre-1913 phenomenon. However, in some national case studies the Kuznets swing may be relevant over a longer period. For example, in America a Kuznets swing pattern is observed throughout the period 1870–1937 and possibly 1870–1973. To this extent Kuznets swings form an interesting phenomenon for understanding the past and the present, since America has been a dominant economic force in the developments of the twentieth-century world economy.

In focusing attention on Kondratieff waves and Kuznets swings the aim of this book is twofold: first, to assess the specific usefulness of these long-cycle ideas for understanding economic trends since 1850, and, secondly, to establish the kind of variables that have influenced historical growth variations.

Acknowledgements

In writing this book I have received valuable help from D.J. Coppock, Charles Feinstein, Chris Freeman, Wendy Guise, Istvan Hont, Robin Matthews, Brian Mitchell, Donald McCloskey, Hashem Peseran, Bob Rowthorn, John Solomos, Nick von Tunzelmann and three anonymous publisher's readers. I am grateful to Charles Feinstein for allowing me to use his recently constructed capital stock figures and John Odling-Smee for supplying me with his calculations for British profitability trends. I must also express my gratitude to the SSRC, Girton College, The Master and Fellows of Peterhouse and The Ellen McArthur Fund for financial assistance at different stages of the research.

Perspectives on long-term economic growth variations

Economic growth has not been steady over long periods throughout history. This empirical observation, which shall be examined in the chapters that follow, has given rise to a number of frameworks aimed at explaining the nature of non-steady growth. Each of the various approaches emphasises differing phases of growth and, moreover, relies on a differing causal mechanism to explain the movement from one phase to another.

In this chapter I shall discuss three of these approaches; the traverse perspective of growth models, the Kondratieff wave and the Kuznets swing.[1] The aim is to use these ideas as a starting point in the study of historical trend periods.

The traverse perspective

Growth models of the economy generally have been developed in terms of steady-state solutions. The traverse in growth models represents the transition phase from one steady-state growth path to another. Thus, a traverse is a change in the rate of change of an equilibrium growth path, combined with structural changes.

A frequent criticism of neoclassical growth models is that they fail to take account of the real world by imposing the conditions of balanced[2] and steady growth. Hahn and Matthews (1965) observe in their survey of growth theory:

the general preoccupation with the case of steady-state growth and also, perhaps, an unduly restricted and over-simplified background concept of the phenomenon to be explained ... have drawn the theory into directions which severely limits its direct empirical application or usefulness. (1965, p. 112)

Clearly, traverse analysis allows neoclassical models to break away from many of these restrictive assumptions; providing the emphasis is on the traverse, neither balanced nor steady growth are necessary features of neoclassical models. Thus, once the steady state growth path is perceived only as a reference point, traverse analysis provides a link between equilibrium and history.

Nevertheless, the link is not easy to capture. As Hicks (1965) observes, by perceiving the traverse as a transition phase from one equilibrium path to another, 'we do not greatly diminish the generality of our study of disequilibrium if we regard it in this way' (1965, p. 184). However, modelling the transition is a difficult problem. In the end of his positive growth analysis Hicks concludes that we cannot say very much about the future course of the growth process – we can only prescribe growth paths:

> Though we cannot determine the actual path which the economy (even the model economy) will follow, we can say much more about its optimum path, about the path which will best satisfy some social objective. (1965, p. 201)

As an alternative to prescriptive growth theory, Abramovitz's research strategy for studying economic growth in an historical perspective seems the most fruitful:

> The study of economic growth, therefore, stands closer to history than do other economic subjects... it seems unlikely that for the foreseeable future, the economics of growth can be much more than economic history rationalised here and there to a limited degree as uniformities in the process of development are established. (1951, pp. 177–8)

In this perspective the growth model is seen as a tool for explaining the historical growth path. Thus, a critique of the neoclassical perspective must focus on the equilibrium assumption as an initial condition for analysing the traverse; a dynamic economy is always in a traverse, pinpointing the equilibrium point (or the neighbourhood of equilibrium) is problematic. About one hundred years are required for a neoclassical model to settle on a balanced growth path (Morishima, 1973, p. 120).

Traverse perspectives to economic growth variations perceive shocks as the driving force for movement in the economy. Once the adjustments to a particular shock have taken place the economy settles on a new steady state path. Both Hicks (1965) and Lowe (1976), who are the two main contributors to the modern analysis of the traverse, regard autonomous changes in the rate of change of technology and the labour force as the driving forces for economic growth variations.

Although the traverse perspective to the dynamics of growth represents a major development in growth economics, one important defect stands out clearly – the traverses are seen to be generated by exogenous shocks in the rate of natural growth.[3] However, the growth of labour and technology are not exogenous to the long-run growth path but are an intricate part of it. The classical economists recognised this in their studies of population growth and Schumpeter's (1939) perspective on technology provides a clear critique of the exogenous theory of technical change. Indeed, it seems paradoxical that neoclassical models which sought to endogenise the first difference (the geometric growth rate) of natural growth as a proof of the stability of the growth path, should regard the second difference (the change in the rate of change) as exogenous.

At the heart of traverse growth theory is the question of the stability of the growth path. Without further shocks a neoclassical growth path is a stable equilibrium path. In contrast, both the Kondratieff wave and the Kuznets swing perspectives postulate 'cyclical' theories of long-term growth variations – a slow-growth traverse follows a high-growth traverse in a causally systematic manner.

The Kondratieff wave

Over time the Kondratieff wave has also been referred to as, *inter alia*, major cycle, long wave, long cycle, trend cycle, secular trend, secondary secular movement, secondary deviation, trend period and *mouvements de longue durée*. The long wave idea refers to the dynamics of capitalist development. The wave is seen as either:

(i) An irregular sinusoidal wave with a length of approximately fifty to sixty years. Kondratieff (1979) argued that pre-1920 variation in prices showed this pattern. *or*

(ii) A trend variation wave that averages an approximate length of fifty to sixty years. The high-growth path is postulated as being significantly higher than the low-growth path. Such variations can be described as square waves.

The periodisation developed in Kondratieff (1979) is as follows:

1st Long wave:	upswing	1780s – 1810/17
	downswing	1810/17 – 1844/51
2nd Long wave:	upswing	1844/51 – 1870/75
	downswing	1870/75 – 1890/96
3rd Long wave:	upswing	1890/96 –1914/20
	downswing	1914/20 – ?

The development of the long-wave framework has an inductive foundation. The Russian Marxist, A. Helphand, writing under the pseudonym of Parvus, pointed to the existence of a long cycle at the turn of the century. In a study of agricultural crises, published in 1901, *Die Handelskrisis und die Gewerkschaffen*, he analysed agricultural secular trends in a framework that emphasised the long-term variations of technical change, credit, trade and colonialism. He drew on Marx's notion of *sturm-und-drang periode* of capital accumulation and applied it to a long-wave perspective.

In 1913 the Dutch Marxist, Van Gelderen, writing under the pseudonym of

J. Fedder, gave an outline of 'springtide' and 'ebbtide' long wave phases in the Socialist monthly, *De Nieuwe Tijd*. Both Helphand and Van Gelderen concentrated on an analysis of price variations in the nineteenth century and dated long-wave phases accordingly, although they both believed the long wave to have real growth implications. In Van Gelderen a long-wave expansion takes place with the opening up of new territories or the development of innovative industries. However, with time, overproduction is the rule for innovative industries and raw material shortages will drive up input costs. The overproduction and rising input costs act to depress profitability leading to a slow-growth phase. Van Gelderen did not analyse the lower turning point (Tinbergen, 1981; Van Duijn, 1983).

A long cycle in prices was also observed in the work of Aftalion (1913), Lenoir (1913), Tugan-Baranowsky (1894) and Wicksell (1898). Even earlier, Hyde Clarke (1847) had argued the case for the existence of a fifty-four year cycle linked to astronomical and meteorological variations.

These early studies have not had a long-lasting impact on the development of long-wave ideas. The major contributions to the long-wave framework are to be found in the work of Kondratieff (1979) and Schumpeter (1939). Nevertheless, even in these much more thorough studies, the use of price and monetary data was dominant. In his first study of long waves Kondratieff (1922) referred exclusively to literature dealing with price movements. Even though he added some production data to his later work, it never formed the core of his analysis. Similarly Schumpeter's empirical observations were generally drawn from monetary and price trends.

Kondratieff's 1925 study of long waves is the most well known in the English speaking world, having been translated into English in 1935. The study is mainly an empirical exercise to test for the existence of price and output long waves. The empirical methodology of this paper implies a perspective on the nature of long waves. Kondratieff fitted ordinary least squares (OLS) trends to per capita data and then used a nine year moving average of the deviations to eliminate the Juglar cycle.[4] These filtered deviations were supposed to describe the long-wave pattern. The statistical methodology employed is a reflection of his 1924 paper on static and dynamic equilibrium. In this paper Kondratieff distinguished between reversible (wavelike movements) and non-reversible (trend) processes. Moreover, the trend could be removed by OLS estimation because Kondratieff viewed wavelike movements as occurring around an equilibrium path. Kondratieff distinguished between three types of equilibria – what he called first, second, and third order equilibria. These are equivalent to Marshall's distinction between market, short-term and long-term equilibria:

The wavelike fluctuations are processes of alternating disturbances of the equilibrium of the capitalistic system; they are increasing or decreasing deviations from the equilibrium levels. (Garvy, 1943, p. 207).

Such a methodology implies that the equilibrium structure of capitalist economies remained unchanged over the period of his empirical work (c. 1780–1920).

Kondratieff's early work had little to say on the generating processes for long waves; the emphasis was on the description of long-wave variations. Five descriptive characteristics of long waves were noted:

(i) During the upswing phases, years of prosperity are more numerous, whereas years of depression predominate during the downswing phases;

(ii) The problems of agriculture are particularly severe during long-wave downswings;

(iii) Innovations (what he calls inventions) cluster during the downswing phases, and their large-scale application is evident during the next long upswing;

(iv) Gold production increases during the beginning of the long upswing, and the world market for goods is generally enlarged by the assimilation of new, and especially of colonial, countries;

(v) Wars and revolutions occur during upswing phases.

All of these five characteristics are part of an endogenous long-wave process and not the exogenous causal explanations for long waves. Even war is part of an endogenous long wave; wars originate from the 'increased tension of economic life, in the heightened economic struggle for markets and raw materials' (Kondratieff, 1979, p. 539).

Kondratieff's theory of the generating process for long waves was developed in a paper read before the Economic Institute in Moscow in 1926. The theory was a long duration investment cycle, similar to Marx's ten year investment cycle:

The material basis of long cycles is the wear and tear, the replacement and the increase of the fund of basic capital goods, the production of which requires tremendous investment and is a long process. (Garvy, 1943, p. 208)

To explain the discontinuities in re-investment, Kondratieff introduced Tugan-Baranowsky's theory of free loanable funds. Lumpy investments require large amounts of loanable capital and, therefore, the following preconditions are needed for the upswing:

(i) a high propensity to save;

(ii) a large supply of loan capital at low rates of interest;

(iii) the accumulation of loan capital at the disposal of powerful entrepreneurial and financial groups; and

(iv) a low price level to induce saving.[5]

The expansion has its limits in the increased interest rate and the resulting capital shortage. Thus, Kondratieff has a monetary overinvestment theory[6] of the upper turning point, similar to Spiethoff (1925). The lower turning point was not explained (Garvy, 1943). Kondratieff's long-wave framework borrowed ideas extensively from the existing trade cycle and crisis literature.

Kondratieff's generating process for the long wave is similar to that of De Wolff (1924) who perceived the long wave as an echo wave, caused by the replacement of capital goods of a long lifetime, averaging thirty-eight years. The replacement cycle was seen to be endogenous once set in motion by the industrial revolution of the eighteenth century.

Kondratieff's ideas stand out as preliminary and incomplete. The concentration on the price long wave can be very misleading; the relationship between price and output variations is neither theoretically clear nor empirically simple. The waves are supposed to reflect the development path of the capitalist world economy; 'The long waves that we have established above relating to the series most important in economic life are international; and the timing of these cycles corresponds fairly well for European capitalistic countries' (Kondratieff, 1979, p. 535). However, as will be shown in later chapters, national growth paths were neither synchronised nor balanced. Under such conditions the growth path of the world economy could differ significantly from the growth path of nation states. Moreover, the existence of a scale of relative backwardness in the world economy has significant implications for Kondratieff's generating mechanism. Funds did not remain idle during depressed eras in the leading economies but flowed to the relatively high growth regions of the world economy. The inverse pattern between long-term British home and overseas investment trends has been widely noted in the literature (Cairncross, 1953). I argue later that an inverse pattern is also observed for France and Germany (see Chapter 7). Thus, the closed capitalist economic system assumed by Kondratieff to represent the pre-1920 era is not a valid assumption. Only if the long wave influences all of the world economy will excess funds accumulate at a world level. Kondratieff did recognise that America was in many ways out of line with some of his long-wave evidence but he did not stress the implications of this within a world economy perspective.

Credit creation was never made an alternative to savings in Kondratieff's explanation. If the innovational opportunities exist these should be able to generate the necessary funds to finance the projects, assuming a certain degree of flexibility in the monetary system. The gold standard did impose some restrictions on the bounds of credit creation but the historical evidence suggests wide flexibility even before 1913 (Rostow, 1980).

Schumpeter popularised Kondratieff's ideas in the English speaking world and also refined the generating process for the wave. Schumpeter (1911) developed his ideas with reference to the trade cycle and established a framework for analysing innovational investment and credit creation around an equilibrium growth path. In his later work (Schumpeter, 1939) he applied this framework to explaining long waves.

The first major development of Schumpeter over Kondratieff was to view the cycle in a four phase schema of prosperity, recession, depression and recovery around an equilibrium path. With respect to the price long wave the classification of the four phases can be interpreted in modern economic terminology. However, since Schumpeter worked within an Austrian economic framework the pattern of real economic growth differs significantly from that postulated by Kondratieff. In Schumpeter the economy is modelled as consisting of a producer goods and consumer goods sector. During the prosperity phase, output growth in fact remains unchanged – only the structure of production changes, with the producer goods sector expanding relative to the consumer goods sector (Hayek, 1935). Aggregate output only expands during the recession phase as the gestation of the new investment generates increased productivity. Thus, over time, because of the impact of technical progress in a competitive environment, the price long wave is centred around a downward trend while output growth follows discrete upward steps.

The Schumpeterian long wave is an innovation-induced cycle.[7] Schumpeter developed his theory of Kondratieff waves via a number of approximations. The first approximation is the prosperity–recession cycle first analysed in *The Theory of Economic Development* (1911). The cycle is started off at equilibrium; at this point profit calculation is made easier and expectations of profit are seen with greater certainty. The entrepreneur borrows to introduce the innovations. In this first approximation credit is, in fact, limited to the entrepreneur. The increased purchasing power of the innovating entrepreneurs bids factors and resources away from the old firms. Thus, the price level increases. Output growth remains unchanged, but the need for producer goods to introduce the innovations implies a change in the structure of production in favour of producer goods (the 'roundaboutness' of the production structure increases). During the recession phase the innovations are diffused further as old firms strive to maintain profitability. The price level falls as credit is contracted when entrepreneurs repay old loans from their new incomes. In summary form the two traverses satisfy the following conditions:

$$PQ = x$$
$$P'Q' = x$$
$P' < P$ and $Q' > Q$ (where P = price level, Q = output and x is a scalar value index)

The second approximation allows old firms to participate in the growth process. Expectations are formed that current rates of change (e.g. of profitability) will continue indefinitely and thus Schumpeter introduces the classic overinvestment assumption. The period of prosperity also implies that people are prepared to borrow for unproductive (consumption) purposes and banks are willing to lend. These new assumptions generate the four phase cycle of prosperity, recession, depression and recovery. The resulting 'abnormal liquidation' gives rise to the depression phase, and the tendency to equilibrium generates the recovery. Schumpeter assumes, rather than proves, the tendency to equilibrium.

The third and final approximation aims to explain the historical specificity of different cyclical lengths. Schumpeter considered Kitchins, Juglars and Kondratieffs and explained their varying lengths in terms of the gestation lags and the lumpiness of different investments.[8] If the innovation gives rise to lumpy, long gestation investment, the long wave will be generated. Schumpeter talked of cotton, railways and electricity as the major innovations behind the Kondratieffs he analysed.

In many ways Schumpeter's formalisation represents a major development in understanding the causal processes for long waves. Nevertheless, Schumpeter added little to Kondratieff's price-dominated empirical work. The critical question that remains unanswered, beyond circular reasoning is, as Kuznets (1940) observed, why the major innovational bunching should occur cyclically every fifty years or so. Another important question arises from the critical role assigned to gestation lags during the long wave. Gestation lags of twenty-five years are difficult to interpret and to observe. Capitalist economies are unlikely to be dominated by such lags, except perhaps by error. The long gestation lags can only be meaningful in terms of the spread of the innovation into the whole economy or in terms of the average gestation period being higher over the upswing of the Kondratieff than in the downswing. Thus, the expansive effects of an upswing in investment are expected during the upswing of the Kondratieff, via inter-sectoral multiplier–accelerator effects, not after long lags. Much of the recent work along a Schumpeterian perspective (Freeman et al., 1982; Mensch, 1979; Van Duijn, 1983) recognises this problem and assumes a pro-cyclical price–output relationship, although employing the innovation framework.

Both Kondratieff and Schumpeter worked with a long-run equilibrium dynamics framework. In their methodology, equilibrium is not just a deductive construct (a reference point) but is also meant to describe the actual growth path. The only long-run disequilibrating effects were found in the dynamics of innovation and its diffusion, or in re-investment cycles. As an explanation of historical events, and this is clearly what the framework was meant for, their methodology tends to the historicist perspective. An explanatory framework that concentrates on traverses can offer greater flexibilities for understanding the historical growth path if the causal factors behind different growth variations have varied over time.

The long-wave framework, as outlined so far, has little role for history. Growth variations are viewed as taking place within an unchanged economic structure for national economies and the world economy. However, if the long wave has any historical validity it must be in terms of a specific historical structure; as the structure changes, so will the growth variations. Frisch (1933) has recognised this in deriving his models of the trade cycle and Abramovitz (1968) has noted significant structural breaks in long-swing growth variations. With the kind of structural changes that have been observed since 1780 (Hoffmann, 1958) it would be surprising to observe an unchanged long-wave growth path.

Thus, given the theoretical weaknesses of the long-wave perspective, and its inductive origins, what is most needed from new work along these lines is a test for the existence of a long-wave economic growth pattern, given the much wider availability of output and price data.

The recent revival of interest in long waves is an aspect of the dissatisfaction with present economic paradigms. Much of the recent work has served the purpose of disseminating the old ideas on long waves rather than in critically analysing and developing the framework. Rostow (1975, 1980) and Rostow and Kennedy (1979) have concentrated their analysis on price variation, including relative price variation, and have provided little evidence on the relationship between price and output changes. Wallerstein's (1979) work is mainly a popularization of trend ideas and is recognised to be such. Lewis (1978) has suggested that long waves are not observed in output variations. Forrester (1977, 1978, 1981) has shown that the System Dynamics National Model of the US economy is capable of simulating a long-wave growth path – simulation is one thing, the empirical verification of a long-wave something very different. Freeman (1979) and Freeman et al. (1982) have verified a long-wave innovation pattern for the postwar period but have little to say on the long wave as an historical phenomenon.

A basic problem of much of the recent work is that the existence of long waves as an historical phenomenon is accepted on inadequate and prima-facie evidence. Mandel notes, 'The existence of these long waves in capitalist development can hardly be denied in the light of overwhelming evidence' (1980, pp. 1–2). I would argue that it is this basic defect that needs to be corrected before any progress can be made in developing the long-wave framework. The long-wave perspective is an historical perspective and needs to be tested against the empirical evidence. A re-evaluation of historical trends is needed not only because much of the new output data has not been carefully examined within the long-wave framework, but also because the testing for the issue of existence has been undertaken casually. An example of this is the total neglect of the Kuznets swing in long-wave statistical analyses. Following in the tradition of Kondratieff and Schumpeter, only the trade cycle has been incorporated in the recent statistical work on the issue of existence (Van Duijn, 1983; Bieshaar and Kleinknecht, 1984). While the early work can be excused for neglecting the Kuznets swing, Kondratieff being unaware of its existence and Schumpeter having only Kuznets' early work to go on, the recent neglect of the Kuznets swing is unacceptable. As will be shown in later chapters, the long swing has both statistical and methodological implication for the Kondratieff wave perspective.

The long-swing perspective

The long-swing or Kuznets swing perspective to trend period analysis has a history distinctly different from the long-wave perspective. The two approaches are explicitly or implicitly assumed to be mutually exclusive. In an un-published manuscript, quoted in Easterlin, Abramovitz has defined such movements as:

swings in the level or rate of growth of a variable with a duration longer than the normal business cycles but shorter than the very long swings with which Kondratieff, Schumpeter and others have been concerned. To permit ample room to consider all the possibly relevant evidence, we might set the minimum at five years and the maximum at thirty. (Easterlin, 1968, p. 6).

Those working in the long-swing perspective have analysed a long-term growth phase that has two characteristic aspects:
  (i) as Abramovitz has observed, it is a swing greater in length than the trade cycle but shorter than the Kondratieff wave; and
  (ii) the swing is seen to be generated by population sensitive investments.
  The swings are perceived either as irregular sinusoids of approximately twenty years or trend variation waves in growth rates of the same periodicity. The length of the swings found varies with different authors. Kuznets (1958) found an average length of twenty-two years, Abramovitz (1959) found an average length of fourteen years and Lewis and O'Leary (1955) found swings of sixteen to twenty-two years. As shown in Chapter 2, the different trends found are the result of the different smoothing and trend elimination techniques employed, but the existence of the swings is not critically dependent on the statistical techniques used to analyse them, since most series exhibit long swings in the original data. More will be said on the statistical problems of studying long swings in the next chapter.
  Most of the past work on long swings has been undertaken with an emphasis on the British and American economies, with the aim of explaining the inverse pattern between British home and overseas investment. Only the Lewis and O'Leary (1955) study includes a long-swing analysis of France and Germany. The empirical evidence, to be presented in the chapters that follow, suggests that long swings are a generalised phenomenon in the economies under consideration. Long-swing variations are observed in aggregate output,

productivity, the money stock, investment, profitability, the sectoral terms of trade and many other variables. The emphasis of much of the past literature has been on the role of migration in generating long swings via its effects on population sensitive investments. The evidence that the swings were generalised suggests that much has been left unexplained. Moreover, migration cannot be assumed to be an exogenous variable given that there exists strong evidence for widespread aggregate economic variations across economies (see Chapter 3).

The evidence for an inverse overseas–domestic investment path in the British economy does not clarify the issue of causality. The emphasis on the Anglo-American inversities has been misleading. Inversities were also striking between the French and American economies; however, these two economies did not have strong links either via trade or factor movements. Thus, the swings can be better understood by including France and Germany as case studies and breaking away from simple causality assumptions.

A second point of departure of this study with respect to the existing long-swing literature is the emphasis on the relevance of the long-swing growth process for understanding the interwar world depression. Most of the literature has stressed that long swings are relevant only for the pre-1913 economic structure (Abramovitz, 1968). It is argued in Chapter 8 that because the long swing continued to operate as a relevant growth variation in the American economy after 1913, combined with marked changes in world economic leadership, the 1930s downswing can be partly understood in terms of the severity of the long-swing contraction in America. In much of the past literature it has been argued that since migration patterns changed in the interwar years the long swing pattern of economic growth is not important after 1913. However, since the evidence suggests that a monocausal framework is not valid even for the pre-1913 era, the idea of a changed migration structure is not serious.

The methodological framework for analysing long swings has been developed in the monocausal tradition. Thomas (1954) argued that long swings are generated by exogenously determined migration waves; Cairncross (1953) saw long swings as being the result of variations in the relative profitability between manufactures and primary commodities, as signalled by the variations in the sectoral terms of trade. Many American studies have assumed a purely American centric pull explanation for the swings observed in the various European economies (Kuznets, 1958). The evidence does not support any of these simple ideas; the swings were generated by a more complicated historical process than has been recognised. In my opinion long swings are generated by the economic system in a process that entails a series of shocks feeding through the economy in a system of organic causation. The swings are aggregate and generalised. Moreover, the evidence presented in later chapters suggests that the impact of a series of comparable shocks is critical to sustaining this pattern of economic growth. When the shocks change, the long-swing pattern can change, as is observed after 1950, when the long swing is marked by its absence from all the European economies over the period 1950–73. When the nature of shocks changes, the resulting initial conditions may generate new types of growth variations.

The perspective of the young Kuznets needs to be revived. Kuznets (1930) analysed long swings in terms of price, output and profitability variations on an aggregate level without reference to the importance of population sensitive investment. The recent literature has developed this one aspect to the detriment of studying everything else.

This outline of long-swing ideas is far from being complete. Long-swing studies have been undertaken in an empirical tradition and the ideas can be better discussed in the chapters that follow.

Conclusions

It is clear that long-wave and long-swing studies need to be re-evaluated. Many of the early ideas on these themes were derived in the inductive historical methodology. As such there is a need for continuous re-evaluation to include better data for real and other indicators of economic change. Moreover, many long-wave studies are flawed in that they have failed to consider the question of *existence* allowing for the possibility that the Kuznets swing is a lower-order growth variation. Beginning with Kuznets' (1930) work there is now extensive evidence for the existence of growth swings of the twenty to thirty year periodicity (Abramovitz, 1959; Easterlin, 1968; Kuznets, 1958; Thomas, 1973). Even if the Kondratieff wave is assumed to be generated by differing causal processes from the Kuznets swing, the latter needs to be considered in the statistical analyses of long waves.

The existing studies of Kuznets swings have focused on the Anglo-American economies, emphasising the role of international migration. The evidence to be presented in the following chapters suggests that long swings are a far more generalised growth phenomenon than has previously been recognised. The monocausal perspective to long swings is misleading. Long swings can only be understood within a framework of circular or organic causality; although not endogenous cycles, the swings are generated by shocks within a given economic structure.

The traverse literature has focused on changes in the rate of change of technology and labour supply. To the extent that Kondratieff waves and Kuznets swings are episodic phases of historical change rather than *cycles* of growth, they can also be viewed as traverses in economic growth. In this respect the traverse literature is incomplete. As will be argued later, historical growth variations are best understood in a complex model of interaction between various patterns of change at the national and international economy level of analysis.

2

Statistical methodology

This chapter outlines a statistical methodology for phasing historical trend periods. The first section is a review of the statistical methodology that has been employed to analyse long-term growth phases in previous literature. The next section outlines the statistical methodology followed in this study.

The existing statistical methodology

The statistical methodology of the early work on trend periods was mechanistic in nature, neglecting the economic implications of the statistical transformations. Kondratieff's (1979) methodology was to fit ordinary least squares (OLS) trend lines to time series data and take a nine-year moving average of the residuals to eliminate the Juglar cycle. The idea that the trend line was constant over the period of his study (1780–1920) assumes that the economic structure remained unchanged. The nine-year moving average assumes that trends and cycles are additive and one can be removed from the other. Even if this assumption holds, the use of the nine-year moving average will serve its purpose only if the cycle is, in fact, exactly nine years. The actual cycle is variable in length and random variation. In such cases the moving-average process will only serve to produce longer cycles. A fixed moving-average process is being applied to an irregular cycle and, thus, will capture the summation of random factors. Slutsky (1937) has shown that the moving-average process when applied to random numbers may create cyclical fluctuations where none existed before.[1] If a cycle already exists, the effect will be to generate a longer cycle. Simulated examples of this process can be found in Bird *et al.* (1965, pp. 233–7).

As was noted in Chapter 1 the length of the long swings found varies widely in the different studies. The difference arises not so much from differences in the data as from differences in the data doctoring (Adelman, 1965; Adelman and Adelman, 1965). Given that the swing talked of by some studies is only fourteen to sixteen years, the use of such long-moving averages is clearly capable of generating statistical artefacts.

Kuznets (1952, p. 240) presented his original national income data in the form of overlapping decadal averages. This is equivalent to a fixed moving average process to smooth out the short-run fluctuations. It can be proved that employing this method will also give rise to statistical artefacts. Bird *et al.* (1965, pp. 229–31) found that for a cycle with an exact periodicity of four years, the use of overlapping decades will give rise to a twenty-year cycle in growth rates. Consider a sinusoid with a four year periodicity, as shown in Figure 2.1. Starting with a peak and collecting every fifth observation, as is done in the overlapping decade method, points 2, 7, 12, 17, 22 . . . are collected. The first peak after 2 that is collected with be 22, giving a periodicity in growth rates of twenty years (see Figure 1). Such a periodicity is clearly a statistical artefact.

The method employed by Abramovitz (1958, 1959) involves calculating average per annum rates of change between successive peak-to-peak and trough-to-trough average reference cycle standings (the ARCS method). The inter-cycle rates of change obtained from peak-to-peak and trough-to-trough cycles are intermixed to form a series of rates of change during overlapping inter-cycle intervals. Each rate of change is centred on the midpoint of the midpoints of the two relevant cycles. The reference cycles are those of

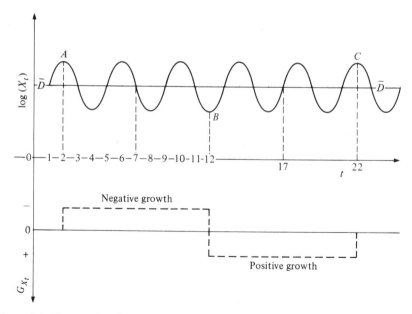

Figure 2.1 The overlapping decadal method and artefact swings

the National Bureau. Since there is not an exact lag between the peaks (troughs) of the reference cycles and the specific cycles, a random element is being introduced into the calculations. This problem can be overcome with Abramovitz's specific cycle standing method which makes no use of reference cycle turning points (ASCS method). Bird *et al.* (1965, pp. 237–9) found that although the ASCS method performs better in predicting long-swing turning points, both methods are still biased towards giving rise to a long cycle. However, the bias in the Abramovitz ASCS method is much reduced from that of the Kuznets method of overlapping decades. This can explain the difference in the empirical findings of Kuznets (1958) and Abramovitz (1959) – Kuznets's average swing is twenty-two years while Abramovitz's average swing is only fourteen years.

Thus, the statistical methodology employed by the early analysts of long waves and long swings is based on arbitrary assumptions about the additive and stable nature of the trend-cycle relationship. The Abramovitz ASCS method of trend variation comes out as the least defective.

By perceiving the trend-cycle relationship as one of independence, the early long-term phase studies lost a lot of information in the study of the different Juglars as a means of discerning growth phases. The interdependence of the trend-cycle relationship seems a more valid and flexible assumption to make (Kalecki, 1968; Spiethoff, 1953). As Svennilson (1952, p. 4) has observed in his study of the interwar European economy: 'Long term changes manifest themselves in the disguise of short term cyclical variations.'

Studies of trend periods that employ spectral analysis are faced with similar problems. The spectral analysis of time series is perhaps the most sophisticated technique presently available. Its major advantage over more traditional time-series approaches is that processes that are not of interest need not be smoothed over (Granger and Hatanaka, 1964; Soper, 1975). Thus if the concern of the researcher is with the Kondratieff wave, the Kuznets swing need not be filtered out of the data.

As in traditional time series the components of a time series are analysed in terms of trend, cyclical, seasonal and random variation. In spectral analysis the usual rule of thumb is to define as trend all disturbances with a period greater than $N/2$ (where N is the sample size). Given this definition of trend the need for a large sample in the study of long waves and long swings is clear. Granger and Hatanaka (1964) state as a rule of thumb that the number of observations should equal at least seven times the average duration of the fluctuation examined; they also add that no other technique will find cycles correctly with less data.

Since reliable time-series data can only be found for the post-1850 period, or later in many cases, spectral methods are inadequate for discussing the issues under consideration. However, a more important reason for rejecting the use of spectral methods is that the growth variations under discussion do not take place under an unchanged economic structure. My concern here is with describing the historical growth path; spectral analysis seeks the existence of average cyclical paths. Since the issue of cycles of growth cannot be resolved with either spectral or more traditional time-series analysis, the focus of this study is on phasing and explaining historical growth. As the economic structure changes, spectral analysis will generate artefact periodicities. One major conclusion of this study is that both on a national and a world economy perspective, the structure of growth has undergone significant change over time. Similar conclusions have also been drawn by others working in this field: Abramovitz (1968) has argued that the Kuznets swing is a pre-1913 growth phenomenon; the nature of the short trade cycle has changed significantly in the postwar period compared to the pre-1937 era.

The statistical framework

I wish to develop a phasing of trend variations based on the Juglar cycle as the unit of the trend phases. The Juglar is a cyclical process that is long enough to capture trend variations in growth and changes in the structure of the economy. Both Kondratieff (1979) and Spiethoff (1953) noted that prosperous years tended to predominate during long-wave upswings, whereas years of depression predominate during the downswings. One way to test this would be to take the proportion of years of prosperity to years of depression within the long wave. However, this implies that all cycles designated by turning points are comparable units of similar amplitudes and rates of change. Since this is not necessarily so, a more valid test would be to calculate the actual rates of change over complete Juglar phases; this has the additional advantage of preventing non-comparable growth measures from generating statistical artefacts; moreover, a priori information about the long wave is not required. It should be emphasised that in using the trade cycle as the unit of trend variations I do not assume a fixed generating mechanism for the cycle.

Growth rate measures must be made on a consistent basis – i.e. two points must be comparable in time. Cyclical growth measures can be made on a peak-to-peak, trough-to-trough, or equilibrium-to-equilibrium basis. I shall employ a peak-to-peak Juglar measure because the peaks are more easily comparable, having the common link of a capacity constraint. A trough-to-trough measure would also serve the purpose of studying the long-run growth path, but there will be less comparability since depressions do not have a common low level. Defining equilibrium (beyond the mechanistic trend definitions) for the Schumpeterian phasing of the cycle is not clear.

My major concern is with real-growth processes; hence, the phasing I shall develop is independent of the long-term price variations. Peak-to-peak cycle growth measures have also been employed by others working on trend periods (Lewis, 1978; Mandel, 1980; Matthews *et al.*, 1982; Van Duijn, 1983). The long-wave and long-swing ideas outlined in Chapter 1 can be stated in the following statistical hypotheses.

The Kondratieff long-wave hypothesis

Kondratieff's long-wave hypothesis postulates a pattern of Juglars that traverses a high-growth path being followed by a pattern that traverses a low-growth path. Given that the long wave is postulated to have a length of approximately forty to sixty years, the number of Juglars in the wave is expected to be approximately four to six. The null and alternative hypotheses can be stated thus:

$$H_0 : g_Y(J_{H_i}) = g_Y(J_{L_j})   i = 1,2,(3)$$

$$H_1 : g_Y(J_{H_i}) > g_Y(J_{L_j})   j = 1,2,(3)$$

(H1)

where

$g_Y(J_{H_i}) =$ peak-to-peak growth over high-growth Juglars.

$g_Y(J_{L_j}) =$ peak-to-peak growth over low-growth Juglars.

The Schumpeterian long-wave hypothesis

As was noted in Chapter 1, Schumpeter developed his model of the Kondratieff wave in terms of the Austrian school, employing the concepts of long gestation lags and the roundaboutness of the production process as his analytical tools. The recent Schumpeterian revival has dropped the Austrian language and has substituted in its place the Keynesian multiplier–accelerator framework, generating a four-phase output wave where prosperity, recession, depression and recovery have a modern meaning (Mensch, 1979; Van Duijn, 1980). For simplicity I will assume that a Kondratieff is approximated by four Juglars, as a means of capturing the four-phase cycle. Starting the process off in the prosperity phase of the wave, the following Juglar growth pattern is expected:

$$g_Y(J_1) > g_Y(J_2) > g_Y(J_3)$$
$$g_Y(J_4) > g_Y(J_2) > g_Y(J_3)$$
$$g_Y(J_4) \geq g_Y(J_1)$$

(H2)

where the subscripts 1, 2, 3 and 4 stand for prosperity, recession, depression and recovery respectively.

Thus, the null and alternative hypotheses can be specified as:

$$H_0 : g_Y(J_4) = g_Y(J_1) = g_Y(J_2) = g_Y(J_3)$$
$$H_1 : g_Y(J_4) \geq g_Y(J_1) > g_Y(J_2) > g_Y(J_3)$$

(H3)

The long-swing hypothesis

The length of the long swing implies that it will be approximated by two Juglar cycles. Thus, the long-swing null and alternative hypotheses can be stated as:

$$H_0 : g_Y(J_H) = g_Y(J_L)$$
$$H_1 : g_Y(J_H) > g_Y(J_L)$$

(H4)

Hypotheses (H4) are clearly in conflict with the long-wave hypotheses (H1) and (H3). The existence of Kuznets swings imposes restrictions on the testing of hypotheses (H1) and (H3). Consider a long-swing process with the following regular characteristics (see Figure 2.2):

$$g(J_{H_i}) = \bar{a} \qquad i = 1,3,5$$
$$g(J_{L_j}) = \bar{\gamma} \qquad j = 2,4,6$$

Assuming a Kondratieff wave consists of six Juglars, an artefact Kondratieff can be generated from the above regular long-swing growth process,

$$\sum_{i=a}^{d} g_i > \sum_{j=d}^{g} g_j$$

Thus, the existence of a long-swing growth path implies that the only consistent growth measure for trend variations longer than the swing, is one

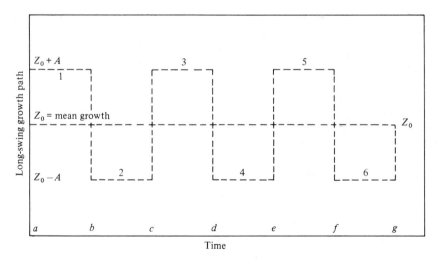

Figure 2.2 A regular long swing growth process

that considers the Juglar cycle and the long swing – growth measures must be taken over complete Juglars and complete swings. As pointed out in Chapter 1 the total neglect of the long swing by long-wave analysts is clearly unjustified. With the exception of studies employing spectral analysis, the only long-wave study I have been able to find that explicitly considers the statistical implications of a long swing in the analysis of long-wave growth variations is that of Van Ewijk (1981). If there exist growth variations longer than the long swing, then traverses in the long-swing growth path should be observed. A Kondratieff pattern in the swing traverses would postulate that, for complete swing growth phases, a pattern of alternating traverses are observed:

$$\mu_1 > \mu_2 < \mu_3 > \mu_4 < \mu_5 \ldots$$

where μ $(i = 1, 2 \ldots, n)$ represents complete-swing growth measures in ordered time.

Thus the Kondratieff wave null and alternative hypotheses that consider the long swing can be stated as:

$$H_0 : \mu_1 = \mu_2 = \ldots = \mu_5$$
$$H_1 : \mu_1 > \mu_2 < \ldots < \mu_5 \qquad \text{(H5)}$$

It may be argued that longer trend phases have an independence from shorter trend phases – the Kondratieffs being independent of the Kuznets swings and the Juglars; and the Kuznets swing being independent of the Juglars. This kind of argument gives rise to statistical artefacts in many historical studies of growth phases. A growth measure can only have meaning if it is consistent. Moreover, the idea that Juglar cycles. Kuznets swings, Kondratieff waves and trends are independent of each other is clearly unfounded. Unless the generating mechanisms of the cycles are completely independent, the various cycles will have a degree of interdependence. Since all these cycles are supposed to affect the aggregate path of the economy, each is bound to affect the others, at least via aggregate income and multiplier effects. Hence, the variation of the short cycles can be used to proxy the variation in the long cycles (Matthews, 1959, p. 214).

Having outlined a methodology for phasing historical trend periods, I will now outline a methodology for discerning significant trend variations. A number of significance tests may be undertaken:

(i) Significance tests on the *pattern* of growth to establish the cyclical nature of a growth path. The kind of tests I have in mind are non-parametric runs tests (Siegel, 1956). To test for the significance of a particular pattern of growth variation, the minimum number of half swings required is nine. Clearly, the significance of the Kondratieff wave cannot be examined in these terms because of data limitations.

(ii) Significance tests on the differences in the growth paths of different periods. This approach to significance clearly does not aim to seek a test for the existence of a cyclical process, but only to test a much weaker hypothesis that some periods have been historically different from others. Thus, the Kondratieff wave and the Kuznets swing are viewed as historical eras rather than cycles of growth.

At first glance, undertaking significance tests on the differences in growth paths seems a straightforward application of the significance tests for differences in means in two samples. The usual justification for using time-series analysis as just another example of random sampling is that the observed time series is viewed as one example from an infinite set of time series which might have been observed (Chatfield, 1980, p. 34). This metaphysical abstraction is unconvincing. The only practical justification for using statistical sampling techniques in time series is that they may help us understand and describe regular relationships. For example, astronomers use time-series data successfully to predict Earth–Sun movements. Such a presumed constancy of natural laws is unlikely to hold for economic data, but as long as a degree of homogeneity holds, time series methods can be used to describe the economy. For example, in testing for significant differences in two sample means for two long periods a t-test could be employed, based on the following formula:

$$t = \frac{\bar{g}_{y_1} - \bar{g}_{y_2}}{\left\{ \frac{\Sigma(g_{Y_i} - \bar{g}_{Y_1})^2 + \Sigma(g_{Y_i} - \bar{g}_{Y_2})^2}{n_1 + n_2 - 2} \left(\frac{1}{n_1} + \frac{1}{n_2} \right) \right\}^{1/2}} \qquad (1)$$

where g_Y represents growth rates and n_i $(i = 1,2)$, the sample size.

Such calculations are easy to compute for data satisfying the following conditions:

(i) the variances of the two period growth rates are equal;
(ii) the observations are independent, i.e. non-autocorrelated; and
(iii) the observations are normally distributed.

Conditions (i) and (ii) are also referred to as stationarity in variance and mean respectively.

For reasonably large samples (iii) presents the least problem. The central limits theorem implies that the sample mean will be asymptotically normal. The assumption of equal variances is more critical. If the two variances are unequal and if the sample sizes are unequal then the denominator of the two sample t-test is not an estimate of the standard error of the numerator which can give rise to serious errors. The failure of this assumption to hold, assuming everything else is in order, can be overcome by undertaking non-parametric tests on the sample means, such as the chi-square test, the median test and the Wald–Wolfowitz runs test which do not rely on the assumption of equal variances (Siegel, 1956). An alternative procedure would be to adjust the t-test accordingly (Welch, 1938). For the autocorrelated time series under consideration, such tests are not optimal since the calculated standard errors are invalid. The basic problem is that the process generating these samples is dynamic and the data needs to be doctored to eliminate the autocorrelation before such tests, based on the assumption of stationarity, can be applied.

The methodology of classical regression analysis can be used to resolve the problem. Assume that a time series can be approximated by a long-run exponential trend:

$$Y_t = A\exp(\alpha \text{TREND})\exp(u_t) \tag{2}$$

Taking logs, (2) can be estimated employing least squares,

$$\log Y_t = \log A + \alpha \text{TREND} + u_t \tag{3}$$

Taking first differences of (3) eliminates some of the autocorrelation and we have an easier working model,

$$\Delta \log Y_t = \alpha \Delta \text{TREND} + \Delta u_t \tag{4}$$

Since $\Delta \log Y_t$ is the growth rate (g_{Y_t}), $\Delta \text{TREND} = 1$ since we are looking at growth per annum and $\Delta u_t = u'_t$ (4) can be expressed as,

$$g_{Y_t} = \alpha + u'_t \tag{5}$$

The process of taking first differences can eliminate some of the autocorrelation in the original series; in some cases this is all that is required to satisfy the stationarity condition. If the data set in (5) is still autocorrelated, further operations are needed to eliminate the problem. Assume the simplest case, where the autocorrelation process is a first-order Markov process:

$$u'_t = \rho u'_{t-1} + \varepsilon_t \tag{6}$$

$$\varepsilon_t \sim N(0, \sigma_\varepsilon^2) \tag{7}$$

Lagging (5) and multiplying by ρ gives,

$$\rho g_{Y_{t-1}} = \rho \alpha + \rho u'_{t-1} \tag{8}$$

Subtracting (8) from (5) gives,

$$g_{Y_t} - \rho g_{Y_{t-1}} = (1 - \rho)\alpha + u'_t - \rho u'_{t-1} \tag{9}$$

$$\Rightarrow g_{Y_t} - \rho g_{Y_{t-1}} = \alpha' + \varepsilon_t \tag{10}$$

Thus the data can be doctored in the form of (10) allowing the use of conventional tests for significance; ρ can be estimated by regressing (6) or from the d-statistic in (5). Alternatively ρ may be estimated in the more direct form,

$$g_{Y_t} = \alpha' + \rho g_{Y_{t-1}} + \varepsilon_t \tag{11}$$

It should be noted that in model (11) g_Y plays the simultaneous role of dependent and independent variable. Hence, asymptotic results have to be relied on. Since $\varepsilon_t \sim N(0, \sigma_\varepsilon^2)$ equation (11) gives asymptotically unbiased estimates of α' and ρ. Mann and Wald (1943) have also shown that the OLS standard error formulae will be asymptotically valid.

A major problem in testing the stationarity condition is that classical asymptotic theory, which has been developed for stationary models, is not valid for testing the hypothesis of the existence of a unit root. The standard expression for the large sample variance of the least squares estimator $\hat{\rho}$ is $(1 - \rho^2)/T$ which would be zero under the null hypothesis of $\rho = 1$. If $\rho < 1$ the OLS estimators of (11) are normally distributed; if $\rho > 1$ the OLS estimators are not normally distributed; but if $\rho = 1$ the distribution is not determined theoretically.

A number of recent studies have tried to derive the distribution of $\hat{\rho}$ when $\rho = 1$. Evans and Savin (1981) found that the distribution of $\hat{\rho}$ is heavily skewed to the left of 1; two-thirds of the estimates of $\hat{\rho}$ are distributed to the left of 1. Moreover, this limited distribution holds irrespective of sample size. Such a skewed distribution for $\hat{\rho}$ implies that for much of the time classical tests would fail to reject the stationarity assumption when in fact $\rho = 1$.

Another problem that arises from the simple model in (11) is that the distribution of α' and ρ are conditional on each other. This can be illustrated by dividing (11) by σ (a standard error term) and subtracting g_0 from both sides of the equation, i.e.

$$\frac{g_{Y_t} - g_0}{\sigma} = \frac{\alpha' - g_0}{\sigma} + \frac{\rho g_{Y_{t-1}}}{\sigma} + \frac{\varepsilon_t}{\sigma} \tag{12}$$

Adding and subtracting $\rho g_0/\sigma$ from the RHS of (12),

$$\frac{g_{Y_t} - g_0}{\sigma} = \frac{\alpha' - g_0}{\sigma} + \frac{\rho(g_{Y_{t-1}} - g_0)}{\sigma} + \frac{\rho g_0}{\sigma} + \frac{\varepsilon_t}{\sigma} \tag{13}$$

$$\Rightarrow Z_t = \frac{\alpha' + g_0(1 - \rho)}{\sigma} + \rho Z_{t-1} + W_t \tag{14}$$

that is

$$Z_t = \gamma + \rho Z_{t-1} + W_t \tag{15}$$

where Z_t is defined as the LHS of equation (13) and W_t as ε_t/σ.

The conditional distribution of α' and ρ can be seen clearly in equation (14). Thus, any test for the existence of a unit root needs to consider this dependency. Dickey and Fuller (1981) have defined a maximum likelihood ratio test for the unit root that allows for these problems. Consider the following first-order autoregressive model:

$$Y_t = \alpha^* + \beta^* \text{TREND} + \rho^* Y_{t-1} + \varepsilon_t^* \tag{16}$$

The test 'ϕ_3' is aimed to test for the following constraint:

$$H_0 : (\alpha^*, \beta^*, \rho^*) = (\alpha^*, 0, 1) \tag{17}$$

The test can be undertaken by comparing the maximum likelihood ratio statistic with the relevent ϕ_3 calculations in Dickey and Fuller (1981, p. 1063).

Since the Dickey and Fuller ϕ_3 statistic aims to test a joint restriction, I also employ the Fuller $\hat{T}\tau$ statistic which is only concerned with testing for $\rho^* = 1$. The test is undertaken as a t-test on $\rho^* = 1$, except that significance is found not from the t tables but from Fuller's empirical distribution assuming the true $\rho = 1$ (Fuller, 1976, Table 8.5.2).

If the autocorrelation process is of a more general order than the first-order Markov process of equation (6), similar transformations can be undertaken. Consider a general autoregressive scheme of order n [AR(n)],

$$u_t' = \sum_{i=1}^{n} \rho_i u_{t-i}' + \varepsilon_t \tag{18}$$

$$\varepsilon_t \sim N(0, \sigma_\varepsilon^2)$$

Equations (5) and (18) imply

$$g_{Y_t} = \alpha \left(1 - \sum_{i=1}^{n} \rho_i \right) + \sum_{i=1}^{n} \rho_i g_{Y_{t-i}} + \varepsilon_t \tag{19}$$

Such transformations imply that classical significance tests may be applied assuming that the stationarity condition is satisfied. The stationarity condition for a first-order autoregressive series has already been discussed. The stationarity condition for a second-order autoregressive scheme, AR(2), will also be outlined. Consider the following AR(2) scheme:

$$g_{Y_t} = \alpha(1 - \rho_1 - \rho_2) + \rho_1 g_{Y_{t-1}} + \rho_2 g_{Y_{t-2}} + \varepsilon_t \tag{20}$$

Employing the backward shift operator, B,

$$(1 - \rho_1 B - \rho_2 B^2) g_{Y_t} = \alpha(1 - \rho_1 - \rho_2) + \varepsilon_t \tag{20a}$$

Box and Jenkins (1976) have shown that stationarity requires that the roots of the equation,

$$\phi(B) = (1 - \rho_1 B - \rho_2 B^2) = 0 \tag{21}$$

must lie inside the unit circle. Hence the stationarity region is the triangular region satisfying:

(i) $\rho_1 + \rho_2 < 1$

(ii) $\rho_1 - \rho_2 > -1$

(iii) $\rho_2 > -1$

If $[\rho_1^2 + 4\rho_2] > 0$, the autocorrelation function implied is declining exponentially; if $[\rho_1^2 + 4\rho_2] < 0$ the autocorrelation function is a damped cosine wave.

The assumption of the equality of sample variances is easier to test. Suppose $\hat{\sigma}_1^2$ and $\hat{\sigma}_2^2$, the two sample variances, are independent estimates of σ_1^2 and σ_2^2, the true variances. Then it can be shown that the distribution of

$$\frac{\hat{\sigma}_1^2/\sigma_1^2}{\hat{\sigma}_2^2/\sigma_2^2} \sim F(v_1, v_2)$$

where $v_1 = n_1 - 1$ and $v_2 = n_2 - 1$, the degrees of freedom. To test the null of equality in the variances against the alternative of differences in the variances:

$$H_0 : \sigma_1^2 = \sigma_2^2$$
$$H_1 : \sigma_1^2 \neq \sigma_2^2$$

A variance ratio test can be defined from the above F-distribution:

$$V = \frac{\hat{\sigma}_1^2}{\hat{\sigma}_2^2} \tag{22}$$

where, $\hat{\sigma}_1^2 > \hat{\sigma}_2^2$.

If the calculated F-statistic for the variance ratio is greater than the significant $F(v_1, v_2)$, the null is rejected in favour of the alternative.

Having checked the conditions for employing classical testing procedures, I propose to carry out the required significance tests by two alternative means. Where all the conditions are satisfied, regression analysis will be employed using dummy variable tests to discern significant growth traverses. The choice of using dummy variables to test for significant breaks in the growth path has the disadvantage of viewing change as dramatic. The change could be viewed as being continuous by employing Poirier's cubic splines which both maintains continuity in the relationship and allows tests for structural change (Buse and Lim, 1977; Poirier, 1977). However, the output and productivity variables considered here did change significantly over an annual basis, allowing the use of dummy variables. In any case the simplicity of such tests outweighs any gains in technical sophistication.

The significance of growth variations may be tested by introducing a dummy variable into the relevant AR scheme. Since the principle is the same I shall illustrate how it operates in the simplest model possible, AR(0). Let

$$g_{Y_t} = a + \varepsilon_t \tag{23}$$
$$\varepsilon_t \sim N(0, \sigma_\varepsilon^2)$$

Consider two growth paths; one for period $1 \ldots T_1$ and one for $T_1 + 1 \ldots T_2$. Let these two growth paths be characterised by a and b respectively. Therefore,

$$g_{Y_{t_a}} = a_1 + \varepsilon_{t_a} \tag{24}$$

and

$$g_{Y_{t_b}} = a_2 + \varepsilon_{t_b} \tag{25}$$

Define vectors $\mathbf{Z}_a = \binom{1}{0}$ and $\mathbf{Z}_b = \binom{0}{1}$ for the relevant sample periods.
The null under consideration is the equality of the growth paths:

$$H_0 : a_1 = a_2$$

Equations (24) and (25) can be combined as

$$g_{Y_t} = a_1(\mathbf{Z}_a + \mathbf{Z}_b) + (a_2 - a_1)\mathbf{Z}_b + \varepsilon_t \tag{26}$$

or

$$g_{Y_t} = a_1 + d\mathbf{Z}_b + \varepsilon_t \tag{27}$$

(27) implies that if the null holds $a_1 = a_2 = a \Leftrightarrow d = 0$. Thus, the null can be rejected if the dummy, proves significant in equation (27).

Where the equal variance assumption is not satisfied I will undertake calculations based on a different test statistic. The new statistic which allows for differences in variances is

$$t' = \frac{\bar{g}_{Y_{t_1}} - \bar{g}_{Y_{t_2}}}{\left(\dfrac{\hat{\sigma}_1^2}{n_1} + \dfrac{\hat{\sigma}_2^2}{n_2}\right)^{1/2}} \tag{28}$$

Its distribution is still approximated by the t-distribution but with degrees of freedom depending on the variance ratio (Wetherill, 1967, p. 160). The degrees of freedom (f) of t' can be calculated from

$$\frac{1}{f} = \frac{\hat{\sigma}_1^4}{k^2 n_1^2(n_1 - 1)} + \frac{\hat{\sigma}_2^4}{k^2 n_2^2(n_2 - 1)} \tag{29}$$

where

$$k = \frac{\hat{\sigma}_1^2}{n_1} + \frac{\hat{\sigma}_2^2}{n_2}$$

This completes the presentation of the statistical methodology. In the chapters that follow I shall develop a phasing of the historical growth process that allows for these problems.

3

Production trends in the world economy

As was noted in Chapter 1 the empirical study of trend periods is in need of further analysis. This chapter outlines a phasing of historical growth paths for the period 1856–1973 in Britain, France, Germany, America and the world economy. The chapter deals with output and productivity trends; other aspects will be dealt with in later chapters.

For clarity I shall present the evidence in terms of five case studies; each case study is further divided into two parts, dealing with the pre- and post-1913 eras respectively.

Britain

Pre-1913

Despite the existence of an extensive literature on the theme of pre-1913 British economic growth, a consensus on the phasing of growth does not exist. The existing research has been undertaken on an *ad hoc* basis, investigating trend periods within a partial perspective. The Kondratieff wave phases of 1850–1873–1896–1913 have been discussed in the literature without any clearly set out theoretical or empirical hypotheses. Both Church's (1975) study of the 'Mid Victorian Boom' and Saul's (1969) study of the 'Great Depression' have neglected the importance of inter-period comparisons in discussing these phases of growth and have drawn most of their inferences from evidence referring to within-period variations. Long-swing analyses are still based on the work of Cairncross (1953) and Thomas (1954), despite the wider availability of better production data. Recent literature has also drawn attention to the existence of a climacteric stepping down of long-term economic growth, with 1873, 1890 and 1899 chosen as possible transition dates (Aldcroft, 1974; Crafts, 1979; Feinstein *et al.* 1982; Lewis, 1978). However, with the exception of Feinstein *et al.* (1982) the climacteric evidence has been presented without any

Table 3.1 *Peak-to-peak growth measures and related calculations: the compromise estimate of GDP, 1845–1913 (growth/annum)*

(1) t	(2) $\bar{g}_{Y_t}$	(3) $\hat{\sigma}_{gY_t}$	(4) $\hat{\sigma}_{gY_t}/\bar{g}_{Y_t}$	(5) $\Delta\bar{g}_{Y_t}$	(6) Characteristic of growth path
1845–1856	0.0251	0.0200	0.79	—	H
1856–1865	0.0186	0.0100	0.54	−0.0065	L
1865–1873	0.0227	0.0243	1.07	+0.0041	H
1873–1882	0.0188	0.0159	0.85	−0.0039	L
1882–1889	0.0220	0.0227	1.03	+0.0032	H
1889–1899	0.0219	0.0275	1.26	−0.0001	H
1899–1907	0.0118	0.0170	1.44	−0.0101	L
1907–1913	0.0155	0.0290	1.87	+0.0037	L
Long periods					
1845–1913	0.0199	0.0205	1.03	—	
1856–1913	0.0193	0.0206	1.07	—	
1856–1873	0.0205	0.0177	0.86	—	
1873–1899	0.0209	0.0219	1.05	+0.0004	
1899–1913	0.0134	0.0220	1.64	−0.0075	

$\bar{g}_Y$ = mean geometric growth rate of GDP
$\hat{\sigma}_{gY}$ = standard deviation of the geometric mean
Δ = first difference operator
H = high-growth path
L = low-growth path
Source: Feinstein (1976, Table 6, T18–T20).

consideration for either long waves or long swings. As was pointed out in Chapters 1 and 2, historical studies of long-term economic growth variations can only be undertaken within a generalised perspective; only then can long waves be distinguished from long swings and long-swing low-growth phases from climacterics.

Although the data sets analysed here have existed for some time, they have not been widely used in these discussions. Most of the literature has focused attention on the compromise estimate[1] of gross domestic product (GDP), on the assumption that the errors of the various series composing the compromise estimate are averaged out over time. It will be shown below that such an assumption is misleading for studies dealing with trend periods as short as the Kuznets swing.

The data sources to be analysed in this section are the GDP estimates presented in Feinstein (1976) and the industrial production indices presented in Lewis (1978). Although the GDP estimates measure the same variable, different trends are observed for the output, income, expenditure and the compromise estimates.

The peak-to-peak cycle growth calculations for the compromise estimate are presented in Table 3.1. The dominant variation of this series is observed over the inter-period comparison of 1856–99 and 1899–1913; the inter-cycle variations during the period 1856–99 are small. Although there is some evidence for a Kuznets swing pattern of inter-cycle variations, the range in growth rates is only 0.4 per cent, a statistically insignificant magnitude.[2] The only statistically significant growth variation over 1856–1913 is the transition to a low-growth phase during the Edwardian era.[3] Not only does such evidence negate the significance of the long-swing pattern of economic growth, it also negates the relevance of the Kondratieff wave perspective since the inter-period variations of 1856–73 and 1873–99 are marginal.[4]

The GDP series measured from the output side shows very low long-term variation; the whole period 1856–1913 is best represented as following a steady growth path.[5] Two reasons have been given for this linearity. Firstly, the extensive use of linear interpolation in the construction of the series may be generating the artefact of steady growth. Secondly, and probably more importantly, there is no inventory adjustment involved in calculating the series.[6] Given this bias the output estimate is the least suited for analysing either the issue of the Kuznets swing or the Edwardian climacteric. However, since interpolations are rarely made over very long-run periods the trends in the output estimate may be used as evidence in presenting the case against a Kondratieff wave phasing of 1856–1913.

The industrial production indices are also constructed with extensive linear interpolation and also fail to show up any significant long-term growth variation over the period 1850–1913.[7] This conclusion applies to Lewis' (1978) manufacturing and mining index and his total industrial production index, including construction.

The relevant peak-to-peak growth calculations for the income estimate are presented in Table 3.2. The income estimate of GDP does not rely on extensive linear interpolation and Feinstein (1972) suggested that it provides the best guide to cyclical movements. A long-swing phasing of the income estimate is significant throughout the period 1856–1913.[8] Obviously a sample of two and one-half complete swings does not allow one to label the observed path as a statistically cyclical growth path. Nevertheless it remains an historically significant growth pattern that is in need of explanation. Both the complete swings and the half swings are variable in length with the following periodicity:

Period	Length (in years)
1856–73	18
1873–99	27
1899–1913	14 (half swing)

Table 3.2 also suggests a prima-facie case for a climacteric in the performance

Table 3.2 *Peak-to-peak growth measures and related calculations: the income estimate of GDP, 1856–1913 (growth/annum)*

(1) t	(2) $\bar{g}_{Y_t}$	(3) $\hat{\sigma}_{g_{Y_t}}$	(4) $\hat{\sigma}_{g_{Y_t}}/\bar{g}_{Y_t}$	(5) $\Delta\bar{g}_{Y_t}$	(6) Characteristic of growth path
1856–1865	0.0177	0.0139	0.78	—	L
1865–1873	0.0282	0.0247	0.88	+0.0105	H
1873–1882	0.0164	0.0209	1.28	−0.0118	L
1882–1889	0.0274	0.0282	1.03	+0.0110	H
1889–1899	0.0235	0.0338	1.44	−0.0039	H
1899–1907	0.0099	0.0294	2.97	−0.0136	L
1907–1913	0.0117	0.0342	2.91	+0.0018	L
Long periods					
1856–1913	0.0195	0.0263	1.35		
1856–1873	0.0227	0.0198	0.88		
1873–1913	0.0181	0.0287	1.59		
1882–1899	0.0251	0.0307	1.22		
1899–1913	0.0107	0.0302	2.83		

Source: Feinstein (1976, Table 6, T18–T20).

of the economy over the period 1899–1913, or sampling over complete swings during the period 1882–1913. However, in both cases the null hypothesis specifying equality of growth paths fails to be rejected, negating the idea of an Edwardian climacteric.[9] The long-period variation between the periods 1856–73 and 1873–99 is also insignificant, negating the idea of a Kondratieff wave periodisation.

A long-swing pattern of growth is also observed in the expenditure estimate but with a different phasing from that observed for the income estimate. Although the expenditure estimate has similar linear artefacts imposed in its construction to those of the output estimate of GDP, the growth path of the series is far more variable. This would suggest that the errors in the British national income figures are more fundamental and need to be resolved with new data.[10] The relevant calculations are presented in Table 3.3 for the post-1870 period when the expenditure estimate is available. The peak-to-peak cycle calculations suggest the existence of one and one-half swings – with 1874–99 as a complete swing and 1899–1913 as a half swing. All these variations are statistically significant.[11] There also exists some prima-facie evidence for a climacteric effect in the Edwardian period since the low-growth phase of 1899–1913 is more depressed than the slow-growth phase during the period 1874–91. However, the difference in growth is not statistically significant over the two phases.[12]

Productivity trends also need to be analysed to gain an insight into the productive potential of the economy. I shall consider the trends in labour

Table 3.3 *Peak-to-peak growth measures and related calculations: the expenditure estimate of GDP, 1874–1913 (growth/annum)*

(1) t	(2) $\bar{g}_{Y_t}$	(3) $\hat{\sigma}_{g_{Y_t}}$	(4) $\hat{\sigma}_{g_{Y_t}}/\bar{g}_{Y_t}$	(5) $\Delta\bar{g}_{Y_t}$	(6) Characteristic of growth path
1874–1883	0.0197	0.0293	1.49	—	L
1883–1891	0.0159	0.0194	1.22	−0.0038	L
1891–1899	0.0272	0.0312	1.15	+0.0113	H
1899–1906	0.0101	0.0175	1.73	−0.0171	L
1906–1913	0.0160	0.0321	2.01	+0.0059	L

Source: Feinstein (1976, Table 6, T18–T20).

Table 3.4 *Peak-to-peak growth measures in labour productivity (income estimate) 1858–1913 (growth/annum)*

(1) t	(2) $\bar{g}_t$	(3) $\hat{\sigma}_{g_t}$	(4) $\hat{\sigma}_{g_t}/\bar{g}_t$	(5) $\Delta\bar{g}_t$
1858–1862	0.0093	0.0394	4.25	—
1862–1868	0.0097	0.0242	2.50	+0.0004
1868–1873	0.0186	0.0191	1.03	+0.0089
1873–1881	0.0123	0.0377	3.07	−0.0064
1881–1889	0.0144	0.0216	1.50	+0.0022
1889–1899	0.0122	0.0252	2.07	−0.0023
1899–1907	0.0025	0.0238	9.64	−0.0097
1907–1913	0.0054	0.0129	2.41	+0.0029

Source: Feinstein (1976, Table 6, T18–T20 and Table 57, T125–127).

productivity and total factor productivity (TFP). Labour productivity growth is defined as the difference between the growth rate of output and that of labour input. Labour input is taken to be the Feinstein (1976) labour force figures adjusted for unemployment. Given that specific peak-to-peak cycle phases for output and labour input rarely coincide it was chosen to work with the peaks in the labour productivity index.

Employing the output and compromise estimates of GDP as the numerator of the labour productivity index results in eliminating the long-swing growth pattern altogether. Both productivity indices capture a downward step after the early 1880s in line with the more rapid growth of labour input.

The income estimate of labour productivity growth captures only part of the Kuznets swing variations observed in the GDP estimate. The relevant trends are presented in Table 3.4. During the period 1856–81 the growth path is similar to that observed for output trends. However, the growth path of the 1870s is insignificantly different from that of the 1880s and 1890s since the

Table 3.5 *Peak-to-peak growth measures in labour productivity (expenditure estimate), 1871–1913 (growth/annum)*

(1) t	(2) $\bar{g}_t$	(3) $\hat{\sigma}_{g_t}$	(4) $\hat{\sigma}_{g_t}/\bar{g}_t$	(5) $\Delta\bar{g}_t$
1871–1880	0.0145	0.0219	1.51	—
1880–1884	0.0127	0.0308	2.43	−0.0018
1884–1891	0.0026	0.0197	7.58	−0.0101
1891–1899	0.0139	0.0207	1.49	+0.0113
1899–1913	0.0040	0.0167	4.17	−0.0099

Source: Feinstein (1976, Table 6, T18–T20 and Table 57, T125–127).

Table 3.6 *Peak-to-peak growth measures for total factor productivity: the income estimate of GDP (growth/annum)*

(1) t	(2) $\bar{g}_t$	(3) $\hat{\sigma}_{g_t}$	(4) $\hat{\sigma}_{g_t}/\bar{g}_t$	(5) $\Delta\bar{g}_t$
1858–1865	0.0022	0.0229	10.29	—
1865–1873	0.0146	0.0202	1.38	+0.0124
1873–1881	0.0033	0.0278	8.51	−0.0113
1881–1889	0.0123	0.0194	1.58	+0.0090
1889–1899	0.0096	0.0279	2.91	−0.0027
1899–1913	−0.0032	0.0244	−7.68	−0.0128

Sources: Feinstein (1976, Table 6, T18–T20); Feinstein (1976, Table 57, T125–127); Feinstein's revised (unpublished) capital figures.

higher labour input growth after 1884 reduces the labour productivity growth rate for the last two decades of the nineteenth century. This also makes the retardation of the Edwardian era more striking. In fact, the dominant growth variation of this series is the Edwardian climacteric.[13]

In contrast to the income estimate, the long swing observed in the expenditure estimate of GDP is transformed into a more regular long swing in labour productivity (see Table 3.5). During the period 1870–1913 the one and one-half swings in output are transformed into two swings in productivity growth.[14] Moreover, as can be seen from Table 3.5 there is no evidence for an Edwardian climacteric; the phase 1899–1913 is comparable to 1884–91. In addition, the complete swing phase of 1871–91 is insignificantly different from that of 1891–1913, further negating a Kondratieff wave phasing of the economy.[15]

Labour productivity measures are partial measures of productivity. Measures of total factor productivity (TFP) give rise to different conclusions. The growth of TFP is defined as the difference between the growth rate of final output and that of a weighted combination of inputs, total factor inputs (TFI).

Table 3.7 *Peak-to-peak growth measures for total factor productivity: the expenditure estimate of GDP (growth/annum)*

(1) t	(2) $\bar{g}_t$	(3) $\hat{\sigma}_{g_t}$	(4) $\hat{\sigma}_{g_t}/\bar{g}_t$	(5) $\Delta\bar{g}_t$
1874–1880	0.0067	0.0149	2.22	—
1880–1891	0.0038	0.0177	4.66	−0.0029
1891–1899	0.0121	0.0238	1.96	+0.0083
1899–1913	0.0008	0.0197	24.02	−0.0113

Sources: As for Table 3.6.

The TFP trends for the income estimate of GDP are presented in Table 3.6. Since TFI grew on an exponentially constant path during 1856–1913[16] the variations in output growth dominated the trend for TFP. These long-swing variations are statistically significant.[17] The long-term variation over the periods 1856–73 and 1873–99 is highly insignificant, negating a Kondratieff wave phasing. Although the retardation of the Edwardian era is marginally greater than the other slow-growing eras the differences are not statistically significant.[18] The expenditure series also follows the long swings in output performance (see Table 3.7). The expenditure estimate of TFP further suggests that the period 1899–1913 was statistically significantly lower than the low-growth phase over the period 1874–91.[19] It should be emphasised that the differences between the income and expenditure series for the TFP measure of the Edwardian era are probably not economically significant since the capital stock series employed is not adjusted for utilisation levels. This would be the result from adjusting for capital utilisation using the Wharton school method of weighting the capital stock by the ratio of actual to trend output, since GDP shows a mild climacteric effect only for the expenditure estimate. Nicholas (1982) calculated a TFP growth measure for the expenditure series after adjusting the capital stock by the Wharton method, of 0.333 per cent per annum for 1901–15; this is comparable to the 1874–91 growth path.

1913–1973

The phasing of British economic growth after 1913 poses many problems. The phase 1913–29 is the most difficult to handle. The statistics for 1914–21 are less satisfactory than for other periods (Matthews *et al.*, 1982). Moreover, the variation of growth is very large, with GDP receiving the largest setback since the industrial revolution over the period 1918–21. In terms of a phasing of interwar growth, the cycle peak-to-peak dates popularly chosen are 1924, 1929 and 1937. Although these dates are broadly comparable in some aspects of economic activity, such as unemployment levels, they are not strictly compara-

Table 3.8 *Peak-to-peak growth measures and related calculations: the compromise estimate of GDP since* c. *1913 (growth/annum)*

(1)	(2)	(3)	(4)	(5)
t	$\bar{g}_{Y_t}$	$\hat{\sigma}_{g_{Y_t}}$	$\hat{\sigma}_{g_{Y_t}}/\bar{g}_{Y_t}$	$\Delta\bar{g}_{Y_t}$
1913–1925	0.0026	0.0590	22.47	—
1925–1929	0.0202	0.0474	2.34	+0.0176
1929–1937	0.0196	0.0364	1.86	−0.0006
1937–1951	0.0172	0.0432	2.51	−0.0024
1951–1961	0.0271	0.174	0.64	+0.0099
1961–1968	0.0289	0.0151	0.52	+0.0018
1968–1973	0.0307	0.0192	0.63	+0.0018
Long periods				
1913–1937	0.0112	0.0494	4.40	
1937–1973	0.0241	0.0297	1.23	
1925–1937	0.0198	0.0382	1.93	
1951–1973	0.0285	0.0163	0.57	

Source: Maddison (1980, pp. 31–5).

ble to the pre-1913 peak-to-peak output cycles. In particular, 1924 is far too close to 1921 to be a peak year in economic activity. Moreover, in terms of output, 1925 seems to be the relevant specific peak year. As a means of coping with some of these problems I shall work with the benchmark years of 1913 and 1929, both peak years in economic activity. To gain further insight into the growth path of the 1920s I shall also consider the traditional cycle phasing of 1924–9 and 1929–37, but 1924 will be replaced with 1925 as the specific peak in the production series.

The relevant peak-to-peak growth rates for the compromise estimate of GDP are presented in Table 3.8. The low-growth phase of 1899–1913 continued over the period 1913–29. Although the growth rate during the period 1925–9 increased significantly, the period was too short to affect the long-run trends. During 1929–37 economic growth showed signs of traversing onto a higher path, making up for some of the losses of 1899–1929.

This high-growth trajectory continued during the period 1937–51. Such a continuity suggests that the low-growth phase over the period 1913–29 was not related to the war conditions. In fact, between 1913 and 1918 the British economy grew at a rate of 2.5 per cent per annum, a marked gain over the period 1899–1913. Thus the low-growth path of 1913–29 was due to the crisis of 1919–21 and the slow recovery of the 1920s. The postwar era saw further step increases in the growth path.

The conclusions drawn for the period 1913–73 are not dependent on the choice of series; the output, income, expenditure and compromise estimates of GDP all suggest similar trends.

The evidence for a Kuznets swing pattern of growth before 1913 is clearly

Table 3.9 *Peak-to-peak growth measures for the various GDP estimates, the interwar period (growth/annum)*

(1)	(2)	(3)	(4)	(5)
GDP series	1913–1929	1925–1929	1929–1937	(4)–(3)
Income	0.007	0.024	0.019	−0.005
Expenditure	0.005	0.015	0.017	+0.002
Output	0.009	0.021	0.022	+0.001
Compromise	0.007	0.020	0.020	0.000

Table 3.10 *Various long-run growth measures for the UK (growth/annum)*

(1) t	(2) GDP	(3) GKS	(4) TFP	(5) GDP/L
1856–1873	0.022	0.019	0.009	0.013
1873–1913	0.018	0.019	0.005	0.009
1924–1937	0.022	0.018	0.007	0.010
1937–1951	0.018	0.011	0.014	0.010
1951–1973	0.028	0.032	0.023	0.024

GDP = gross domestic product
GKS = gross capital stock
TFP = total factor productivity
GDP/L = labour productivity
Source: Matthews *et al.* (1982)

not extendable to the interwar and postwar periods. The economy moved from one mode of growth variations to another. The trend calculations for the various GDP estimates in the interwar years are presented in Table 3.9. Since TFI grew on a constant path over this period (1.4 per cent per annum) similar phases are observed for TFP.

The post-1913 trends also provide further evidence to negate the relevance of the Kondratieff wave phasing of British economic growth. The twentieth century represents an era of trend accelerated growth with significant steps taking place at 1929 and the postwar.

The postwar era grew on a trajectory higher than for any period since 1850.[20] What are even more distinct about this era are the trends in productivity and the growth of the capital stock which are clearly much higher than for the pre-1937 period (see Table 3.10). Thus, the postwar can best be characterised as an era of intensive growth, relying more on technical progress, while the prewar period was one of extensive growth, relying more on the growth of factor inputs.

This outline of British growth trends over the period 1856–1973 has illustrated a diversity of growth patterns, which suggests that the structure of growth has changed significantly over time. Although the division into pre-

and post-1913 eras was chosen for expositional purposes, the evidence suggests that such a phasing can also be justified on analytical grounds.

To the extent that growth varied along trend periods, the dominant growth variation before 1913 was a Kuznets swing with a variable periodicity. The Kuznets swing in aggregate British economic growth has not been recognised in previous literature mainly because most studies have employed the compromise estimate of GDP as a proxy of economic performance. It is quite clear that the choice of working with the compromise estimate of GDP is misleading. Since both the income and expenditure series yield a significant long-swing pattern of growth, but one of a different phasing, averaging the various estimates in fact averages the long swing into insignificance and substitutes in its place the artefact of an Edwardian climacteric. However, the differing trends of the income, expenditure and output estimates suggest that the artefact interpretation of long swings in aggregate output cannot be ruled out at present.[21]

The case against a Kondratieff wave phasing of British growth is supported by all the indicators studied here. The trends since 1913 reinforce the case against a Kondratieff wave and illustrate significant structural change in Britain's growth path after the First World War. Economic growth during the period 1913–73 shows a tendency to trend acceleration, with significant step increases in the growth path after 1929 and the Second World War. The postwar growth boom of 1950–73 is the peak in British economic performance for the whole period 1856–1973. Although the phase of the postwar boom does fall in the Kondratieff wave time band, the total rejection of the Kondratieff wave phasing of growth before 1950 makes this analogy meaningless.

The transition of the British economy from a Kuznets swing mode of growth variations to a trend-acceleration mode suggests that the degree of relative backwardness of the British economy became significant by 1929 and especially by 1950. Moreover, to the extent that there is some evidence for Kuznets swings in British economic growth, it suggests that long swings were specific to the period 1856–1913. This suggests that the two and one-half swings should be explained within an historical model emphasising the specific conditions of that era rather than a generalised cyclical model. I shall take up both the pre-1913 swings and the trend acceleration of the twentieth century in later chapters.

Germany

Pre-1913

In this section I shall consider the trends in German growth employing the statistical work of Hoffmann (1965) and the adjustments made by Maddison

Table 3.11 *Peak-to-peak growth measures and related calculations: German net domestic product, 1850–1913 (growth/annum)*

(1) t	(2) $\bar{g}_{Y_t}$	(3) $\hat{\sigma}_{g Y_t}$	(4) $\hat{\sigma}_{g Y_t}/\bar{g}_{Y_t}$	(5) $\Delta \bar{g}_{Y_t}$
1857–1864	0.0261	0.0355	1.36	—
1864–1874	0.0250	0.0311	1.25	−0.0011
1874–1884	0.0127	0.0208	1.64	−0.0123
1884–1890	0.0283	0.0121	0.42	+0.0156
1890–1900	0.0339	0.0147	0.43	+0.0056
1900–1907	0.0268	0.0251	0.94	−0.0071
1907–1913	0.0321	0.0114	0.35	+0.0053
Long periods				
1857–1874	0.0254	0.0319	1.25	
1874–1884	0.0127	0.0208	1.64	
1884–1900	0.0318	0.0137	0.43	
1900–1913	0.0292	0.0194	0.66	
1884–1913	0.0307	0.0162	0.52	

Source: Maddison (1980, pp. 32–5).

(1980) and Lewis (1978). The peak-to-peak cycle calculations for German net domestic product (NDP) are reported in Table 3.11. The existence of a major German depression during the period 1874–84 suggests a prima-facie case that the era 1857–1913 is best described as following a Schumpeterian four-phase Kondratieff wave. In fact, although the depression phase of 1874–84 stands out as a low-growth phase at the 5 per cent significance level, the four-phase Kondratieff wave over the period 1857–90 is not statistically significant.[22] Thus, a Kuznets swing periodisation of 1857–90 is possible with the following half swings:

1857–74	High growth
1874–84	Low growth
1884–90	High growth

The acceleration of economic growth after 1890 is more marked. The low-growth phase of 1874–90 is distinguished from the high-growth phase, 1890–1913, at the 5 per cent significance level. The trend increase of growth after 1890 is also associated with a reduction in the long-swing output variations of the economy. Although there exists a pattern of Kuznets swing variations over the period 1884–1913, the magnitude of the inter-cycle variations are small and insignificant.

Nevertheless, although a Kuznets swing pattern of growth is not significant for the output performance of the economy, there seems to be far more variation in labour productivity growth. Employing Maddison's labour input figures for Germany, I was able to trace a rough picture of productivity trends

Table 3.12 *Man-hour and man-year labour productivity over the specific peak-to-peak phases of German NDP (growth/annum)*

(1) t	(2) $\bar{g}_{Y_t}$	(3) $\bar{g}_{L_{t_1}}$ (years)	(4) $\bar{g}_{L_{t_2}}$ (hours)	(5) $\bar{g}_{Y_t} - \bar{g}_{L_{t_1}}$	(6) $\bar{g}_{Y_t} - \bar{g}_{L_{t_2}}$
1874–1884	0.0127	0.0079	0.0048	0.0048	0.0079
1884–1890	0.0283	0.0087	0.0058	0.0196	0.0225
1890–1900	0.0339	0.0139	0.0110	0.0200	0.0229
1900–1907	0.0268	0.0172	0.0142	0.0096	0.0126
1907–1913	0.0321	0.0172	0.0142	0.0149	0.0179

Sources: Maddison (1980, pp. 33–5), and Maddison (1979, pp. 41–2).

since 1870 (see Table 3.12). What distinguishes the productivity trends from the output trends is the retardation of productivity during the period 1900–13. Thus, the Kuznets swing in output observed for the period 1857–90 continued after 1890 only as a productivity swing.

Before proceeding further it should be noted that the Hoffmann data poses many problems for the 1870–84 period (Lewis, 1978, 1981). Hoffmann's output data is mainly derived from import information. However, the basis of recording German imports changed several times during this period, the biggest change occurring in 1879. Between 1872 and 1879 the transit trade is included (but not always) in import statistics but not fully in export statistics. Thus, published import figures show a fall of 25 per cent between 1879 and 1880 and Hoffmann translated this into a constant price fall of 24 per cent. But the evidence shows that 1880 is, in fact, a prosperous year. Hoffmann's index of manufacturing (excluding building and mining) fell 3 per cent over the period 1879–80. During the same period his indices for minerals, metal production and railway traffic rose by 12 per cent, 16 per cent and 13 per cent respectively – all these series were not affected by customs statistics.[23] Thus, the severity of the depression of 1874–84 could clearly be an artefact.

Lewis (1978) has put forward the artefact interpretation of the German depression of the 1870s. To derive this conclusion Lewis notes that an index of German coal production, including lignite, grew at the same rate as the index of manufacturing between 1884 and 1913 and also between 1866 and 1871. He then substituted the coal production index over the years 1871–84 for Hoffmann's manufacturing index between those dates. Lewis (1978) presents three indices relating to industrial production from 1865, covering manufacturing and mining, total industrial production (including construction) and construction. The peak-to-peak cycle calculations for total industrial production are reported in Table 3.13. The period 1873–1913 shows a pattern of steady growth and the depression of the 1870s is noted only by its absence. The phase 1869–73 is clearly on a significantly higher growth path but is too

Table 3.13 *Peak-to-peak growth measures and related calculations: Lewis's German total industrial production index (growth/annum)*

(1) t	(2) $\bar{g}_{Y_t}$	(3) $\hat{\sigma}_{g_{Y_t}}$	(4) $\hat{\sigma}_{g_{Y_t}}/\bar{g}_{Y_t}$	(5) $\Delta\bar{g}_{Y_t}$
1869–1873	0.0685	0.0524	0.76	—
1873–1883	0.0366	0.0462	1.26	−0.0319
1883–1889	0.0379	0.0308	0.81	+0.0013
1889–1899	0.0401	0.0157	0.39	+0.0022
1899–1913	0.0381	0.0220	0.58	−0.0020

Source: Lewis (1978, p. 271).

Table 3.14 *Peak-to-peak growth measures and related calculations: Lewis's German manufacturing and mining production index (growth/annum)*

(1) t	(2) $\bar{g}_{Y_t}$	(3) $\hat{\sigma}_{g_{Y_t}}$	(4) $\hat{\sigma}_{g_{Y_t}}/\bar{g}_{Y_t}$	(5) $\Delta\bar{g}_{Y_t}$
1869–1873	0.0826	0.0475	0.58	—
1873–1883	0.0429	0.0423	0.99	−0.0397
1883–1890	0.0399	0.0283	0.71	−0.0030
1890–1898	0.0421	0.0204	0.49	+0.0022
1898–1907	0.0379	0.0225	0.59	−0.0042
1907–1913	0.0440	0.0275	0.62	+0.0061
1873–1890	0.0417	0.0358	0.86	—
1890–1913	0.0409	0.0222	0.54	−0.0008

Source: Lewis (1978, p. 271).

short to form any conclusions about a possible climacteric around 1873. The manufacturing and mining index follows the same growth path as is observed for total industrial production (see Table 3.14).

However, Lewis' (1978) revision of the Hoffmann data is inadequate. Although Lewis is correct in saying that manufacturing and coal production grew at the same rate from 1866 to 87 and from 1884 to 1913 they did not do so before 1866. Moreover, although the two indices averaged the same growth over the period 1884–1913 the time path of the growth variations was different. In fact, since Lewis is in effect using coal production as a proxy for the overall growth performance of the German economy, it would be more fruitful to employ this index throughout its availability; using it only for the period 1871–84 makes it an inefficient and arbitrary proxy.

The specific peak-to-peak cycle measures for coal production are reported in Table 3.15. The trends provide a prima-facie case for the existence of a long-wave downswing during the period 1873–91. This low-growth phase is statistically significant at the 5 per cent level, both when compared to the period

Table 3.15 *Peak-to-Peak growth measures and related calculations: German coal production (including lignite), c. 1845–1913 (growth/annum)*

(1) t	(2) $\bar{g}_{Y_t}$	(3) $\hat{\sigma}_{g_{Y_t}}$	(4) $\hat{\sigma}_{g_{Y_t}}/\bar{g}_{Y_t}$	(5) $\Delta\bar{g}_{Y_t}$
1846–1857	0.0848	0.0528	0.63	—
1857–1864	0.0764	0.0534	0.70	−0.0084
1864–1873	0.0611	0.0465	0.76	−0.0154
1873–1883	0.0423	0.0352	0.83	−0.0188
1883–1891	0.0364	0.0224	0.62	−0.0059
1891–1900	0.0513	0.0336	0.66	+0.0149
1900–1907	0.0456	0.0402	0.88	−0.0057
1907–1913	0.0498	0.0308	0.62	+0.0042

Source: Mitchell (1981, pp. 381–91).

1857–73 and the mean growth path during the period 1857–1913. As can be seen from Table 3.15 the equal-variance assumption is a valid approximation for the post-1873 era but breaks down when a comparison is made between the pre- and post-1873 eras. However, the unequal variance over the 1857–91 phases is not critical to this significance result. Although the unequal variance reduces the degrees of freedom to 23, the 't' value is still significant at the 5 per cent level.

No doubt much of the extreme severity of the depression of the 1870s is an artefact resulting from Hoffmann's use of import data to calculate production trends. Nevertheless, the available non-import dependent data (the coal production index) suggests that a less severe depression is likely to have occurred in the German economy of the 1870s. The production evidence available at present is inadequate to set the bounds of the magnitude of this retardation. It should be emphasised that the coal production index was analysed as a means of showing the limits of Lewis' assumptions; the index does not seem to be a good proxy of aggregate production movements. The further retardation of coal production in the 1880s is not observed in either industrial production or the GDP trends.

1913–1973

German output trends for the period 1913–73 are easier to phase then pre-1913 trends mainly because of the greater availability of data. Peak-to-peak cycle calculations for Maddison's GDP series are presented in Table 3.16. Output growth grew very slowly during the period 1913–28; from 3 per cent per annum growth achieved during the period 1884–1913 the economy retarded to 1.2 per cent during the period 1913–28. The cycle of 1928–38 saw an acceleration of growth, averaging 3.3 per cent per annum.

Table 3.16 *Peak-to-peak growth measures and related calculations: German gross domestic product, c. 1913–1973 (growth/annum)*

(1) t	(2) $\bar{g}_{Y_t}$	(3) $\hat{\sigma}_{g_{Y_t}}$	(4) $\hat{\sigma}_{g_{Y_t}}/\bar{g}_{Y_t}$	(5) $\Delta\bar{g}_{Y_t}$
1913–1925	0.0025	0.1194	48.47	—
1925–1928	0.0554	0.0356	0.64	+0.0529
1928–1938	0.0330	0.0712	2.16	−0.0224
1938–1952	0.0096	0.0211	2.19	−0.0234
1952–1956	0.0841	0.0203	0.24	+0.0745
1956–1960	0.0653	0.0217	0.33	−0.0188
1960–1965	0.0484	0.0132	0.27	−0.0169
1965–1969	0.0398	0.0350	0.88	−0.0086
1969–1973	0.0434	0.0120	0.28	+0.0035
Long periods				
1925–1938	0.0381			
1952–1973	0.0551			
1884–1913	0.0307			
1913–1938	0.0210			
1938–1973	0.0369			

Source: Maddison (1980, pp. 33–5).

Thus, German long-term growth followed a similar pattern to Britain in the twentieth century. The low-growth path of productivity between 1899 and 1928, and of output between 1913 and 1928 was followed by a stepping up of growth in the 1930s and 1950s. The twentieth century is best described as an era of trend acceleration. As can be seen from Table 3.16 trend acceleration is observed even if allowance is made for the war shocks of 1913–25 and 1938–52 – the growth path during the period 1913–38 was significantly lower than that of 1938–73. Although the high growth of the 1950s and 1960s was partly catching-up growth, making up for the losses of 1899–1928 and 1938–52, the high-growth path of the postwar period was more than a catching-up process – even by the 1960s and early 1970s the growth rates observed were much higher than long-run historical trends.

Labour productivity trends also vindicate the trend acceleration perspective for the twentieth century. The slow productivity growth of 1899–1928 was reversed during the 1930s, with a productivity growth above pre-1899 trends. Further gains in labour productivity were made during the postwar era with a growth rate of labour productivity above 5 per cent per annum (see Table 3.17). Such rapid labour productivity growth rates suggest that the postwar is best perceived as an era of intensive growth, based on unprecedented productivity increases. The pre-1938 growth path can best be characterised as

Table 3.17 *Growth of German labour*
productivity per man-hour (growth/annum)

(1)	(2)	(3)
t	$\bar{g}_P$	Δg_P
1880–1913	0.0199	—
1913–1938	0.0173	−0.0026
1938–1973	0.0379	+0.0207
1913–1929	0.0137	—
1929–1938	0.0236	+0.0099
1952–1956	0.0601	—
1956–1960	0.0681	+0.0080
1960–1965	0.0559	−0.0122
1965–1969	0.0477	−0.0082
1969–1973	0.0507	+0.0030

Source: Maddison (1979).

extensive growth, based on factor input increases. Even the rapid product-ivity increases of the 1930s only served to make up for the losses of 1899–1928.

This brief synopsis of German output and productivity trends suggests that the German economy does not fit into a simple long-wave or long-swing growth pattern. Output trends followed a Kuznets swing pattern during the period 1857–90; after 1890 the output growth path is characterised by rapid growth throughout the period 1890–1913. However, in terms of productivity, the retardation of 1899–1913 means that the Kuznets swing pattern is obser-ved throughout the period 1857–1913. The evidence on German investment trends, which will be presented in Chapter 7, gives further support to this interpretation. Lewis' (1978) conclusion that German economic growth was steady during the period 1873–1913 is unfounded; a careful examination of coal production suggests that Lewis has misinterpreted the evidence. The results presented here agree with Metz and Spree (1981) that Kuznets swings are a relevant growth variaton for the pre-1913 German economy.

A Kondratieff wave phasing of German economic growth is not a good description of the observed trends. Only for output is there some evidence of a stepping up of long-term economic growth after1890. Productivity and invest-ment trends yield a Kuznets swing pattern of development. The twentieth century evidence further reinforces the case against a Kondratieff wave phasing of economic growth. The twentieth century follows a pattern of trend accele-ration, with significant step increases in growth during the 1930s and the postwar. Such evidence also suggests a structural break in the Kuznets swing pattern of productivity and investment variations of the pre-1913 era.

France

Pre-1913

This section provides an analysis of trends in French GDP, industrial production and commodity production, a weighted index of industrial and agricultural output. Peak-to-peak cycle calculations for Maddison's (1980) GDP series are presented in Table 3.18. A long-wave growth pattern is observed with the following phases:

1852–69   High growth
1869–92   Low growth
1892–1912   High growth

The cycle of 1869–75, which embraces the Franco-Prussian War may be placed in either the high- or low-growth phase but this does not critically affect the long-run trends.

Allowing for autocorrelation and the unequal variances during the phases 1852–69 and 1875–92 the null hypothesis specifying equality of growth paths fails to be rejected. Only the trend acceleration of the phase 1892–1912 stands out as significant at the 5 per cent level. Given the evidence to be presented later in this section and the evidence on French investment trends, presented in Chapter 7, I wish to emphasise the structural change taking place in the French growth path after 1892, rather than seeing the phase 1892–1912 as following a Kondratieff wave pattern of development.

Table 3.18 *Peak-to-peak growth measures and related calculations:*
Maddison's French GDP estimate, c. 1850–1913 (growth/annum)

(1) t	(2) $\bar{g}_{Y_t}$	(3) $\hat{\sigma}_{g_{Y_t}}$	(4) $\hat{\sigma}_{g_{Y_t}}/\bar{g}_{Y_t}$	(5) $\Delta\bar{g}_{Y_t}$
1852–1863	0.0182	0.0548	3.01	—
1863–1869	0.0186	0.0618	3.32	+ 0.0004
1869–1875	0.0122	0.0958	7.86	− 0.0064
1875–1882	0.0078	0.0379	4.89	− 0.0044
1882–1892	0.0035	0.0198	5.72	− 0.0043
1892–1899	0.0200	0.0404	2.02	+ 0.0165
1899–1904	0.0130	0.0318	2.45	− 0.0070
1904–1912	0.0215	0.0296	1.38	+ 0.0085
Long periods				
1852–1912	0.0147	0.0467	3.18	—
1852–1869	0.0183	0.0573	3.13	—
1875–1892	0.0069	0.0269	3.91	− 0.0114
1892–1912	0.0188	0.0326	1.73	+ 0.0119

Source: Maddison (1980, pp. 32–5).

Table 3.19 *Peak-to-peak growth measures and related calculations: French commodity production, c 1850–1913 (growth/annum)*

(1) t	(2) $\bar{g}_{Y_t}$	(3) $\hat{\sigma}_{g_{Y_t}}$	(4) $\hat{\sigma}_{g_{Y_t}}/\bar{g}_{Y_t}$	(5) $\Delta\bar{g}_{Y_t}$
1850–1858	0.0229	0.0221	0.97	+0.0117
1858–1863	0.0171	0.0435	2.55	−0.0058
1863–1869	0.0158	0.0335	2.12	−0.0013
1869–1875	0.0080	0.0916	11.48	−0.0078
1875–1882	0.0141	0.0480	3.41	+0.0061
1882–1892	0.0008	0.0240	31.33	−0.0133
1892–1899	0.0177	0.0322	1.82	+0.0169
1899–1907	0.0067	0.0302	4.51	−0.0110
1907–1912	0.0331	0.0363	1.09	+0.0264

Source: Lévy-Leboyer (1978, Table 60, pp. 292–5).

Table 3.20 *Complete swing growth measures for French commodity production (growth/annum)*

(1) t	(2) $\bar{g}_Y$	(3) $\Delta\bar{g}_Y$
1869–1882	0.0113	—
1882–1899	0.0078	−0.0035
1899–1912	0.0178	+0.0100

Source: Lévy-Leboyer (1978, Table 60, pp. 292–5).

The peak-to-peak cycle measures for Lévy-Leboyer's (1978) commodity production series are reported in Table 3.19.[24] The series shows a very different pattern from the GDP estimate. The differences are accounted for by a different peak-to-peak phasing of the pre-1863 era and the fact that 1875–82 is perceived as a slow-growing era in Maddison's series and a high-growing era in Lévy-Leboyer's series. The latter difference is explicable in terms of the wider scope of the GDP series which includes a measure for services derived from linear interpolation across census years. Since the era 1875–82 is a short phase placed between the war cycle of 1869–75 and the severe depression of the 1880s, any interpolations would act to depress the growth path during those years. In this respect the commodity production series is superior to the GDP series when discussing trend period variations. The dominant growth variations of this series is a Kuznets swing pattern observed during the period 1875–1913. Looking at complete swing variations illustrates the trend acceleration of 1899–1912 (see Table 3.20).

The French industrial production series also suggests that the Kuznets swing was the dominant growth cycle of the French economy after 1850. Only

Table 3.21 *Peak-to-peak growth measures and related calculations: French industrial production, c. 1850–1913 (growth/annum)*

(1) t	(2) $\bar{g}_{Y_t}$	(3) $\hat{\sigma}_{g_{Y_t}}$	(4) $\hat{\sigma}_{g_{Y_t}}/\bar{g}_{Y_t}$	(5) $\Delta \bar{g}_{Y_t}$
1850–1856	0.0283	0.0435	1.54	+0.0211
1856–1860	0.0091	0.0515	5.69	−0.0192
1860–1866	0.0153	0.0295	1.92	+0.0062
1866–1874	0.0056	0.0947	16.92	−0.0097
1874–1882	0.0255	0.0331	1.30	+0.0199
1882–1892	0.0077	0.0347	4.49	−0.0178
1892–1899	0.0163	0.0421	2.58	+0.0086
1899–1907	0.0129	0.0331	22.55	−0.0034
1907–1912	0.0461	0.0363	0.79	+0.0332
Long periods				
1856–1882	0.0145			
1882–1899	0.0113			
1899–1913	0.0257			

Source: Lévy-Leboyer (1978, Table 60, pp. 292–5).

Table 3.22 *Trends in labour productivity over peak-to-peak growth measures for GDP (growth/annum)*

(1) t	(2) $\bar{g}_{Y_t}$	(3) $\bar{g}_{L_t}$	(4) $\bar{g}_{Y_t} - \bar{g}_{L_t}$	(5) $\Delta(\bar{g}_{Y_t} - \bar{g}_{L_t})$
1875–1882	0.0078	0.0014	0.0064	—
1882–1892	0.0035	0.0026	0.0009	−0.0055
1892–1899	0.0199	0.0027	0.0172	+0.0163
1899–1912	0.0182	0.0017	0.0165	−0.0007

Sources: Maddison (1980, pp. 32–5), and Maddison (1979, pp. 41–2).

during the period 1899–1912 is there evidence of a step acceleration of long-term industrial production growth (see Table 3.21).

It is impossible to derive a TFP series given the absence of a reliable capital stock series for the nineteenth century. Finding reliable labour force figures is also a problem. The census data is clearly inaccurate since the definition of labour participation is uncertain for family helpers, especially in agriculture. An examination of the sex and age breakdown in the agricultural labour force shows some changes that appear manifestly artificial – e.g. the number of women per hundred men was forty-eight in 1895 and 1901 and sixty in 1906. The labour force as a whole appears to have been considerably underestimated in the 1896 census. The activity rates for men in age groups 25–34, 35–44 and 45–54 were 92, 92 and 99 per cent in 1896; at the 1901 census these rates were

96, 97 and 95 per cent and they remained the same (within 1 per cent) at all the next censuses (Carre *et al.*, 1976).

Employing Maddison's labour input figures, which are an improvement on the census data and give a similar growth rate to that calculated by Carre *et al.* (1976) for 1896–1911, the aggregate labour productivity trends are presented in Table 3.22. The trend acceleration during the period 1892–1912 is also observed in labour productivity trends.

1913–1973

Peak-to-peak cycle calculations for GDP are presented in Table 3.23. The presence of two world wars complicates matters. Treating the war years as separate phases and concentrating on the peacetime cycles of 1924–37 and 1950–73 clearly illustrates the uniqueness of the postwar era in a long-run perspective. Alternatively, the wars could be perceived as part of the growth process; certainly the reconstruction cycle immediately after a war will affect the growth performance of an economy (Jánossy, 1971). Nevertheless, even if the war years are included, the uniqueness of the postwar era is striking – the postwar was more than a catching up phase. This is also illustrated by the fact that the growth path of the 1960s and early 1970s was higher than the 1950s.

The pattern of growth in the interwar years needs to be placed in a long-run perspective. It was argued above that a Kuznets swing phasing of French economic growth is significant during the period 1856–1912. Hence, although

Table 3.23 *Peak-to-peak growth measures and related calculations: Maddison's GDP estimate after 1913 (growth/annum)*

(1) t	(2) $\bar{g}_{Y_t}$	(3) $\hat{\sigma}_{g_{Y_t}}$	(4) $\hat{\sigma}_{g_{Y_t}}/\bar{g}_{Y_t}$	(5) $\Delta\bar{g}_{Y_t}$
1912–1924	0.0066	0.0739	11.25	—
1924–1929	0.0301	0.0387	1.29	+0.0235
1929–1937	−0.0051	0.0386	−7.60	−0.0352
1937–1950	0.0138	0.1687	12.19	+0.0189
1950–1956	0.0431	0.0130	0.31	+0.0293
1956–1960	0.0465	0.0194	0.42	+0.0034
1960–1969	0.0537	0.0088	0.16	+0.0072
1969–1973	0.0549	0.0036	0.07	+0.0012
Long periods				
1912–1937	0.0076	0.0578	7.65	
1937–1973	0.0369	0.1008	2.73	
1924–1937	0.0085	0.0386	4.54	
1950–1973	0.0499	0.0120	0.24	

Source: Maddison (1980, pp. 32–5).

the inter-period variation of growth was far greater during the period 1912–1937 this may be explicable in terms of the magnitude of the shocks rather than a basic change in the underlying growth structure of the French economy. The war shock of 1912–24 gave rise to very low growth and served to lay the basis for the high-growth path of the 1920s. Hence, although the downswing of 1929–37 was exceptional by long-run historical standards, it was only exceptional in terms of the magnitude of the growth retardation not in terms of the nature of growth variations. It was also noted earlier that French production and productivity showed a tendency to trend acceleration over the period 1899–1912; in fact, this acceleration continued over the period 1912–29. Thus, the greater severity of the 1930s depression could be partly explained by the changed structure of growth during the period 1899–1929, a path that combines long swings with trend acceleration.

As a means of gaining an insight into the catching-up growth of the postwar era, Carre *et al.* (1976) compared the growth path across the benchmark years of 1896, 1913, 1929, 1938 and 1969. Carre *et al.* found that the whole of the postwar rapid growth could be explained in terms of a catching-up growth process, making up for the losses of the 1930s and the world wars. However, when 1912–73 is compared to 1892–1912 there occurs a 1 per cent annum stepping up of long-term growth rates. The Carre *et al.* conclusion is dependent on the choice of 1969 as the final benchmark year. Hence, the rapid growth rates of the postwar are more than catching-up growth; nevertheless, the catching-up aspect was strong during the 1950s and early 1960s.

A study of labour productivity trends further illustrates the uniqueness of the postwar growth path. Production per man-hour increased by 5.2 per cent per year in all productive sectors from 1949 to 1969. The highest earlier growth was 2.5 per cent per year during the period 1913–29 (Carre *et al.*, 1976).

French production trends illustrate the existence of a diversity of growth patterns. The dominant growth variation before 1937 was a long-swing pattern. The evidence does not give support to a Kondratieff wave phasing of French economic growth. Although Maddison's GDP series does suggest a prima-facie case for the existence of a long-wave phasing during the period 1850–1913, the inter-period variations are not statistically significant. Moreover, the use of linear interpolation to derive a GDP series biases downwards the long-term growth path of the 1870s cycle. Only the trend acceleration of 1899–1912 is statistically significant.

This trend acceleration continued over the period 1912–29, combined with a war-induced long-swing process. Despite the greater amplitude of the 1930s downswing, compared to previous long-swing downswing phases, the 1930s depression follows a pattern of Kuznets depressions.

The postwar era sees a break from the Kuznets swing growth pattern. The

Kuznets swing gives way to an era of trend-accelerated growth over the period 1950–73. Although the rapid growth of the postwar was partly catching-up growth, by the mid-1960s trend acceleration had found a momentum of its own.

Thus, as was observed for Britain and Germany, the structure of growth variations has not remained constant over time. The postwar boom signalled the end of the Kuznets swing growth pattern. Moreover, already by 1899 there is evidence of trend acceleration of French growth, despite the continuance of a Kuznets swing growth pattern. The French pattern of growth was very different from Britain and Germany which suggests that national specific aspects are an important influence on long-term economic growth.

America

Pre-1913

Output data for America have been placed on a reliable annual basis only from the 1870s (Maddison, 1980). This section gives an outline of the output and productivity trends observed in the GDP series put together from a variety of sources by Maddison (1980) and Lewis' (1978) adjustments to the Frickey indices of industrial production (Nutter, 1962, p. 382). The implications of the recent revisions to the American GDP series suggested by Romer (1985, 1986) are then considered.

Peak-to-peak cycle growth rate calculations for Maddison's GDP series are reported in Table 3.24. A long-swing pattern of growth is observed throughout the period 1873–1912. The significance tests for these phases of growth suggest that the swings are significant at the 5 per cent level (see Appendix Table A3.10). The variations over complete swings are small and statistically insignificant, suggesting that a Kondratieff wave pattern of economic growth is not observed (see Appendix Table A3.9).

Labour productivity growth rates for man-years and man-hours have also been calculated using Maddison's (1979) labour input figures. Labour productivity growth has been calculated over the specific peak-to-peak cycle of the GDP series (see Table 3.25). The evidence suggests that the long swings observed in aggregate output are also observed in aggregate labour productivity growth. The long-period measures covering complete swings suggest that productivity growth was centred around a constant exponential growth path.

Lewis' (1978) industrial production indices also suggest the existence of a long-swing growth pattern but one of a slightly different phasing from GDP swings. Peak-to-peak cycle calculations for Lewis' manufacturing and mining index are presented in Table 3.26. The growth path of the 1870s is not

Table 3.24 *Peak-to-peak growth measures and related calculations: US gross domestic product, c. 1870–1913 (growth/annum)*

(1) t	(2) $\bar{g}_{Y_t}$	(3) $\hat{\sigma}_{g_{Y_t}}$	(4) $\hat{\sigma}_{g_{Y_t}}/\bar{g}_{Y_t}$	(5) Δg_{Y_t}
1873–1884	0.0403	0.0118	0.29	—
1884–1892	0.0533	0.0206	0.39	+0.0130
1892–1899	0.0305	0.0665	2.18	−0.0228
1899–1906	0.0513	0.0469	0.91	+0.0208
1906–1912	0.0222	0.0650	2.93	−0.0291
Long periods				
1873–1892	0.0458	0.0169	0.37	—
1892–1906	0.0410	0.0563	1.37	−0.0048
1884–1899	0.0427	0.0474	1.11	—
1899–1912	0.0379	0.0556	1.47	−0.0048

Source: Maddison (1980, pp. 32–5).

Table 3.25 *Man-hour and man-year labour productivity over the specific peak-to-peak phases in US GDP, 1873–1912 (growth/annum)*

(1) t	(2) $\bar{g}_{Y_t}$	(3) $\bar{g}_{L_{t_1}}$ (years)	(4) $\bar{a}_{L_{t_2}}$ (hours)	(5) $\bar{g}_{Y_t}-\bar{g}_{L_{t_1}}$	(6) $\bar{g}_{Y_t}-\bar{a}_{L_{t_2}}$
1873–1884	0.0403	0.0248	0.0217	0.0155	0.0186
1884–1892	0.0533	0.0246	0.0217	0.0287	0.0316
1892–1899	0.0305	0.0202	0.0172	0.0103	0.0133
1899–1906	0.0513	0.0215	0.0184	0.0298	0.0329
1906–1912	0.0222	0.0215	0.0186	0.0007	0.0036

Long period measures	$\bar{g}_{Y_t}-\bar{g}_{L_{t_1}}$	$\Delta(\bar{g}_{Y_t}-\bar{g}_{L_{t_1}})$	$\bar{g}_{Y_t}-\bar{g}_{L_{t_2}}$	$\Delta(g_{Y_t}-\bar{g}_{L_{t_2}})$
1884–1899	0.0201	—	0.0231	—
1899–1912	0.0164	−0.0037	0.0194	0.0037
1873–1892	0.0211	—	0.0241	—
1892–1906	0.0201	−0.0010	0.0231	−0.0010

Sources: Maddison (1980, pp. 32–5), and Maddison (1979, pp. 41–2).

distinguishable from the 1880s in either the mean or the variance. The pattern of growth during the period 1892–1913 is similar for both the GDP series and industrial production. Thus, during the period 1872–1913 two complete swings are observed instead of two and one-half as in the GDP series. The pre-1872 phase is on a high-growth path but is too short for any sound conclusions to be drawn.

Table 3.26 *Peak-to-peak growth measures and related calculations:
US manufacturing and mining, 1865–1913 (growth/annum)*

(1) t	(2) $\bar{g}_{Y_t}$	(3) $\hat{\sigma}_{g_{Y_t}}$	(4) $\hat{\sigma}_{g_{Y_t}}/\bar{g}_{Y_t}$	(5) $\Delta\bar{g}_{Y_t}$
1866–1872	0.0664	0.0553	0.83	—
1872–1882	0.0493	0.0662	1.34	−0.0177
1882–1892	0.0485	0.0614	1.27	−0.0008
1892–1899	0.0339	0.0884	2.61	−0.0146
1899–1906	0.0675	0.0705	0.95	+0.0336
1906–1913	0.0339	0.1119	3.30	−0.0336
Long periods				
1872–1899	0.0450	0.0689	1.53	—
1899–1913	0.0507	0.0915	1.80	−0.0057

Source: Lewis (1978, p. 273).

Table 3.27 *Peak-to-peak growth measures and related calculations: US total
industrial production 1865–1913 (growth/annum)*

(1) t	(2) $\bar{g}_{Y_t}$	(3) $\hat{\sigma}_{g_{Y_t}}$	(4) $\hat{\sigma}_{g_{Y_t}}/\bar{g}_{Y_t}$	(5) $\Delta\bar{g}_{Y_t}$
1866–1872	0.0701	0.0345	0.49	—
1872–1881	0.0457	0.0980	2.14	−0.0244
1881–1892	0.0456	0.0730	1.61	−0.0001
1892–1899	0.0274	0.1121	4.09	−0.0182
1899–1906	0.0699	0.0909	1.30	+0.0425
1906–1913	0.0263	0.1199	4.56	−0.0436
Long periods				
1866–1881	0.0555	0.0779	1.40	—
1881–1899	0.0385	0.0875	2.27	−0.0177
1899–1913	0.0481	0.1047	2.18	+0.0096
1872–1892	0.0456	0.0827	1.81	—
1892–1906	0.0487	0.1005	2.06	+0.0031

Source: Lewis (1978, p. 273).

A similar pattern of growth is also observed for total industrial production,
including construction (see Table 3.27). As in the manufacturing and mining
series only two complete swings are observed during the period 1872–1913.
The complete swing growth calculations for this series provide some prima-
facie evidence for the existence of a long-wave pattern of long-period growth
variations. The complete swing phases show an inter-period variation of
growth rates of between +1 per cent and −2 per cent growth per annum.
Nevertheless, the variation of the series as a whole is extremely large and the

Table 3.28 *Peak-to-peak growth measures and related calculations:*
US construction activity (growth/annum)

(1) t	(2) $\bar{g}_{Y_t}$	(3) $\hat{\sigma}_{g_{Y_t}}$	(4) $\hat{\sigma}_{g_{Y_t}}/\bar{g}_{Y_t}$	(5) $\Delta\bar{g}_{Y_t}$
1866–1871	0.0861	0.1104	1.28	—
1871–1881	0.0314	0.2353	7.49	−0.0547
1881–1892	0.0299	0.1537	5.14	−0.0013
1892–1899	0.0007	0.2086	298.00	−0.0292
1899–1906	0.0804	0.2062	2.57	+0.0797
1906–1912	0.0024	0.1856	77.33	−0.0780
Long periods				
1866–1881	0.0574	0.1940	3.38	—
1881–1899	0.0185	0.1720	9.29	−0.0389
1899–1912	0.0444	0.1930	4.35	+0.0259
1881–1902	0.0336			
1902–1912	0.0206			

Source: Lewis (1978, p. 273).

inter-period variations are not statistically significant. Indeed, the variation of the series is so large that substituting the peak of 1902 for that of 1899 generates a growth pattern that suggests long-term retardation throughout the period 1866–1913, not a Kondratieff wave pattern. Given that these variations are not statistically significant, total industrial production can also be viewed as following a constant long-run exponential growth path. Construction activity also followed the swing pattern observed for the other industrial production series (see Table 3.28).

The most recent revisions of American data have been undertaken by Romer (1985, 1986). Romer has revised the existing series on the assumption that they have an artificially high variance. Kuznets estimated an annual series of GDP using regression analysis. The regression series was constructed by taking the period 1909–38, a period when fairly reliable estimates of GDP are obtained using the income-payments approach. Kuznets regresses the percentage deviations from trend of aggregate GDP to the percentage deviations from trend of aggregate commodity output. He then uses the estimated coefficient to form an estimate of GDP for the period 1869–1918. However, since the 1909–38 period is dominated by the depression of the 1930s, the coefficient relating GDP to commodity output may be biased to generate large cyclical responses. GDP and commodity output move much closer to one-for-one during the 1930s than other periods. During the period 1909–28 the coefficient relating the deviations of the two series is substantially less than one (0.6). Romer uses the period 1909–28 to estimate the relevant coefficient. This

Table 3.29 *Peak-to-peak growth measures and related calculations: Romer US gross domestic product, c. 1870–1913 (growth/annum)*

(1) t	(2) $\bar{g}_{Y_t}$	(3) $\hat{\sigma}_{g_{Y_t}}$	(4) $\hat{\sigma}_{g_{Y_t}}/\bar{g}_{Y_t}$	(5) $\Delta\bar{g}_{Y_t}$
1873–1882	0.05438	0.03015	0.55	—
1882–1892	0.02963	0.02056	0.69	−0.0248
1892–1899	0.03189	0.03790	1.19	+0.0023
1899–1906	0.04775	0.02761	0.58	+0.0159
1906–1912	0.02535	0.03617	1.43	−0.0224

Source: Romer (1985, pp. 170–1).

yields a substantially less volatile GDP series before 1909, where volatility is measured by the standard deviation of growth rates or the amplitude of cycles.

Although the Romer revised GDP series is less volatile than the old Kuznets series, the long-swing behaviour of the American economy is not invalidated (see Table 3.29). The inter-period variations allow for the following long-swing phasing of the economy:

1873–82   High growth
1882–99   Low growth
1899–1906   High growth
1906–13   Low growth

All these swings are statistically significant from the mean growth path during the period 1873–1913 at the 1 per cent level (see Appendix Table A3.11). Thus, although Romer's revisions suggest that growth was far less variable than previously thought, the growth swings are still large and statistically significant.

1913–1973

Twentieth-century US trends form an interesting case study because of their marked contrast with the trends observed for the European economies. The first noteworthy difference is that the wars were markedly favourable for the US economy. Both wars gave a boosting shock to the economy, bringing it out of excess capacity. The First World War occurred during a long-swing downswing phase and the Second World War during the major depressed swing of the 1930s. The wars being European wars, also placed the US in the favourable position of undisturbed production. Over the 1912–23 war cycle, growth accelerated from the long-swing depression phase of 1906–12; during the period 1937–45 the US GDP grew at the unprecedented rate of 7.4 per cent per annum. Although such rapid rates of growth were not maintained after the war (mainly because by 1945 the favourable growth impact of excess capacity had been used up), the favourable effect of the war shock on US

Table 3.30 *Peak-to-peak growth measures and related calculations: US gross domestic product c. 1912–1973 (growth/annum)*

(1)	(2)	(3)	(4)	(5)
t	$\bar{g}_{Y_t}$	$\hat{\sigma}_{gY_t}$	$\hat{\sigma}_{gY_t}/\bar{g}_{Y_t}$	Δg_{Y_t}
1912–1918	0.0295	0.0752	2.55	—
1918–1923	0.0308	0.0596	1.94	+0.0013
1923–1929	0.0328	0.0233	0.71	+0.0020
1929–1937	−0.0016	0.1006	−62.08	−0.0344
1937–1951	0.0441	0.0844	1.91	+0.0457
1951–1959	0.0279	0.0306	1.10	−0.0162
1959–1966	0.0433	0.0167	0.39	+0.0154
1966–1973	0.0331	0.0198	0.60	−0.0102
Long periods				
1912–1937	0.0206			
1937–1959	0.0382			
1959–1978	0.0297			

Source: Maddison (1980, pp. 32–5).

growth is seen right up to 1951, when a more normal peacetime growth path had started (see Table 3.30).

During the period 1912–37 growth followed a long-swing pattern but with greater variation than was observed during pre-1913 swings. The favourable war shock and the reconstruction cycle of the 1920s made the 1912–29 upswing phase particularly long when compared to the upswing phases of the 1880s and 1899–1906.

The American economy also shows signs of an aggregate long-swing growth process continuing into the period 1937–73, although this continuity is critically dependent on the inclusion of the war cycle of 1937–51. Such evidence suggests that the war shocks of the twentieth century were critical to sustaining the long-swing growth process in the American economy. Moreover, the postwar catching-up boom of the European economies is not observed in the American economy. This further suggests that, without a technological gap, growth spurts are limited to a long-swing periodicity.

American economic growth was not above long-term trends. Although the growth path during the period 1937–73 was above that of 1912–37 (3.8 per cent per annum as against 2.1 per cent per annum) this was due to the effect of the 1930s depression. In fact, economic growth during the period 1912–29 was of the same magnitude as that of 1929–73 (3.1 per cent per annum). In a longer-run perspective the postwar growth path of America was clearly below the trend growth rate between 1872 and 1912.

Labour productivity trends on a per-worker and per-hour basis are reported in Table 3.31. The trends suggest that labour productivity growth followed a

Table 3.31 *Man-hour and man-year labour productivity over specific peak-to-peak phases of US GDP, 1912–1973 (growth/annum)*

(1)	(2)	(3)	(4)	(5)	(6)
t	$\bar{g}_{Y_t}$	$\bar{g}_{L_{t_1}}$ (years)	$\bar{g}_{L_{t_2}}$ (hours)	$\bar{g}_{Y_t} - \bar{g}_{L_{t_1}}$	$\bar{g}_{Y_t} - \bar{g}_{L_{t_2}}$
1912–1929	0.0310	0.0142	0.0082	0.0168	0.0228
1929–1937	−0.0016	−0.0106	−0.0247	0.0090	0.0231
1937–1951	0.0441	0.0236	0.0151	0.0205	0.0205
1951–1959	0.0279	0.0081	0.0043	0.0198	0.0236
1959–1966	0.0433	0.0172	0.0147	0.0261	0.0286
1966–1973	0.0331	0.0191	0.0097	0.0140	0.0234

Sources: Maddison (1980, pp. 32-5) and Maddison (1979, pp. 41–2).

similar long-term path as was observed for output growth. The gains in labour productivity per man-year during the period 1937–73 were mainly due to making up the losses incurred during the depression of the 1930s. Allowing for this the growth path between 1912 and 1929 is comparable to that of the period 1929–73.

In measuring labour productivity trends we are faced with the problem of dealing with the rapid growth of the government and service sector. Output of government services is usually measured by the growth of labour input and, hence, shows no productivity change except in so far as labour inputs are weighted by skill or education. With the rapid growth of the government sector in the postwar period, productivity growth would be biased downwards in relation to the past. A way to overcome this problem is to eliminate the government output and employment figures altogether and consider only the private domestic economy. Kendrick's (1977) data for this variable which stretch back to 1889, are reported in Table 3.32. Over the period 1889–1919 labour productivity (per man-hour) grew at 2 per cent per annum and over the period 1919–48 at 2.2 per cent per annum. Thus, the postwar growth rate of 3.2 per cent is significantly higher.

American growth during the period 1870–1973 suggests that the dominant growth variation was a Kuznets swing pattern of 20–30 year growth variations. The continuity of this pattern into the twentieth century is dependent on the impact of the world wars. During the pre-1913 era the complete swing growth measures suggest the existence of a constant exponential long-run growth trend. The evidence is against a Kondratieff wave phasing of economic growth.

The long-swing pattern continued into the 1912–73 era, with a significant change in amplitude over time – increasing during the period 1912–37 and falling during the period 1937–73. The continuity of a long-swing pattern during the period 1870–1973 is in marked contrast to the other economies

Table 3.32 *Various growth trends in Kendrick's figures for the US private domestic economy (growth/annum)*

(1)	(2)	(3)	(4)	(5)
t	g_1	g_2	g_3	g_4
1889–1919	0.039	0.020	0.005	0.013
1919–1948	0.028	0.022	0.015	0.018
1948–1969	0.039	0.032	0.003	0.023
1948–1953	0.046	0.041	0.003	0.028
1953–1957	0.025	0.027	−0.012	0.019
1957–1960	0.026	0.026	0.003	0.023
1960–1966	0.052	0.036	0.018	0.029
1966–1969	0.034	0.019	−0.010	0.011
1969–1973	0.038	0.029	0.002	0.021

g_1 = real product
g_2 = labour productivity (man-hours)
g_3 = capital productivity
g_4 = total factor productivity

Source: Kendrick (1977, p. 31).

under consideration. Both Britain and Germany traversed from a long-swing mode of growth variations to a trend-acceleration mode in the twentieth century; France followed suit in the postwar era.

The evidence also suggests a mild and discontinuous American postwar upswing in comparison to the European economies. Britain, Germany and France witnessed their highest output and productivity growth rates since 1850 in the postwar era; in terms of productivity the differences were even more spectacular. In America both the output and productivity growth paths were comparable to long-run trends before 1929.

The world economy

Pre-1913

Although the production trends in the major parts of the world economy have been outlined, it is also necessary to give separate consideration to the aggregates for the world economy since countries were growing on differential trajectories. Amongst those who have argued the case for a Kondratieff wave pattern of growth, it is widely believed that the strongest evidence for existence is provided by the trends in the world economy. Jaap Van Duijn has recently expressed this view:

Great Britain, the USA, Germany and France each have their own histories, in which

Table 3.33 *Peak-to-peak growth measures and related calculations: world industrial production, c. 1850–1913 (growth/annum)*

(1) t	(2) $\bar{g}_{Y_t}$	(3) $\hat{\sigma}_{g Y_t}$	(4) $\hat{\sigma}_{g Y_t}/\bar{g}_{Y_t}$	(5) Δg_{Y_t}
1856–1866	0.0272	0.0695	2.56	—
1866–1872	0.0439	0.0550	1.25	+0.0167
1872–1883	0.0267	0.0321	1.20	−0.0172
1883–1892	0.0330	0.0381	1.15	+0.0063
1892–1899	0.0458	0.0436	0.95	+0.0128
1899–1907	0.0396	0.0329	0.83	−0.0062
1907–1913	0.0372	0.0662	1.78	−0.0024
Long periods				
1856–1872	0.0335	0.0630	1.88	—
1872–1892	0.0295	0.0341	1.16	−0.0040
1892–1913	0.0410	0.0454	1.11	+0.0115

Source: Kuczynski (1980, pp. 309–16).

the S-shaped life cycle of economic development may be more conspicuous than long wave fluctuations. The industrialized world as a whole, or even the four core countries taken together, moves forward along a long wave path. (1983, p. 154)

The peak-to-peak cycle growth calculations for world industrial production are presented in Table 3.33. During the period 1856–92 there exists much inter-cycle variation in growth with a periodicity that falls in the Kuznets swing time band of approximately twenty-year variations. However, there does not exist any significant variation in the world growth path over complete swings (i.e. 1856–72 compared to 1872–92). During the period 1892–1913 the level of growth increased by 1.2 per cent per annum compared to that of 1872–92.[25] Thus, only if history is truncated at 1872 would it be possible to talk of a Kondratieff wave phasing of world economic development. The arbitrariness of this approach suggests that a more valid perspective is to view the world economy as moving onto a structurally different growth path after the 1880s, a traverse distinguished from the whole period 1856–92.[26] The upswing in growth after 1892 did not follow a Kondratieff depression during the period 1872–92. The upswing in growth after 1892 was also associated with the ending of the long-swing pattern of growth observed during the period 1856–92; the growth variations during the period 1892–1913 are not statistically significant.

The accelerating world growth path after 1892 and the failure to observe a Kondratieff wave pattern of growth for the dominant economies suggests that over time the summation of differential national growth paths generated an accelerating trend for the world economy.[27] The observed growth path since 1850 is distinguished from long waves by describing these trends with the phrase 'shocked Gerschenkronian catching-up waves' (henceforth abbreviated G-waves). This phrase is employed not because Gerschenkron (1962) analysed such trends but because he was one of the first to formalise a framework for modelling the characteristics of the growth path of the 'relatively backward' economies. Relative backwardness and differential growth rates across nations were the main determinants of the world-growth path.

As a means of gaining further insight into G-waves I analysed Maddison's (1980) data for sixteen capitalist countries during the period 1870–1913.[28] The various national figures are made comparable and additive by changing them into constant 1970 dollars based on the Kravis *et al.* (1978) international GDP for that year. I divided Maddison's sample into four categories:

  (i) the aggregate for the sixteen (the world);
 (ii) the aggregate for Britain, France, Germany and America (the core);
(iii) the aggregate for Britain, France and Germany (the European core); and
 (iv) the aggregate for the rest of the world (the ROW, defined as category (i) minus (ii)).

As can be seen from column (7) of Table 3.34 the acceleration of growth observed for world industrial production is also observed for world GDP trends.[29] Table 3.34 also suggests that the growth variations of the world economy are explained by a number of diverse trends. The step of the 1880s is mainly accounted for by America, Germany and Britain (in order of importance). The ROW had a negative influence and France showed no significant variation. The step of the 1890s is explained by the growth variation of France, Germany and the ROW (all of about the same order of importance). The growth path of 1899–1913 is fully accounted for by the variations of America and the ROW.

Thus, the G-wave growth path of the world economy after 1872 was the result of (a) structural change in the distribution of world production, due to countries growing at differential rates; (b) the effect of new countries, mainly in the ROW category, joining the world growth leagues on a significant scale after 1890; and (c) random variations in national growth paths.

The structural change effect has been separated from the other aspects of the growth acceleration by calculating the growth path of the world economy and the growth path of the core on variable and fixed 1870 weights[30] (see Table 3.35). With the exception of the inter-cycle variation of 1882–99 the structural change effect had a large impact on the observed G-wave. Nevertheless, even with fixed weights the world growth path moved onto a higher trajectory during the period 1890–1913. However, this was due entirely to the effect of the highly significant trend increase in growth for the ROW. The fixed-weight growth path of the core was constant during the period 1872–1913.

Table 3.34 *Weighted growth rates for various parts of the world economy: peak-to-peak phases for world economy (growth/annum)*

(1) t	(2) Britain	(3) France	(4) Germany	(5) USA	(6) Rest of world	(7) World[a]
1872–1882	0.00370	0.00176	0.00289	0.00930	0.00634	0.023634
1882–1890	0.00456	0.00186	0.00415	0.01152	0.00573	0.025900
1890–1899	0.00419	0.00249	0.00467	0.01120	0.00624	0.028094
1899–1907	0.00182	0.00106	0.00392	0.01503	0.00968	0.031128
1907–1913	0.00214	0.00259	0.00445	0.00839	0.00868	0.025906
Inter-cycle variations						
1872–1882	—	—	—	—	—	—
1882–1890	+0.00086	+0.00010	+0.00126	+0.00222	−0.00061	+0.002266
1890–1899	−0.00037	+0.00063	+0.00052	−0.00032	+0.00051	+0.002194
1899–1907	−0.00237	−0.00143	−0.00075	+0.00383	+0.00344	+0.003034
1907–1913	+0.00032	+0.00153	+0.00053	−0.00664	−0.00100	−0.005222
Shares in world production (%)						
1872–1882	18.95	16.14	13.83	22.70	28.35	100
1882–1890	18.14	13.71	13.61	26.87	27.67	100
1890–1899	17.83	12.31	13.99	29.63	26.24	100
1899–1907	16.12	10.77	13.84	33.02	26.24	100
1907–1913	14.55	10.08	14.13	33.61	27.62	100

[a] Rounding-up errors mean that column (7) is not the exact sum of columns (2), (3), (4), (5) and (6).
Source: Maddison (1982, Appendix A, pp. 158–77).

Table 3.35 *Peak-to-peak variable and fixed weighted growth steps in the world economy*

	g_{Y_V}	g_{Y_F}	Δg_{Y_V}	Δg_{Y_F}	$(\Delta g_{Y_V} - \Delta g_{Y_F})/\Delta g_{Y_V}$
1872–1882	0.023634	0.023085	—	—	—
1882–1890	0.025990	0.024126	+0.002356	+0.00104	0.56
1890–1899	0.028094	0.026709	+0.002104	+0.00258	−0.22
1899–1907	0.031128	0.027708	+0.003034	+0.00099	0.67
1907–1913	0.025906	0.025678	−0.005222	−0.00203	0.61

g_{Y_V} = variable weights per annum
g_{Y_F} = fixed (1870) weights

Source: Maddison (1982, Appendix A, pp. 158–77).

Table 3.36 *Peak-to-peak growth measures and related calculations: world industrial production, c. 1913–1973 (growth/annum)*

(1) t	(2) $\bar{g}_{Y_t}$	(3) $\hat{\sigma}_{g_{Y_t}}$	(4) $\hat{\sigma}_{g_{Y_t}}/\bar{g}_{Y_t}$	(5) $\Delta\bar{g}_{Y_t}$
1913–1924	0.0080	0.0995	12.50	−0.0292
1924–1929	0.0582	0.0185	0.32	+0.0502
1929–1937	0.0154	0.0131	8.53	−0.0428
1937–1951	0.0302	0.1539	5.10	+0.0148
1951–1956	0.0509	0.0434	0.85	+0.0208
1956–1960	0.0442	0.0562	1.27	−0.0068
1960–1965	0.0598	0.0174	0.28	+0.0156
1965–1969	0.0557	0.0281	0.51	−0.0041
1969–1973	0.0507	0.0356	0.70	−0.0050
Long periods				
1913–1937	0.0209	0.1000	4.78	—
1937–1973	0.0438	0.0964	2.21	+0.0229
1924–1937	0.0319	0.1032	3.24	—
1951–1973	0.0525	0.0345	0.66	+0.0207

Source: Kuczynski (1980, pp. 309–16).

1913–1973

The production trends for the world economy during the twentieth century have been greatly influenced by the world wars. The dominant position of the European economy in 1913 meant that the First World War had a devastating effect on the world growth path. In contrast, the dominant position of the American economy in the 1930s meant that the effect of the Second World War was more favourable (see Table 3.36).

The world economy failed to recover fully on to the pre-1913 long-run growth trajectory. Although a classic war 'reconstruction cycle' was observed over the period 1913–29, with rapid catching-up growth rates during the period 1924–29, the long-run growth path during the period 1913–29 failed to return to prewar trends. The long-run growth path of world industrial production was only 2.4 per cent, approximately 60 per cent of the growth rate observed for 1892–1913. World GDP trends for Maddison's sixteen capitalist economies averaged 2.2 per cent over the period 1913–29 while it had averaged 2.8 per cent for the period 1890–1913.

It has been argued in the long-wave literature that the failure of the world economy to regain its prewar growth path is evidence of a long-run 'recession' process that culminated in the downswing of the 1930s (Van Duijn, 1983). However, such a perspective is not valid. Not only is the Kondratieff wave phasing of the world economy during the approximate period 1850–1913 invalid but during the period 1913–29 the dominant economies that failed to recover from the effects of the world war were Britain and Germany; excluding these two economies from Maddison's sixteen raises the world economy growth rate to 2.6 per cent per annum for the period 1913–29. Moreover, in both the case of Britain and Germany the trend growth rate did not lapse into depression in the 1930s but recovered significantly to a higher long-run growth path. Thus, the countries that were growing slowly in the 1920s were not the slow-growing economies of the 1930s.

The various European national case studies illustrated the uniquely high-growth path of the postwar era. The pattern of growth for the world economy reflected the dominance of the American economy. The world economy saw retarding growth during the periods 1956–60 and 1965–73, reflecting the American long-swing pattern of growth. Moreover, the high-growth path of 1937–73 was not historically unprecedented – a comparable path was observed during the period 1890–1913. In fact, since the world growth path over the period 1937–73 was partly catching up on the lost growth of the 1930s, it is also meaningful to compare the historical standing of growth throughout the period 1913–73 relative to the past. The growth rate for world industrial production averaged 3 per cent per annum, representing a comparable path to that of 1856–92 but significant retardation when compared to that of 1890–1913. Such a pattern of growth reflects the dominant position of the American economy in the twentieth century. This evidence suggests that an S-shaped pattern of economic development is observed at a world level of analysis where the constraints of the technological frontier are relevant. The European economies were growing at unprecedented rates in the twentieth century, mainly from borrowed technology.

The growth trends of the world economy have not been steady over long periods throughout history. Nevertheless, this should not mislead us into viewing world growth as having followed a Kondratieff wave. The pre-1913 era showed a tendency to trend acceleration rather than a long-wave pattern of growth. The world economy grew on a higher growth path during the period c. 1890–1913 but this did not follow a long-wave contraction phase. The world growth path since 1850 can best be characterised as being domi-nated by a G-wave catching-up process. The evidence presented here also suggests that the postwar upswing for the European economies can be understood as a catching-up wave. In contrast, the world economy and the American economy saw an entirely different growth path – twentieth century trends were not unprecedented by historical standards.

The Kuznets swing pattern of growth has significant implications for an understanding of the world economy. Before 1913 a Kuznets swing pattern is only observed for 1856–92, reflecting the dominance of the British economy in the structure of world production. During the period 1892–1913 the Kuznets swing ceases being a significant growth variation at the world economy level. Thus, despite the existence of marked national growth swings before 1913 the world growth path does not seem to be dominated by such variations in an observed way, partly because pre-1913 swings were not synchronised and partly because no one economy was dominant.

However, after the First World War the structure of the world economy changed significantly. Simply in terms of proportions the world economy was dominated by the trends of the American economy. Thus, the downswing of 1929–37 was as much a US downswing as a world economy downswing. The dominance of the US is also reflected in the growth path of world industrial production in the postwar period. Hence, in a world of changing economic leadership, the Kuznets swing is essential to understanding the growth path of the world economy.

General conclusions

This chapter has focused on the issue of the existence of Kondratieff waves and Kuznets swings. Three important conclusions can be drawn:

First, the evidence rejects the Kondratieff wave phasing of post-1850 econ-omic growth. This conclusion is valid for all the national case studies examined here. Whether one takes the period 1856–1913 or 1856–1973 a Kondratieff wave phasing cannot be supported. The postwar high-growth boom does fall within the Kondratieff time band for high-growth periods but is a unique historical era. The growth path of the world economy is not a simple replication of national growth paths. In fact, non-steady growth over long periods has characterised the world economy throughout the period 1856–1973. Nevertheless, the observed variations do not follow a Kondratieff wave pattern. I have described the actual path as a G-wave path to distinguish it from the long-wave periodisation. G-waves are historical waves of irregular periodicity and amplitude. The era between 1856 and 1937 represents one complete G-wave – with the accelerating growth trajectory of 1856–1913 or 1856–1929 ended by the world depression of the 1930s. The two Kondratieff waves discussed in the long-wave literature for the period 1856–1937 misre-present history.

Secondly, Kuznets swings are a more generalised phenomenon than has been recognized in the past literature. Moreover, the swings I have been analysing are observed at a macroeconomic level. Kuznets swings are observed over specific historical eras and are thus critically dependent on the nature of shocks within a given economic structure. The Kuznets swing for Germany and Britain is limited to the pre-1913 era; in France the swing pattern continued into the inter-war period; in America a swing pattern is observed throughout the period 1870–1973. The past literature has discussed Kuznets swings in terms of the American economy and has failed to recognise the evidence for aggregate swings in the European economies. The historically specific nature of the European swings suggests that the explanatory model for these growth variations must also be historically specific, analysing the particular shocks sustaining or changing the Kuznets swing phases. Such problems will be examined in Chapters 6 and 7, devoted to an historical explanation of the swings.

Thirdly, the structure of growth has not remained constant over time. Britain and Germany traversed from a Kuznets swing mode of growth variations before 1913 to a 'trend-acceleration' pattern of growth in the twentieth century. France followed suit after 1950. Even in America, where a long-swing pattern of growth was observed for a much longer period, the structure of these swing variations changed significantly. The amplitude of the 1930s downswing was much higher than any other period. The idea that economies grow along a regular cycle is not valid either for the Kuznets swing or longer-run growth variations. In much of the literature episodic changes have been mistaken for cycles of economic growth.

Statistical appendix

We can test for variation in the growth path by introducing a dummy variable into the relevant autoregressive (AR) scheme for the growth variable. The relevant AR scheme is chosen empirically. Since the principle is the same I shall illustrate how it operates in the simplest model possible, AR(0). Let

$$g_{Y_t} = a + \varepsilon_t$$
$$\varepsilon_t \sim N(0, \sigma_\varepsilon^2) \tag{1}$$

Consider two growth paths; one for period $1 \ldots T_1$ and one for $T_1 + 1 \ldots T_2$. Let these two growth paths be characterised by a and b respectively. Therefore,

$$g_{Y_{t\,a}} = a_1 + \varepsilon_{t\,a} \tag{2}$$

and

$$g_{Y_{t\,b}} = a_2 + \varepsilon_{t\,b} \tag{3}$$

Define vectors

$$\mathbf{Z}_a = \begin{pmatrix} 1 \\ 0 \end{pmatrix} \text{ and } \mathbf{Z}_b = \begin{pmatrix} 0 \\ 1 \end{pmatrix}$$

for the relevant sample periods.

The null under consideration is the equality of the growth paths:

$$H_0 : a_1 = a_2$$
$$g_{Y_t} = a_1(\mathbf{Z}_a + \mathbf{Z}_b) + (a_2 - a_1)\mathbf{Z}_b + \varepsilon_t \qquad (4)$$

or

$$g_{Y_t} = a_1 + d\mathbf{Z}_b + \varepsilon_t \qquad (5)$$

If the null holds $a_1 = a_2 = a \Leftrightarrow d = 0$. Thus, the null can be rejected if the dummy proves significant in equation (5). It should be noted that the test is one-tailed since the long-wave hypothesis postulates a one-directional difference in growth rates.

Although not reported here I also tested the usual stationarity assumptions. Differences in variances do not critically affect the results and the null hypothesis for the existence of a unit root in the growth process is rejected by both the Dickey and Fuller (1981) ϕ_3 statistic and the Fuller $\hat{\tau}_\tau$ statistic.

The choice of using dummy variables to test for significant breaks in the growth path has the disadvantage of viewing change as discontinuous.

Where the simplicity of dummy variable tests proved inadequate, as in the modelling of the world growth path, I employed a version of Poirier's method of cubic splines, which both maintains continuity in the relationship and allows us to test for structural change (Buse and Lim, 1977; Poirier, 1977).

I will illustrate this method for a two-period case in the more manageable form of restricted least squares. Let

$$y = f_j(X) = a_j + b_j X + c_j X^2 + d_j X^3 \quad j = 1,2 \qquad (6)$$

Let e_1 be the join point between periods 1 and 2 and (e_0, e_k) the end points; $y =$ level series and $X =$ time.

The following restrictions are placed at e_1:

$$f_j(e_1) = f_{j+1}(e_1) \qquad (7)$$
$$f'_j(e_1) = f'_{j+1}(e_1) \qquad (8)$$
$$f''_j(e_1) = f''_{j+1}(e_1) \qquad (9)$$

i.e. the values, first derivatives and second derivatives of adjacent cubic regressions must be equal. Poirier also adds the end-point constraints (10) and (11) to make the system identifiable:

$$f''_0(e_0) = \Pi_0 f''_j(e_1) \qquad (10)$$
$$f''_k(e_k) = \Pi_k f''_j(e_1) \qquad (11)$$

Π_0 and Π_k are chosen a priori.

Poirier observed structural change by comparing the third derivatives of regression pieces at adjacent intervals. Let this difference in third derivatives $= \tau$. If $\tau > 0$ and the second derivative is positive then there has occurred an increase in the rate of acceleration in the function.

To simplify the estimation we employed dummy variables but imposed restrictions (7)–(11) on the estimation.

Let the growth paths of the two periods be

$$Y_1 = a_1 + b_1 X + c_1 X^2 + d_1 X^3 + \varepsilon \tag{12}$$
$$Y_2 = a_2 + b_2 X + c_2 X^2 + d_2 X^3 + \varepsilon \tag{13}$$

(12) and (13) can be estimated by running

$$Y = a_3 + b_3 X + c_3 X^2 + d_3 X^3 + a_3^* Z + b_3^* ZX + c_3^* ZX^2 + d_3^* ZX^3 + \varepsilon \tag{14}$$

where

$$\varepsilon \sim N(0, \sigma_\varepsilon^2), \ Z = (0, 1)$$

Thus, Poirier's test reduces to

$$d_1 = d_2 \text{ iff } d_3^* = 0$$

where the coefficients with an asterisk represent dummy variables. For economic variables, distinguishing structural change at the level of the third derivative may not be very useful. Therefore, an analogous approach will be used for linear and quadratic splines.

Table A3.1 *Significance tests for differences in long-swing phases and complete swings: the compromise estimate of GDP ('t' values in parenthesis)*

Results of regressing $g_{Y_t} = \alpha + dZ + \varepsilon_t$, $Z = (0, 1)$, $\varepsilon_t \sim N(0, \sigma_\varepsilon^2)$

(1) t	(2) $Z = 1$ for	(3) $\hat{\alpha}$	(4) $\hat{d}$	(5) 'H' phase	(6) 'L' phase
Long swings					
1845–1865	1845–1856	0.018752 $(3.23)^a$	0.005705 (0.76)	1845–1856	1856–1865
1865–1882	1873–1882	0.022687 $(3.17)^a$	− 0.00386 − (0.39)	1865–1873	1873–1882
1882–1913	1899–1913	0.022292 $(4.10)^a$	− 0.008896 − $(1.10)^b$	1882–1899	1899–1913
Complete swings					
1845–1882	1845–1865	0.020643 $(4.75)^a$	+ 0.0015313 + (0.26)		
1856–1899	1856–1873	0.020857 $(5.20)^a$	− 0.0003275 − (0.05)		
1865–1913	1865–1882	0.018076 $(4.55)^a$	− 0.0031038 − (0.47)		

[a] Significant at 1 per cent significance (two-tailed test).
[b] Significant at a value near 10 per cent (one-tailed test).

Table A3.2 *Significance tests for the existence of low-growth phases: the compromise estimate of GDP* ('t' *values in parenthesis*)

Results of regressing $g_{Y_t} = a + dZ + \varepsilon_t, Z = (0, 1), \varepsilon_t \sim N(0, \sigma_\varepsilon^2)$
or $\quad g_{Y_t} = a + dZ_t + u_t, \qquad u_t = \rho u_{t-1} + \varepsilon_t$

(1) t	(2) $Z = 1$ for	(3) $\hat{a}$	(4) $\hat{d}$	(5) AR coefficient
1845–1913	1873–1882	0.020091 $(7.5)^a$	− 0.0012635 − (0.17)	
1845–1913	1899–1913	0.020522 $(7.48)^a$	− 0.007310 $(1.23)^b$	0.013497 (2.2)

^{a} 't' values are significant at 1 per cent (two-tailed test).
^{b} 't' values are significant at a value near 10 per cent (one-tailed test).

Table A3.3 *Significance tests for differences in long-swing phases: the output series of GDP* ('t' *values in parenthesis*)

Results of regressing $g_{Y_t} = a + dZ_t + \varepsilon_t, Z = (0, 1), \varepsilon_t \sim N(0, \sigma_\varepsilon^2)$

(1) t	(2) $Z = 1$ for	(3) $\hat{a}$	(4) $\hat{d}$
1857–1874	1857–1866	0.019892 $(2.68)^a$	0.0008334 (0.08)
1866–1883	1866–1874	0.017726 $(1.74)^b$	0.002165 (0.15)
1883–1899	1883–1890	0.01964 $(2.53)^a$	− 0.00319 − (0.27)
1890–1907	1890–1899	0.01657 $(2.46)^a$	0.00307 (0.33)
1899–1913	1899–1907	0.01719 $(2.03)^b$	− 0.00617 − (0.06)
1874–1899	1874–1883	0.018244 $(2.74)^a$	−0.00519 − (0.05)
1856–1913	1899–1913	0.01879 $(3.96)^a$	− 0.00196 − (0.25)

^{a} Significant at 5 per cent.
^{b} Significant at 10 per cent.

Table A3.4 *Significance tests for differences in long-swing phases: manufacturing and mining ('t' values in parenthesis)*

Results of regressing $g_{Y_t} = \alpha + dZ_t + \varepsilon_t$, $Z = (0, 1)$, $\varepsilon_t \sim N(0, \sigma_\varepsilon^2)$

(1) t	(2) $Z = 1$ for	(3) $\hat{\alpha}$	(4) $\hat{d}$
1853–1889	1853–1873	0.020743 $(2.03)^a$	0.005995 (0.44)
1853–1899	1853–1873	0.021436 $(2.80)^a$	0.005302 (0.45)
1853–1913	1853–1899	0.019321 $(1.90)^b$	0.0044197 (0.37)
1853–1913	1853–1882	0.020177 $(2.90)^a$	0.0052398 (0.52)

^{a} Significantly different from zero at 5 per cent.
^{b} Significantly different from zero at 10 per cent.

Table A3.5 *Significance tests for differences in long-swing growth phases: the income estimate ('t' values in parenthesis)*

Results of regressing $g_{Y_t} = \alpha + d_1 Z_1 + d_2 Z_2 + u_t$
$u_t = \rho_1 u_{t-1} + \rho_2 u_{t-2} + \varepsilon_t$
$\varepsilon_t \sim N(0, \sigma_t^2)$, $Z = (0, 1)$

t	$Z_1 = 1$ for	$Z_2 = 1$ for	$\hat{\alpha}$	$\hat{\rho}_1$	$\hat{\rho}_2$	$\hat{d}_1$	$\hat{d}_2$
1856–1899	1856–1865	1873–1882	0.026664 (5.39)	0.21192 (1.42)	-0.19137 $-(1.28)$	-0.008675 $-(0.90)$	-0.012364 $-(1.27)^a$
1865–1913	1873–1882	1899–1913	0.026974 (5.68)	0.20965 (1.54)	-0.33038 $-(2.43)$	-0.013719 $-(1.45)^a$	-0.15607 $-(1.96)^b$

^{a} Significant at 10 per cent (one-tailed test).
^{b} Significant at near 5 per cent (one-tailed test).

Table A3.6 *Significance tests for differences in long-swing phases: the expenditure estimate ('t' values in parenthesis)*

Results of regressing $g_{Y_t} = \alpha + dZ + u_t$
$u_t = \rho_1 u_{t-1} + \rho_2 u_{t-2} + \varepsilon_t$ or $u_t = \rho_1 u_{t-1} + \varepsilon$
$\varepsilon_t \sim N(0, \sigma_t^2)$, $Z = (0, 1)$

t	$Z = 1$ for	$\hat{\alpha}$	$\hat{\rho}_1$	$\hat{\rho}_2$	$\hat{d}$
1874–1891	1874–1883	0.016625 $(2.63)^a$	-0.35908 $-(1.59)^b$		0.002116 (0.24)
1874–1899	1891–1899	0.016835 $(4.30)^a$	-0.32526 $-(1.69)^b$	-0.27506 $-(1.43)$	0.011058 $(1.53)^b$
1891–1913	1899–1913	0.028284 $(4.74)^a$	-0.38205 $-(1.86)^b$	-0.25872 $-(1.26)$	-0.015042 $-(1.99)^a$

^{a} Significant at 5 per cent (two-tailed test).
^{b} Significant at 10 per cent (two-tailed test).

Table A3.7 *Significance tests for differences in long-wave and long-swing phases in French commodity production* ('t' *values in parenthesis*)

Results of regressing $g_{Y_t} = \alpha + dZ_t + \varepsilon_t$, $\varepsilon_t \sim N(0, \sigma_\varepsilon^2)$
$$g_{Y_t} = \alpha + dZ_t + u_t, \ u_t = \rho u_{t-1} + \varepsilon_t$$

(1)	(2)	(3)	(4)	(5)
t	$\hat{\alpha}$	$\hat{d}$	$\hat{\rho}_1$	$Z = 1$ for
Long waves				
1850–1892	0.016446	− 0.010207		1875–1892
	$(1.86)^a$	− (0.73)		
1875–1912	0.007191	0.009600	0.23031	1892–1912
	(0.71)	(0.70)	(1.44)	
Long swings				
1875–1912	0.02045	− 0.01968		1882–1892
	$(2.66)^b$	− $(1.51)^a$		
1875–1912	0.02045	− 0.01374		1899–1907
	$(2.66)^b$	− (1.0)		

[a] Significant at 10 per cent (one-tailed test).
[b] Significant at 5 per cent.

Table A3.8 *Significance tests for a long-wave phasing of German NDP, 1850–1913* ('t' *values in parenthesis*)

Results of regressing $g_{Y_t} = \alpha + dZ_t + \varepsilon_t$, $\varepsilon_t \sim N(0, \sigma_\varepsilon^2)$

(1)	(2)	(3)	(4)
t	$\hat{\alpha}$	$\hat{d}$	$Z = 1$ for
1857–1913	0.029131	− 0.016436	1874–1884
	$(8.82)^a$	− $(2.09)^a$	
1874–1913	0.030661	− 0.017966	1874–1884
	$(9.47)^a$	− $(2.81)^a$	
1874–1913	0.031282	− 0.01274	1874–1890
	$(8.29)^a$	− $(2.16)^a$	

[a] Significant at 5 per cent.

Table A3.9 *Significance tests for US long-wave phases: Maddison's US GDP, 1870–1913* ('t' values in parenthesis)

Results of regressing $g_{Y_t} = \alpha + dZ_t + \varepsilon_t,\ \varepsilon_t \sim N(0, \sigma_\varepsilon^2)$
or $\qquad\qquad g_{Y_t} = \alpha + dZ_t + u_t,\ u_t = \rho_{1-1} + \varepsilon_t$
or $\qquad\qquad g_{Y_t} = \alpha + dZ_t + u_t',\ u_t' = \rho_1 u_{t-1}' + \rho_2 u_{t-2}' + \varepsilon_t$

(1) t	(2) $\hat{\alpha}$	(3) $\hat{d}$	(4) $\hat{\rho}_1$	(5) $\hat{\rho}_2$	(6) $Z=1$ for
1873–1906	0.041547 (5.83)[a]	0.0029987 (0.32)	− 0.37811 − (2.35)[a]		1873–1892
1884–1912	0.042677 (3.22)[a]	− 0.0048087 − (0.25)			1899–1912
1884–1912	0.042076 (5.91)[a]	− 0.00371034 − (0.35)	− 0.48015 − (2.62)[a]	− 0.23930 − (1.31)	1899–1912

[a] Significant at 5 per cent.

Table A3.10 *Significance tests for US long-swing phases: Maddison's US GDP, 1870–1913* ('t' values in parenthesis)

Results of regressing $g_{Y_t} = \alpha + dZ_t + \varepsilon_t,\ \varepsilon_t \sim N(0, \sigma_\varepsilon^2)$
or $\qquad\qquad g_{Y_t} = \alpha + dZ_t + u_t,\ u_t = \rho_1 u_{t-1} + \varepsilon_t$
or $\qquad\qquad g_{Y_t} = \alpha + dZ_t + u_t',\ u_t' = \rho_1 u_{t-1}' + \rho_2 u_{t-2}' + \varepsilon_t$

(1) t	(2) $\hat{\alpha}$	(3) $\hat{d}$	(4) $\hat{\rho}_1$	(5) $\hat{\rho}_2$	(6) $Z=1$ for
1873–1892	0.053343 (9.42)[a]	− 0.013046 − (1.75)[a]			1873–1884
1873–1913	0.05078 (6.93)[a]	− 0.01897 − (1.43)[a]	− 0.42196 − (2.91)[a]		1892–1899
1873–1913	0.05078 (6.93)[a]	− 0.02737 − (1.96)[a]	− 0.42196 − (2.91)[a]		1906–1913

[a] Significant at 5 per cent.

Table A3.11 *Significance tests for US long-swing phases: Romer's US GDP, 1870–1913* ('t' *values in parenthesis*)

Results of regressing $g_{Y_t} = \alpha + dZ_t + \varepsilon_t, \ \varepsilon_t \sim N(0, \sigma_\varepsilon^2)$
or $\qquad\qquad g_{Y_t} = \alpha + dZ_t + u_t', \ u_t' = \rho_1 u_{t-1}' + \rho_2 u_{t-2}' + \varepsilon_t$

(1) t	(2) $\hat{\alpha}$	(3) $\hat{d}$	(4) $\hat{\rho}_1$	(5) $\hat{\rho}_2$	(6) $Z=1$ for
1873–1913	0.054401 $(7.27)^a$	− 0.02384 $-(2.32)^a$			1882–1899
1873–1913	0.054401 $(7.27)^a$	− 0.02906 $-(2.19)^a$			1906–1913
1873–1899	0.05438 $(5.69)^a$	− 0.02382 $-(2.02)^a$			1882–1899
1882–1906	0.04775 $(4.54)^a$	− 0.01719 $-(1.38)^b$			1882–1899
1899–1913	0.04291 $(4.51)^a$	− 0.01549 $-(2.16)^a$	− 5537 $-(2.51)^a$	− 0.5629 $-(2.55)^a$	1906–1913

[a] Significant at 5 per cent.
[b] Significant at 10 per cent.

Table A3.12 *Significance tests for long waves in world industrial production c. 1850–1913* ('t' *values in parenthesis*)

Results of regressing $g_{Y_t} = \alpha + dZ_t + \varepsilon_t, \ \varepsilon_t \sim N(0, \sigma_\varepsilon^2)$
or $\qquad\qquad g_{Y_t} = \alpha + dZ_t + u_t', \ u_t' = \rho_1 u_{t-1}' + \rho_2 u_{t-2}' + \varepsilon_t$

(1) t	(2) $\hat{\alpha}$	(3) $\hat{d}$	(4) $\hat{\rho}_1$	(5) $\hat{\rho}_2$	(6) $Z=1$ for
1856–1892	0.033470 $(2.73)^a$	−0.0039452 $-(0.24)$			1872–1892
1856–1913	0.031540 $(5.64)^a$	+0.0094995 $(1.02)^b$	−0.11606 $-(0.91)$	−0.25724 $-(2.01)^a$	1892–1913
1856–1907	0.031514 $(5.69)^a$	+0.011921 $(1.20)^b$	−0.07846 $-(0.58)$	−0.25484 $-(1.88)^b$	1892–1907

[a] Significant at 5 per cent.
[b] Significant at 10 per cent.

Table A3.13 *Significance tests for differences in growth path employing Poirier's spline method: world industrial production, 1856–1913* ('t' *values in parenthesis*)

Results of estimating
$y_T = a_3 + b_3 X + c_3 X^2 + a_3^* Z + b_3^* ZX + c_3^* ZX^2 + \varepsilon$
Estimated subject to $b^* e_1 + c^* e_1 = 0$
$U_t = AR(2) + \varepsilon_t$
$\varepsilon_t \sim N(0, \sigma_\varepsilon^2), Z = (0, 1)$

$\hat{a}_3$	$\hat{b}_3$	$\hat{c}_3$	$\hat{b}_3^*$	$\hat{c}_3^*$
3.6398	0.0247	0.0002	0.0003	− 0.00001
$(60.3)^a$	$(4.81)^a$	$(1.70)^a$	(0.07)	− (0.07)

$Z = 1$ for 1892–1913, $R^2 = 0.99$.
[a] Significant at less than 5 per cent.

4

Price trends

Price movements, both absolute and relative, have received much attention in the long-wave literature. In this chapter my concern is with aggregate price variations; in Chapters 6, 7 and 8 I shall consider relative prices. There are a number of approaches to the Kondratieff price wave. At one extreme, price long waves are viewed as complementing real waves. (Bieshaar and Kleinknecht, 1984; Van Duijn, 1983). At the other extreme, price waves are recognised but are not seen to have any real implications (Friedman and Schwartz, 1982; Lewis, 1978; Van Ewijk, 1981). The failure to find a significant Kondratieff wave in output raises strong doubts as to the validity of the former view and the evidence for significant long-run growth variations raises strong doubts as to the validity of the latter idea. Only if price movements are caused purely by monetary variation, without any relative price changes, can one hold to the dichotomy between economic growth trends and price trends. What I wish to do here is to relate price trends to output trends in a consistent historical framework, allowing for both real and monetary influences on prices.

Theoretical aspects

To understand the causes and effects of price variation requires a generalised economic framework (Lange, 1944b). The following are some of the important aspects that need to be considered:
 (i) The market structure needs to be specified. Different relationships are expected to hold under perfect competition, oligopoly and monopoly (Sylos–Labini, 1962).
 (ii) The degree of full employment needs to be considered. A full employment framework immediately rules out many of the aggregate demand effects of price variations.
 (iii) The nature of the monetary system deserves careful consideration. If the money supply (M) and velocity (V) are both inflexible then an exogenous

variation in M or V can affect prices. At the other extreme of assuming an endogenous money supply, real explanations have to be sought for price changes.

To assume an endogenous money supply and the absence of aggregate demand problems means that price variations are entirely dependent on the market structure. In a competitive market structure the fall in the costs of production due to technical progress sooner or later results in a lowering of prices of production via the mechanism of entry (Schumpeter, 1939, Ch. 4). Excess profits are only made during a transition period as new firms enter the market. Similarly, in this framework any variations in production due to the forces of nature (e.g. the harvest) will affect prices and, depending upon weights, the price level.

Under monopoly the reduction in costs may have no effect at all on prices, unless the monopolist who introduces the technical process finds it profitable to alter the volume of output; this being dependent on the elasticity of demand.

Under oligopoly Sylos-Labini (1962) has shown that price reduction follows only from those cost reductions that are due to innovations accessible to firms of all sizes and/or to a fall in variable factor prices. Cost reductions due to new methods, which because of technical discontinuities are not within the reach of enough (big) firms to create competition, lead not to price reductions but to increased profits. Trade union pressure or government intervention may cause cost reductions to be translated into higher wages also. In this situation nominal income increases with real income.

Specifying when a certain market structure was operative, or the particular mix of market structures, is a difficult task. However, there are a number of general considerations that eliminate some possibilities. Free trade in the international economy prevents monopoly from arising. For much of the nineteenth century, cost reducing innovation resulted in raw material cost reductions which, either under perfect competition or oligopoly, would result in price falls. Since raw materials formed a high proportion of the costs of production for nineteenth-century economies, it can be postulated that there existed a direct relationship between costs and prices.

During the twentieth century the concentration of firms has resulted in an oligopolistic structure in the product market. An increased oligopolistic structure of labour markets has also taken place. The greater capital intensity of production processes and the falling share of raw materials in the overall costs of production has resulted in an inverse (or non-responsive) relationship between prices and costs when costs fall, and a positive relationship when costs increase. The interwar protectionist atmosphere reinforced these tendencies. The openness of the world economy in the postwar created a more competitive atmosphere in the product market, but it had little effect on the labour market, where international competition is limited.

Such arguments imply that a direct relationship between costs and prices should be observed for the nineteenth century, while the oligopolistic tendencies of the twentieth century have given rise to a changed price–cost structure, with an inflationary bias. Hence, the paradox of the postwar being one of the fastest technological progress eras and yet the one with the highest price level, and inflation rate, can be resolved.

How do changes in the price level affect the level of aggregate demand? In Keynes (1936) a price level fall will increase the real value of money. Thus, the transactions demand for cash would be smaller and the excess stock of cash would bid up the prices of interest-bearing securities and lower the rate of interest. At lower interest rates real investment would be higher; thus, aggregate demand, further boosted by the multiplier, would expand output and employment. Assuming a phase of falling prices, the Keynes effect would yield the result that income levels increase. The Keynes effect will be operative in the long run only if the analysis can be undertaken in terms of discrete price level changes. Once a continuous phase of deflation or inflation is postulated price expectations become important and the result is inconclusive (Tobin, 1975).

Pigou (1943) generalised the Keynes effect by making consumption a function of wealth which, in turn, depends on real money balances. Fisher (1933) took an entirely different approach to the problem. Since a price-level fall imposes a burden on debtors, corporations, proprietors, home owners and farmers, the effect on the economy is adverse. This conclusion is justified only if the spending propensities are assumed to be greater for debtors. The spending propensities are not distributed randomly between debtors and creditors; debtors should have a higher marginal propensity to spend, since they borrowed for the specific purpose of spending. It should be noted that Pigou was talking about the 'Classical Stationary State' while Fisher was analysing the immediate effects of depression. Hence, the Fisher effect seems to be more relevant for understanding actual historical downswings.

An important defect in all these approaches is a failure to discuss the role of expectations. In a long phase of deflation or inflation, expectations will become important in any rational decision making. The direction of intertemporal substitution depends on whether a change in the current price of a good (or price level) over the discounted expected price change (or price level) is more than, exactly, or less than proportional – i.e. on whether the elasticity of expectation of the discounted price (ε_p) is $\gtreqless 1$. If the price of all goods falls (all except interest in a general equilibrium framework), and all fall in the same proportion, to prevent any intratemporal substitutions, the following results are obtained depending on the elasticity of price expectations:

(i) If $\varepsilon_p = 1$ intertemporal substitution is absent. The demand for cash balances falls in exact proportion to prices – the current demand for real cash balances is thus constant. Static expectations are a special case of unit elastic expectations.

(ii) If $\varepsilon_p < 1$ a shift in planned purchases from the future to the present and a shift of planned sales from the present to the future takes place. Hence the demand for cash balances diminishes more than in proportion to the fall in prices – i.e. the real demand for cash balances falls.

(iii) If $\varepsilon_p > 1$ there is a shift of planned purchases from the present to the future and a shift of planned sales from the future to the present – i.e. the real demand for cash balances increases.

Given that elasticities vary across commodities, in an aggregate analysis Lange's (1944) concept of ε_p being *prevailingly* inelastic and prevailingly elastic is useful. If the assumption of a constant price change for all commodities does not hold, the analysis needs to allow for both intratemporal and intertemporal substitutions.

Clearly, price trends will have important real effects. What is required from an empirical analysis is to determine the nature of the price phases. Critically, are they continuous long waves of inflation and deflation or are they best analysed as discrete price-level changes? If price phases are continuous, the role of price expectations needs to be discussed.[1]

In order to emphasize the importance of the monetary system, assume that the money supply is exogenous and velocity is inflexible within a full-employment growth path. Given these assumptions, only in the chance event of $\Delta \log M = \Delta \log Y$ will the money supply not impose any bounds for price variations. In any other situation the relationship between the growth of the money supply and prices is a direct one:

$$\Delta \log M \gtrless \Delta \log Y \Rightarrow \Delta \log P \gtrless 0$$

where, M = money supply, Y = monetary income and P = price level.

Assuming an exogenous M and an inflexible V are obviously very extreme assumptions. The monetary institutions have undergone greatest change during phases of rapid growth when finance was most needed. In the 1850s and 1860s Europe saw the creation of many credit institutions to finance industrialisation (Cameron, 1961). Similar changes were occurring in the 1950s and 1960s to finance the vast investment undertakings and the rapid growth of international trade (Dupriez, 1978). While the debates as to the exogeneity of the money supply are at a very confused stage of development, it is clear that over the very long run there can be no doubt that the money supply is not perfectly exogenous. This would be true even under a gold standard, since trends in the price level affect the profitability of gold mining.

The aim of the present section has been to show that postulating the existence of price waves is tantamount to an internal contradiction for all but the pure monetarist models. Price and output variations need to be studied in a general framework: if price long waves exist, it is highly likely that they will have real influences on the economy. Given the earlier rejection of production long waves, this chapter provides further evidence on the issue of existence.

Empirical aspects

The focus of this section is on the question of the existence of price long waves. The British wholesale price index is presented in Figure 4.1. Kondratieff price waves are observed only after 1873. What stands out from Figure 4.1 are the following phases:

  1800–1813 War inflation
  1813–1822 Deflation
  1822–1848 Low price level
  1848–1857 Inflation
  1857–1873 High price level
  1873–1897 Deflation
  1897–1920 Inflation
  1920–1933 Deflation
  1933–1973 Inflation

Although the trends for other countries differ, in general, the differences were not large. International competition worked to equalize price movements. This is less true for the pre- than the post-1850 period. In addition, the weighting of commodities is not uniform in the various series. Thus, small differences in wholesale price trends should not be emphasised.

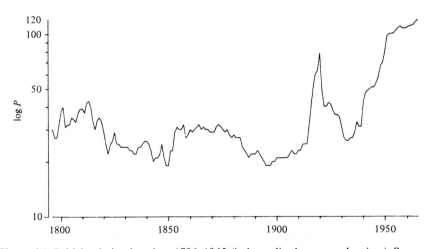

Figure 4.1 British wholesale prices 1796–1965 (index spliced at several points). Source: Mitchell (1981, pp. 771–6)

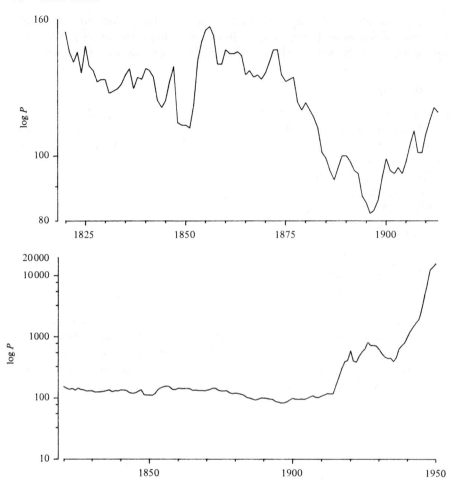

Figure 4.2 (a) French wholesale prices 1820–1913 (1901–1910 = 100); (b) French wholesale prices 1820–1950 (1901–1910 = 100). Source: Mitchell (1981, pp. 771–6)

French wholesale prices are presented in Figure 4.2. The significant differences in relation to the British trends are:
(a) the post-Napoleonic war deflation lasted until 1831;
(b) the war-revolution era of *c*. 1848 resulted in a rapid price level fall that was
    maintained until 1851;
(c) the First World War inflation continued until 1926; and
(d) the deflation after 1929 was far more severe, and continued until 1935.
   German wholesale prices (see Figure 4.3) followed a similar path to the
British with a few exceptions:

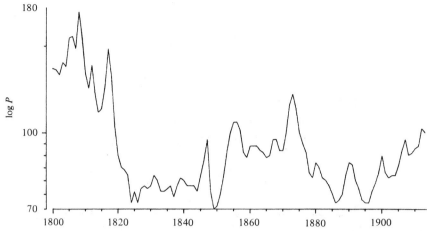

Figure 4.3 German wholesale prices 1800–1913 (1913 = 100). Source: Mitchell (1981, pp. 771–6)

(a) the trough-to-trough cycle in the late 1840s was more marked in Germany;
(b) the years 1871–4 were a period of marked inflation, explicable in terms of the Franco-Prussian war and reparation payments to Germany;
(c) the downswing in prices from 1873 was limited to the period 1873–86.

American wholesale prices (see Figure 4.4) followed a similar path to the European trends over 1800–50 and the post-1873 era. The Civil War generated major differences for the 1850–73 period. The inflation of 1850–7 accelerated during 1862–4 as the price level reached unprecedented magnitudes. The post-bellum readjustments resulted in rapid deflation during 1864–73.

The British and German aggregate gross domestic product (GDP) deflators are presented in Figures 4.5 and 4.6. The movement of these series is significantly different from wholesale prices. In the British case the post-1873 deflation was restricted to the 1873–82 cycle. Similarly, the German deflator captures marked deflation over the cycle of 1874–82 but a constant price level from 1882 to 1900 (see Appendix Table A4.1).

This overview suggests that although the price level has been displaced on many occasions, prices have not followed a Kondratieff long wave. This conclusion conforms with the work of Beenstock (1983, pp. 137–47) who analysed Kondratieff's original price data using spectral analysis and found no evidence of a significant long wave. Van Ewijk (1981, p. 494) found 'a weak but stable indication of a Kondratieff Cycle' for wholesale prices during 1790–1930. The evidence presented here suggests that this result is dominated by the 1873–1930 era. In the pre-1913 era most of the aggregate price adjustment took place over short periods. The Napoleonic wars clearly represented a long-run shock to the price level. However, the post-war deflation was short-

Figure 4.4 (a) US wholesale prices 1800–1914 (1910–1914 = 100); (b) US wholesale prices 1914–1950 (1947–1949 = 100). Source: US Department of Commerce, *Long Term Economic Growth* (1978, pp. 222–3)

lived, lasting until the early 1820s. During the period 1822–48 the British price level settled on a constant low level; a trend is statistically insignificant (see Appendix Table A4.1). The German price level was, in fact, rising on trend during the same period. The French price level was constant during the period 1831–48. The inflation of the 1850s was even more short lived, lasting over the period 1850–7. The British price level was constant during the period 1857–73; the German was constant during the period 1857–71; and the French was actually falling during the period 1856–71. Similar observations apply to the

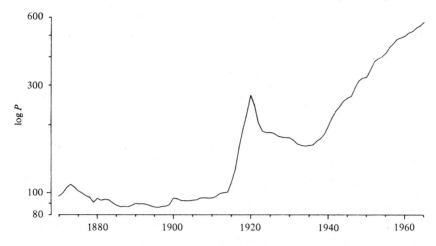

Figure 4.5 Implicit GDP deflator for UK 1870–1965 (1913 = 100). Source: Feinstein (1976, Table 61, T 132–3)

late nineteenth century. The deflation of the late nineteenth century was limited to the tradable sector. Both the British and German GDP deflators suggest that the deflation was limited to the 1873–82 cycle; during the cycles of the 1880s and 1890s the price level settled on a low plateau (see Appendix Table A4.1). The inflation of the Edwardian era was the longest peacetime inflation since the Napoleonic Wars. The deflation of 1920–33 was partly policy induced, as countries strove to return to the prewar gold standard in the

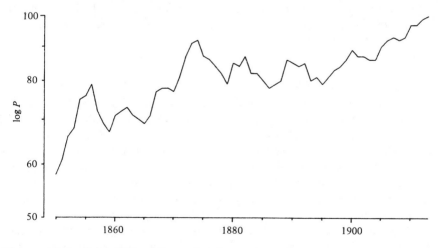

Figure 4.6 Implicit GDP deflator for Germany 1850–1913 (1913 = 100). Source: Mitchell (1981, pp. 817 and 821)

1920s, and partly the result of the world depression during the period 1929–33. The inflation of the late 1930s and 1940s was mainly accelerating war inflation. The rate of inflation moderated significantly in the 1950s and early 1960s. Allowing for the inflationary bias of the twentieth century and the flexibility created by the abandonment of the gold standard, the constant and moderate inflationary path of the 1950s and 1960s could be seen as stable in the growth rate of the price variable.

Thus, the whole of price history during the nineteenth and twentieth centuries can be conceptualised as a series of shocks followed by long eras of price stability. The structure of price adjustment has also changed over the long period comparisons of the nineteenth and twentieth centuries. In the nineteenth century the aggregate price variable can best be seen as having followed a series of 'square waves' in the price level, with short adjustment phases placed between price plateaux. In the twentieth century, apart from shocks, there also exists an inflationary bias pushing up the price level.

Such evidence suggests that for most of the nineteenth and twentieth centuries, expectations have not been destabilizing over long periods. During the nineteenth century the underlying expectational pattern sustained a constant price level for much of the time. During the peacetime inflations of the Edwardian era and the 1950s and 1960s most of the price adjustment took place with unit elastic price expectations.

Explanations for price phases

Having argued the case for shocked price phases as against a long-wave interpretation I will now proceed to justify this perspective by explaining the shocks of the post-1850 era as unique historical events, examining both monetary and real explanations.

The inflation of 1850–1856

Given that the phase was so short a real explanation is to be found within variations in aggregate demand rather than aggregate supply. The pre-1850 data needed to test this idea are subject to a wide margin of error. The British data, which are probably the best, suggest that although the growth rate of the 1845–56 cycle was higher than the growth rate for 1856–73 it was comparable to that of 1825–45 (Crafts, 1983; Harley, 1982; Williamson, 1984). During the early 1850s world industrial production grew on a comparable path to the cycle of 1866–72 (see Chapter 3). Thus, the idea that this inflation was the result of an aggregate demand shock is not supported by the evidence. Moreover, it should be noted that, even if the data was compatible with an output shock, an asymmetry in how this argument operates needs to be accepted. Since the shocked variable adjusted to some normal level, it cannot explain why the price level was sustained at a high plateau for the era 1856–73; only inflexibilities in returning to the old price level could be compatible with this argument.

A strict monetary explanation of such phases would postulate that output is determined independently of the price level, which, in turn, is determined by the money stock of the economy. Data for money stock in this period are limited. World gold production increased on a steady path from 1820–48 (Vilar, 1976, pp. 351–2). The rate of growth increased significantly during the period 1848–53, while during the period 1853–72 gold production was maintained on the level of that of 1852–53.[2] Thus, the world gold stock movements are compatible with explaining the price changes of the early 1850s. The British money stock series further vindicates the idea of a monetary shock in the early 1850s. Collins (1983) calculates the following rate of growth of money stock:

1846/50 – 1856/60   4.8 per cent per annum
1856/60 – 1866/70   3.7 per cent per annum.

The rate of growth of money stock was much higher in the inflationary era than in the plateau phase. However, since income velocity fell from 3.4 in the first period to 2.8 in the second, a *pure* monetary shock is not supported by the evidence.

Rostow (1980, p. 209) uses the fact that prices increased rapidly only over the period 1850–6 to argue against a monetary explanation of this phase. However, the monetary trends adjusted significantly after 1856 which fits the pattern of prices observed. Rostow tries to explain the inflation purely in terms of real variables – the diversion of manpower and resources to gold mining; the rapid increase in the price of food and raw materials during the period 1852–4; the significant military outlays in the Crimean War and the Indian Mutiny.[3] In this framework monetary growth was accommodating real phenomena. However, it is clear that many of the real aspects mentioned by Rostow are related to gold mining as a production activity. The cause for the inflation comes back to the basic fact that a shock occurred to the potential gold stock supplies after 1848. The Rostow perspective has emphasised many aspects missed out by the monetary arguments; however, the fact remains that the monetary variable is also important to the adjustments of the 1850–6 period.[4]

The deflation of 1873–1882

Chapter 3 argued that the 1873–82 cycle represented a depressed long-swing phase in Britain, Germany, America and the world economy. However, this phase was not exceptionally depressed relative to other slow-growing phases; the exceptional severity of the German depression was seen to be an artefact. Thus, the severity of the deflation is difficult to understand purely in terms of a real shock. The deflation is even more interesting given that the terms of trade were moving against Britain and industrial Europe during the period 1873–81 (Kindleberger, 1956), thus placing a potentially inflationary pressure on these economies.

The monetary influences on the deflation seem important. The world stock of gold grew at a lower rate during the period 1873–83. Assuming a relationship between gold and money supply, which under the gold standard is more likely, there may have been monetary pressures on prices in the 1870s. The reduced rate of growth of world gold stock was also associated with an increased demand for gold as both Germany and the Latin Monetary Union[5] changed from silver to gold in the early 1870s.

The various money stock series for Britain throw some light on these debates. A number of money stock series exist. The Collins (1983) series shows the following rate of growth:

1856/60 – 1866/70   3.7 per cent per annum
1866/70 – 1877/80   3.0 per cent per annum

The Friedman and Schwartz (1982) and Bordo (1981) series both show a very low rate of growth for money stock in the 1873–82 cycle relative to the 1880s and 1890s (see Chapter 7).

Thus, the monetary variable was important in accounting for the deflation of the 1870s. However, the severity of the deflation was probably due to a combination of a monetary and output shock, as vindicated by the variations in income velocity during the 1870s (Collins, 1983). The fact that the 1870s were a long-swing depression made the monetary shock even more deflationary.

Rostow's explanation of the 1870s deflation purely in terms of real variables is clearly inadequate. Rostow emphasises the move towards short gestation (home investment) after 1873. However, the long gestation (overseas investment) increased after 1877 and yet prices continued to fall. Similarly in the 1890s investment flows were towards the domestic economy but prices did not follow the expected Rostow path. What is perhaps even more critical is that Rostow cannot explain trends in the international economy since many of the effects he talks of cancel out in a world perspective. It has already been noted that the behaviour of tradable prices was very different from aggregate prices during the period 1873–99. Thus, the explanation for price trends in the tradable sector is different from aggregate movements. Lewis (1978) has provided an explanation of such price variations in terms of output variations in important tradable commodities and shipping costs.

The Edwardian inflation

This inflation is common to all the economies under consideration. However, the output evidence described in Chapter 3 illustrates a variety of national experiences. Both Britain and Germany underwent a productivity retardation; France moved to a higher productivity growth path but only after a large fall in growth during the period 1899–1907; and the American long-run growth rate was little changed. Given that the inflation was an international phenomenon, such a diversity of national growth experiences suggests that the emphasis should be placed on international trends. In fact, as was outlined in Chapter 3, world industrial production and world GDP grew on a higher path during the period 1890–1913 relative to that of 1856–90. Moreover, the period saw a falling off in the rate of growth of the supply of primary products (Lewis, 1978). Such a pattern of international growth helps to explain the adverse terms of trade faced by Britain and other industrial economies during this period. The adverse terms of trade for industrial economies also resulted in much long-gestation investment abroad, although, as noted above, the impact of this should not be overemphasised. In addition there was an increase of military expenditure by the major powers and a number of minor wars were fought, apart from the Boer war. The inflationary pressure may have also been sustained by wage–price adjustments as unions were becoming stronger and more generalised in this period (Lewis, 1980a).

Monetary variations were also important during the period. Between 1890 and 1913 Kitchin's (1930) calculations show the amount of the world monetary gold stock increasing at a rate of 3.47 per cent per annum (after deducting from total production for industrial uses and flows to India, China and Egypt). Although the relationship between the gold stock and money stock was becoming looser, the money-stock evidence for Britain and America does suggest that the rate of growth of money stock was significantly higher between 1890 and 1913 relative to the period 1873–90 (see Chapter 7). However, the evidence for a *pure* monetary explanation of the Edwardian inflation is weak. The structural changes in the international economy, resulting in adverse terms of trade for industrial economies, has already been noted. Moreover, while inflation was fairly constant in the 1899–1913 era the rate of growth of money stock fell markedly during the period 1899–1907 and rose significantly during the period 1907–13. The real money balance trends also suggest that price adjustment was not caused within a *pure* monetary framework. Real money balances grew on a lower path during the period 1899–1913 in both Britain and America. This suggests that price adjustment was influenced by real changes in the international economy outside the quantity theory explanation.

The nineteenth-century price plateaux

It has been argued above that the aggregate price level was unchanged for the trend periods 1822–48, 1857–73 and 1882–1900. It is the shocked adjustment periods that may give rise to the impression of long waves. Such a 'square wave' pattern of price adjustment implies a need to explain the plateaux, not just the shocked periods.

One explanation for the plateaux is that a basic mode of price determination seems to survive throughout the nineteenth century. Shocks may displace the price level and the new price level will be maintained as long as the shock is maintained. Even if the shock is temporary the new price level may be sustained by inflexibilities in the price system. The process of shock and adjustment did not lead to Wicksellian cumulative price changes because the periods were too short for elastic price expectations to be established. Static expectations seem to dominate in the long run.

Shocks were important in displacing a given price level, and their absence was important in maintaining a given price level. Nevertheless, the absence of a major shock can only be seen as a necessary condition for price stability. For sufficient conditions, further requirements were needed. For example, during the period 1856–73 aggregate price stability in Britain was associated with large inter-sectoral variation of prices. The Sauerbeck food price index shows food prices falling by 2 per cent per annum during the period 1857–65 and rising by 2 per cent per annum during the period 1865–73 (Mitchell and Deane, 1962, pp. 474–5). The price of British manufactures, as proxied by export prices, rose by 3 per cent per annum in the first period and fell by 1 per cent per annum in the second. Given that there existed enough monetary flexibility to suggest that these sectoral price inversities were not caused by an aggregate monetary constraint, a realistic explanation for the constancy of aggregate prices during the period 1856–73 is simply the existence of a series of random shocks. The random shocks were the American Civil War, which accounted for the variation of British manufacturing prices, and climatic changes, which help account for the performance of the agricultural sector (see Chapter 6). In these circumstances the inverse sectoral price expectations gave rise to aggregate static expectations. Such a perspective also helps us to understand the relationship between productivity and prices. Although the productivity–price relationship is weak in the aggregate, it is far stronger on a sectoral basis as would be expected within a competitive market structure.

The 1920–1933 deflation

With the exception of France and Germany the 1920s and early 1930s were periods of generalised deflation. The earlier observations on the nineteenth century do not suggest that the deflation of this era was part of a long wave. Moreover, the pattern of price adjustment during the period 1920–33 fits in well with the shock pattern observed during the nineteenth century. In both Britain and America most of the deflation of the 1920s was concentrated in the few years between the periods 1920–3 and 1929–33. In addition, far from being part of an underlying long wave pattern of economic development, much of the deflation of the 1920s was policy induced, as the price level became incompatible with the monetary system in existence.

The deflation of the early 1920s was directly linked to the war inflation. During the period 1918–20 the inflation had reached unprecedented magnitudes. The bad harvests of 1918 and 1919 made the situation worse and added to the shortage of raw materials needed for reconstructing Europe. Thus, many of the factors sustaining the inflation were temporary and the turnaround of prices can be partly understood in such terms. Monetary pressures also played a role in the downturn of prices after 1920. A fear of gold losses by America resulted in high interest rates in 1920 and these remained high (Pilgrim, 1974). During the period 1920–1 the Bank of England also sustained high interest rates.

The deflation of the 1920s is not associated with depressed output conditions in the world economy. As was noted in Chapter 3, the 1920s were a high-growth phase for America and the world economy and a low-growth phase in Britain and Germany. Nevertheless the deflation was observed simultaneously in high-growing and slow-growing economies. Such evidence suggests that policy variables were critical to understanding the deflation of the 1920s. The aim of returning to the gold standard at the prewar parity imposed policy induced deflation on both the British and American price levels, which explains why most of the deflation of the 1920s occurred during the period 1920–4. The analogy with the post-Napoleonic war deflation is striking (Kindleberger, 1982). The inflexibilities of the price mechanism could have sustained the inflation of 1899–1920, as the many labour disputes of the 1920s illustrate; however, the downward adjustment of prices became a necessity for achieving the normalcy of the prewar gold standard.

The deflation of 1929–33 was part of a different process from that of the 1920s. The magnitude of the deflation was greater than that of 1923–9. The severity of this deflation varied across different countries. In the British economy the deflation of the GDP deflator was not much higher than the deflation observed during the period 1924–9. The collapse of German, American and French wholesale prices was far more severe, reflecting the larger output variation in these economies. The deflation was also linked to the degree of monetary collapse. In both America and Germany, where extensive bank failures acted to severely reduce the money stock, deflation was far greater than in Britain. However, the 1929–33 contraction in prices was far more than the result of monetary crisis. In particular, a two-phase schema for the depression seems to help explain the events. The 1929–30 collapse of prices and output was more of a real crisis than a monetary crisis. In America, from August 1929 to October 1930 the money stock declined by only 2.6 per cent.

Thus, real variations were far more important in accounting for the severe deflation during this period (Hicks, 1974; Kindleberger, 1973; Temin, 1976). However, after 1930 financial crises led to a collapse of the money stock and a very severe deflation. Nevertheless, even during the period 1930–3 the monetary contraction was not an autonomous event but formed part of the cyclical path of the economy (Minsky, 1964, 1982). Real problems were at the heart of the German and American banking crises (James, 1984); the problems of primary producers figured centrally in American banking failures and structural problems of the German economy in the 1920s were the underlying causes of the German banking crisis in 1931.

The 1933–1973 inflation

This long era of inflation can be broken up into a number of separate phases. The recovery of prices during the period 1933–7 represented a trade cycle recovery. During the period 1937–48 the inflation rate accelerated due to the effects of war. The inflation rate moderated in the 1950s and early 1960s, after which it began accelerating again. This inflationary era was of unprecedented length; the previous longest peacetime inflation occurred during the period 1899–1913.

The postwar inflation contrasts markedly with the interwar deflation; hence, war cannot provide the explanation for either era. The explanation for the postwar inflation can be found in the inflationary bias noted earlier. The inflationary bias was allowed to manifest itself after the Second World War because of the greater flexibility in the international monetary order. In contrast, after the First World War the policy of deflation was imposed by the policy of returning to the gold standard.

Despite the existence of potentially deflationary effects during the postwar period the underlying trend was towards inflation. The productivity growth path of this era was historically unprecedented, which suggests that a more oligopolistic relationship between prices and costs was operative. The trend of the terms of trade between primary products and manufactures moved consistently in favour of manufactures throughout the 1950s and 1960s (Spraos, 1980). In order eras this would have acted to generate deflationary pressures on the economy. A significant difference between this and other eras is the increasing weight of industry in total world production. Thus, the weight of oligopolistic sectors has increased significantly in recent times, neutralising some of the deflationary terms-of-trade effects.

Another aspect of the inflationary bias in the postwar is that wages tend to move in line with the cost of living, giving rise to a wage–cost spiral. This was clearly not the case before the postwar era (Lewis, 1980a). Such a changed relationship illustrates the importance of the favourable productivity increases and the favourable terms of trade in maintaining a stable inflationary path in the pre-1970 period. As the cost of living increased after 1973 and productivity growth fell, an inflationary spiral was inevitable within the postwar price structure. This relationship between costs, prices and wages accounts for the variations of the inflation rate within the postwar period. Lewis (1980a, p. 426) calculated the following variations in the inflation rate:

1950–1958	5.0 per cent
1958–1966	2.8 per cent
1966–1973	7.6 per cent

The rapid inflation rate during the period 1950–8 is partly explained by the upswing in commodity prices, resulting from the Korean War. Commodity prices rose and wages followed. As commodity prices fell during the period 1958–66, wage growth also fell as did the aggregate inflation rate. The effects of the Vietnam war, the 1972 commodity price increases and the 1973 oil price shock added further inflationary pressures on the price level.

Conclusions

The Kondratieff long wave is not relevant for understanding price trends. However, there exists significant long-term price variation which can only be understood by relating the evidence on Kuznets swings, the G-wave, monetary variations, wars, policies and structural change in the price–cost–productivity relationship. In the nineteenth century, phases of aggregate inflation and deflation were short; the price plateaux of 1856–73 and 1882–1900 are striking. The only long-wave variations that can be identified are not waves of inflation and deflation but square waves in the price level. The wave pattern of wholesale prices during the period 1873–1913 is not part of a generalised long-wave process. A series of shocks added to generate a wave pattern in wholesale prices. The deflationary path during the period 1873–82 was induced by very different factors from those of 1882–90. The fall in prices in the first period was more rapid than the second and mainly reflected the general deflation of that era. The rapid fall of prices in the 1870s was not due to exceptionally rapid output growth of primary commodities. In fact, during the period 1873–82 the sectoral terms of trade moved in favour of primary commodities. In contrast, during the 1880s the rapid increases in the productivity of primary producing sectors and the shipping sector acted to depress wholesale prices.

One general conclusion seems to be that price variation in the long run is large and is the result of the inter-relatedness of various forces: real and monetary, aggregate and sectoral. The evidence presented in this chapter gives support to the econometric evidence of Hendry and Ericsson (1983) showing that the *pure* monetary explanation of price change is invalid. The search for any uniform explanation of price change is simply invalid.

Statistical appendix

Table A4.1 *Significance tests for the existence of a trend in price levels* ('t' *values in parenthesis*)

Results of regressing $P_t = \alpha + \beta \text{ TREND} + \varepsilon_t, \varepsilon_t \sim N(0, \sigma_\varepsilon^2)$
or $\qquad\qquad\quad P_t = \alpha + \beta \text{ TREND} + u_t, u_t = \rho_1 u_{t-1} + \varepsilon_t$
or $\qquad\qquad\quad P_t = \alpha + \beta \text{ TREND} + u_t', u_t' = \rho_1 u_{t-1}' + \rho_2 u_{t-2}' + \varepsilon_t$
$\qquad\qquad\quad$ (in long form)

(1) t	(2) $\hat{\alpha}$	(3) $\hat{\beta}$	(4) $\hat{\rho}_1$	(5) $\hat{\rho}_2$
(A) British wholesale prices				
1822–1848	3.3337	− 0.004377	0.43521	
	$(29.90)^a$	− (1.60)	$(2.51)^a$	
1857–1873	3.3043	+ 0.001429	0.46033	− 0.15058
	$(14.35)^a$	(0.43)	$(1.92)^b$	− (0.63)
1882–1900	4.4888	− 0.001449	0.73381	
	$(9.87)^a$	− $(3.07)^a$	$(4.71)^a$	
(B) British GDP deflator				
1882–1900	4.4908	+ 0.000164	0.83250	
	$(16.32)^a$	(0.06)	$(6.55)^a$	
(C) German wholesale prices				
1822–1848	4.2721	+ 0.002534	0.25186	− 0.38526
	$(93.82)^a$	$(2.05)^b$	(1.42)	− $(2.17)^b$
1857–1871	4.4643	+ 0.001119	0.31275	− 0.52316
	$(36.29)^a$	(0.59)	(1.42)	− $(2.38)^b$
1882–1900	4.0668	+ 0.003231	1.48858	− 0.91507
	$(15.44)^a$	(1.13)	$(16.09)^a$	− $(9.89)^a$
(D) German GNP deflator				
1857–1871	4.0472	+ 0.003888	1.0747	− 0.3943
	$(10.90)^a$	(0.72)	$(4.68)^a$	− (1.72)
1882–1900	4.2609	+ 0.001674	0.55206	
	$(18.27)^a$	(0.69)	$(2.89)^a$	
(E) French wholesale prices				
1831–1848	4.9763	− 0.00322	0.35682	− 0.43578
	$(54.73)^a$	− (1.44)	(1.68)	− $(2.05)^b$
1856–1873	5.2567	− 0.004882	0.84000	− 0.46906
	$(33.32)^a$	− $(2.03)^b$	$(4.04)^a$	− $(2.25)^a$

P_t = price index
[a] significant at 0.01 level.
[b] significant at 0.05 level.

5

Innovation clusters and Kondratieff waves

Chapter 3 examined the issue of the *existence* of Kondratieff waves. Such a pattern of growth was not observed for the period under consideration. This result raises serious doubts as to the validity of the recent long-wave literature that lays stress on the existence of regular long-wave clusters in innovation activity (Graham and Senge, 1980; Mensch, 1979; Van Duijn, 1981, 1983). Given the importance of technical change in accounting for output and productivity growth (Abramovitz, 1956; Solow, 1957), the evidence supporting innovation clusters would contradict the evidence of Chapter 3 and vice versa.

Some theoretical considerations

As was pointed out in Chapter 1, the role of innovation to explain Kondratieff waves was originally emphasised in the work of Schumpeter (1939). Many recent studies have made innovation the cause of a long-wave growth pattern by linking the concept of the product life cycle to the idea of an innovation cluster.[1] Mensch (1979) provides an influential restatement of many of these ideas. Mensch does not postulate a strict long-wave theory but sees economic growth as being characterised by a series of intermittent innovative impulses that take the form of S-shaped growth patterns. He calls this a *metamorphosis model*, depicting long periods of growth and relatively short intervals of turbulence. The analogy with product life-cycle sigmoid curves is clear.

Mensch makes a distinction between minor improvement innovations and what he calls basic innovations. He begins with the following working hypothesis of basic innovations:

A technological event is a technological basic innovation when the newly discovered material or newly developed technique is being put into regular production for the first time, or when an organised market for the new product is first created. (1979, p. 123)

Mensch sees economic development as occurring in one aggregate sigmoid. He argues that there is only limited interest in implementing basic innovation during a prosperous phase of growth – as demand saturates only minor improvements are introduced. In contrast, during a depression phase, when the old technologies have outlived their usefulness in generating growth, there is greater pressure and inducement for basic innovations. Moreover, the new innovation base of society starts a new growth spurt based on the life cycle of new products – innovations overcome depressions.

The introduction of the concept of the product life cycle to the debates of growth and innovation is clearly an important step. However, Mensch's ideas are no more than definitional arguments dependent on proving that regular clusters in basic innovations have been observed. Although the product life cycle is a sound concept, there is no logical reason in Mensch's framework as to why product life cycles should cluster in time. Moreover, even if product life cycles cluster at a point in time, there is no reason as to why the various life cycles should correspond at all points in time. Unsound macro conclusions have been drawn from a micro concept. Mensch also tries to rationalise an a priori framework to explain the clusters. However, his arguments operate within the circular framework of the metamorphosis model. Without assuming the metamorphosis model as a starting point, Mensch has not provided a deductive micro (or macro) economic framework as to why basic innovations should cluster in time.

The Kondratieff wave pattern of innovation specifies a *regular* cluster at approximately fifty- to sixty-year intervals. Since the data available cover only a few complete waves, we cannot talk of cycles of growth. Nevertheless, there remains the possibility of testing a weak Kondratieff wave hypothesis that episodic historical eras of the fifty- to sixty-year periodicity may have existed. As an alternative hypothesis I will specify a random innovation pattern. Random innovation clusters that are not related to a long-wave pattern may result from major shocks to the growth path or structural changes in the determinants of innovation.

Explaining innovation clusters in terms of major shocks to the economy has the advantage that the analytical framework falls in the rational tradition. The type of expectational patterns that give rise to *regular* innovational clusters verge on the irrational. Assuming the aim of a firm is to maintain a normal rate of profit, then it has an interest in innovating at all points in time. This statement can be justified in terms of 'Wolff's law', which argues for diminishing marginal returns to technology.[2] Assuming that the growth path over the long wave is influenced by the technological path of an economy – i.e. diminishing returns to basic innovations are observed over the upswing – old firms would be irrational not to introduce new basic innovation the moment they sense diminishing returns. New firms could also take up innovative opportunities. Waiting for a major depression, as entrepreneurs are supposed to do in Mensch's framework, does not have rational foundations.[3] Of course non-market considerations may be important in preventing a continuous innovative flow. To explain long waves in this framework requires a modelling of such non-market pressures. Assuming a constant flow of basic and minor inventive activity, then the potential for a linear innovative path exists.[4] The question under consideration is empirical and I shall proceed with a discussion of the existence of innovation clusters.

Empirical considerations on innovation clusters

The starting point in this discussion is the influential empirical work of Mensch (1979, Ch. 4). From a list of 127 basic innovations between 1740 and 1955 Mensch postulated that basic innovations have clustered during long-wave depression phases. The major depressions are taken from Kuznets' periodisation of long waves (Kuznets, 1930, 1940). Thus, Mensch postulates basic innovation clusters in the following periods:

(i) 1813–27;
(ii) 1871–85; and
(iii) 1926–38.

In fact, from Figure 5.1 there is a prima-facie case for the existence of clusters within these phases. From this phasing Mensch tries to verify significance by considering whether the pattern of innovations in the sample could have been generated by a random process. He answers this by undertaking non-parametric runs tests based on 1,2,3,..., 10 year classifications. He finds

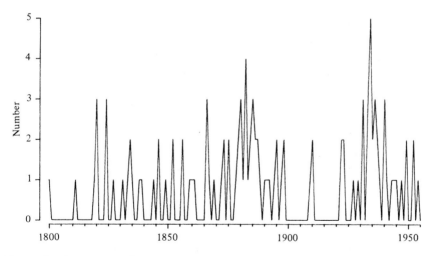

Figure 5.1 Frequency of total basic innovations 1800–1955 (innovations/annum).
Source: Mensch (1979, Tables 4-1, 4-2, 4-3 and 4-4)

that irrespective of the periodisation scheme, the likelihood that the observed discontinuities are simply the work of a random process is well under 5 per cent, fluctuating around 2.5 per cent. Thus, the null postulating randomness is rejected and Mensch concludes:

> The consistent pattern of ups and downs in the innovative stream must therefore be treated as an assured empirical fact. (1979, p. 134)

It is this 'assured empirical fact' that I wish to question.

Much work has already been undertaken along these lines. Freeman *et al.* (1982, pp. 57–64) have provided extensive evidence to criticise Mensch's sampling methods for the twentieth century. I shall extend this criticism by examining the cluster evidence for both the nineteenth and twentieth centuries. Moreover, it should be noted that the empirical conclusions of Freeman *et al.* are based on 200 radical innovations for the UK in the period 1920–80. As will be argued below, given the dominance of America in the world innovation process, conclusions based purely on British data may be misleading. Thus, I shall examine the wider international innovation samples developed by Van Duijn (1981, 1983). Van Duijn's own examination of the Mensch idea rejects the depression cluster framework. Nevertheless, he does not reject the long wave-framework:

> For the long wave periods the null of chance variations in the number of innovations can be rejected at the one per cent level. (1983, pp. 181–2)

Similarly the series of 200 radical innovations developed by Freeman *et al.* (1982) points to a more random distribution of innovations over time. However, Freeman *et al.* still hold to a long-wave framework with the diffusion of innovation being the underlying driving force. The 'New Technology Systems' resulting from the interrelatedness of families of innovations *cause* Kondratieff waves. In this section I question the Mensch conclusions and proceed to argue that neither Van Duijn nor Freeman *et al.* have provided convincing empirical evidence for long waves in innovation processes.

Given that Mensch (1979) draws a distinction between major (basic) and minor innovation there are problems as to what the innovation population is. Even if agreement is reached that basic innovation is a meaningful concept, a weighting structure for these innovations is needed – some are going to be more basic than others if the methodology of ranking innovation is correct. More important, perhaps, is the fact that by its very nature innovation cannot be treated in mechanistic terms; the considerations for introducing major and minor innovations cannot differ greatly. It is only *ex post* that some innovations can be said to have had a greater impact than others.[5]

Such problems imply that the population of basic innovations is an undefined concept. Without knowledge of the population, Mensch cannot claim to have a random sampling procedure – he has an arbitrary selection procedure from an unknown population.[6] The biases in the selection procedure come out clearly in the technological bias of the basic innovation classifications. Despite following in Schumpeter's footsteps the Mensch perception of innovation lacks Schumpeter's commercial orientation to innovation.

As an example of the kinds of biases involved in Mensch's selection procedure I will consider his twentieth-century 'sample'. For a more complete criticism see Freeman *et al.* (1982, pp. 44–57). Mensch takes most of his innovations from Jewkes *et al.* (1969). But Jewkes *et al.* never claimed that their selection of sixty inventions in the first edition (or seventy in the second) was in any sense complete or a random sample.[7] Since Mensch relies mainly on the first edition, his study could not do justice to the innovations of the 1950s. Mensch also omits twenty inventions from the Jewkes *et al.* list (or thirty from the second edition) and almost all of these fall outside the cluster of the 1930s. Moreover, while Jewkes *et al.* were concerned with invention, Mensch was concerned with innovation. Hence, Mensch fails to have a representative sample of innovations in the early twentieth century – during the period 1900–20 Mensch's sample contains only three innovations.[8]

Consistency in the sample is not examined by Mensch. The innovations in the sample will only be comparable over time if the factors determining the propensity to innovate are unchanged in the long run. One of Schumpeter's hypotheses is relevant to this point. Schumpeter argued that large monopolistic firms have more incentive to produce inventions and innovate because they can more easily appropriate the benefits (Schumpeter, 1950, Chs. VII and VIII).[9] Given the changed market structures between the nineteenth and twentieth centuries, long-run innovation series are not strictly comparable. In addition, the Research and Development (R and D) sector has grown rapidly since the 1920s, suggesting different invention–innovation relations from those of earlier periods.[10] Mensch's sample could be capturing structural changes rather than a metamorphosis wave pattern. These structural changes have particular relevance in Mensch's sample. Mensch argued that because Jewkes *et al.* were not concerned with long-term growth phases in deriving their sample, he has a random and indpendent sample. However, since Jewkes *et al.* were concerned with invention and the small firm – the argument of their book being that the small firm is not at a disadvantage – there may be structural biases in the sample given the changed market conditions.

If the population was agreed upon, two relevant questions could be distinguished:
(i) the randomness of the sample; and
(ii) the randomness of the periodisation.

In Mensch's study it is impossible to make this separation. Mensch employs the runs test to determine the significance of a non-random phasing on the

Table 5.1 *Runs test calculations for various sub-periods in Mensch's basic innovation sample*[a]

t	n_1	n_2	r	Z	P_α
1800–1955	67	89	67	1.7	0.09
1800–1900	44	57	44	−1.4	0.17
1800–1849	15	35	21	0.3	0.77
1850–1900	29	22	23	−0.9	0.38
1901–1955	23	32	24	1.3	0.18

[a] n_1, n_2, r and Z are defined as above; P_α is the significance probability of the Z calculation. In this table $n_1 \geq 1$ innovations and $n_2 = 0$ innovations.

assumption that he has a random sample.[11] Given the problems outlined above the assumption of a random sample is clearly unfounded. Instead I shall employ the runs test to test for the randomness of the sample and then proceed to test for significant clusters. It should also be stressed that even if Mensch did have a random sample the runs test is inappropriate as a test for the metamorphosis model. This test cannot distinguish between a metamorphosis model and a shock model – even one major shock, that lasts over a long period, will pick up a non-random process, but this clearly does not justify the metamorphosis model conclusions. Thus a more discerning test is needed.[12]

I first undertook sample runs tests for different sub-periods to test the randomness of Mensch's sample. The runs test for large samples involves calculating the following formula based on the Z-statistic (Siegel, 1956, p. 56):

$$Z = \frac{r - \left\{ \frac{2n_1 n_2}{n_1 + n_2} + 1 \right\}}{\left\{ \frac{2n_1 n_2 (2n_1 n_2 - n_1 - n_2)}{(n_1 + n_2)^2 (n_1 + n_2 - 1)} \right\}^{1/2}} \qquad (1)$$

where, r is the number of runs in the sample; one run is defined as x years of a specified number of innovations; n_1 is the number of elements of one kind (e.g. number of years of ≥ 1 innovation); and n_2 is the number of elements of another kind (e.g. number of years of 0 innovation). The idea behind the test is to test for autocorrelated periodisations (or, at the other extreme, random walk processes) based on the number of runs in the series. The calculations for the Z-statistics from the Mensch sample of basic innovations are presented in Table 5.1.

The results of Table 5.1 suggest that the strongest case for rejecting the null postulating randomness is over the longest period, 1800–1955. In this case the probability that the process was random is only 0.09 – i.e. there is a 9 per cent chance of making the error of saying that the sample is random when, in fact, it is not. This result is in line with Mensch's long-period runs calculations.

Table 5.2 *Runs test calculations for specific a priori historical sub-periods in Mensch's basic innovation sample*

t	n_1	n_2	r	Z	P_α
1813–1870	21	37	29	0.35	0.730
1871–1925	25	30	17	3.09	0.002
1828–1885	28	30	28	0.52	0.603
1886–1938	23	30	21	1.71	0.087
1926–1955(A)	19	11	21	—	—
1926–1955(B)	10	20	12	—	—

However, all the other sub-periods fail to reject the null postulating randomness at a reasonable significance level.

Failing to reject a random process does not mean that clustered periods are not present. In such cases we are basically testing for differences in the probability of occurrence of a certain event from a random sample. Given the failure to reject a random pattern in the Mensch sample of basic innovations over a variety of sub-periods, I undertook a test for the existence of specific historical clusters. The statistic employed for the purpose is the Z-statistic for differences in two sample means:

$$Z = \frac{\bar{x}_1 - \bar{x}_2}{\left\{ \dfrac{\sigma_1^2}{N_1} + \dfrac{\sigma_2^2}{N_2} \right\}^{1/2}} \tag{2}$$

where $\bar{x}_1$ and $\bar{x}_2$ are the sample means; σ_1^2 and σ_2^2 are the sample variances; and N_1 and N_2 are the sample sizes. Before undertaking such calculations I first tested that the innovation pattern for the a priori periods used by Mensch are, in fact, random samples. The runs tests on the relevant Kuznets phases are presented in Table 5.2.

The random null fails to be rejected for the sub-periods 1813–70 and 1828–85. It is rejected for 1871–1925 at a very high significance level, and over the period 1886–1938 at the 9 per cent significance level. Randomness is also rejected for 1926–55 when $n_1 \geq 1$ innovations (case (A) in Table 5.2), but fails to be rejected for $n_1 \geq 2$ innovations (case (B)).[13] Since the sample has a trend the latter inference is more valid. That randomness is rejected for the two phases 1871–1925 and 1886–1938 is to be expected given the criticisms levelled against Mensch's selection procedure.

Where a random sample hypothesis fails to be rejected I proceeded to test for clusters in innovation during long-wave depressions. Equation (2) has been

Table 5.3 *Z-test calculations for Mensch's clusters in innovation activity*[a]

t	$\bar{x}_1$	$\bar{x}_2$	σ_1	σ_2	Z	P_α
1813–1827 1828–1870	0.571429	0.534884	1.08941	0.76684	0.12	0.90
1828–1870 1871–1885	0.534884	1.466666	0.76683	1.24594	2.72	0.01
1926–1938 1939–1955	1.83333	0.82353	1.52753	0.88284	2.10	0.04

[a] Where $\bar{x}_1$, $\bar{x}_2$, σ_1, σ_2, Z and P_α are defined as above.

used to test the null that the expected difference in means is zero, i.e.

$$H_0 : E(\bar{x}_1 - \bar{x}_2) = 0$$

The results are reported in Table 5.3.

Such evidence suggests that the innovation path has not been steady in the long run; nevertheless, the path observed does not fit into a regular Kondratieff wave. Mensch's sample provides evidence for significant innovation clusters in two periods, 1871–85 and 1926–38; the cluster postulated for the period 1813–27 is highly insignificant. Moreover, the results for 1828–85 and 1926–55 cannot be related given the sampling problems outlined above.

As a means of overcoming some of the sampling problems I also undertook a test of the Mensch phases of innovation clusters employing the aggregate Van Duijn (1983) selection for the period 1870–1950 on the assumption that the sample is well covered in this period (Van Duijn, 1983, p. 181). The results are reported in Table 5.4. Employing the Van Duijn selection leaves little of the Mensch hypothesis of a clustering of innovations during major depression phases. Innovation flows have been constant over long periods of time such as 1872–1913 and 1926–50. The innovation path for the 1930s and 1940s was structurally different from the whole era 1872–1925. Such a structural change was due to the effects of war and the development of an R and D sector rather than an underlying long-wave mechanism.

Table 5.4 *The Mensch cluster phasing employing the Van Duijn (1983) Sample, 1872–1950*

t	$\bar{x}$	σ
1872–1885	1.14	1.23
1886–1913	1.11	1.28
1886–1925	1.05	1.20
1926–1938	1.77	2.05
1939–1950	1.75	2.00

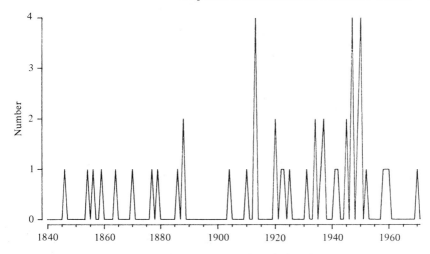

Figure 5.2 Frequency of major innovations in the USA, 1840–1971 (innovations/annum). Source: Van Duijn (1981, Table 4, pp. 271–3)

Given the existence of a leadership structure in the world economy, innovation needs to be looked at on a national level to check that the data is not generating statistical artefacts. Mensch's definition of innovation as the point of introduction of the first production process or the first commodity is not very helpful in this respect. The problems of using 'world' innovation data come out clearly in a study of the Van Duijn (1981, pp. 271–3) sample (see Figures 5.2 and 5.3). Van Duijn has provided a list of eighty-one major

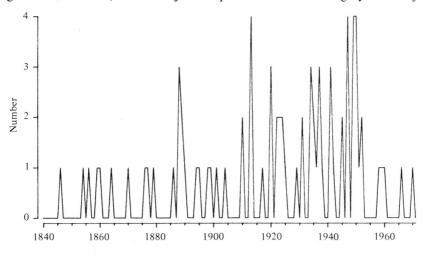

Figure 5.3 Frequency of total basic innovations 1840–1971 (innovations/annum). Source: Van Duijn (1981, Table 4, pp. 271–3)

Table 5.5 *The national distribution of innovations in the Van Duijn (1981) sample, 1840–1971*

Country	Number of innovations[a]	Percentage of total
USA	49	56
Germany	20	23
Britain	10	11
France	9	10

[a] The total number of innovations in all countries is greater than the total in the sample (88 > 81) since some innovations are classified as occurring simultaneously in more than one country because of lack of evidence.

innovations between 1840 and 1971. His lists date the innovation by its point of introduction and also classify the national origins of the innovation. It is clear from his sample that the greatest innovator is the USA (see Table 5.5).

Such an international distribution of innovation is clearly inappropriate to study the non-synchronised growth path of modern economies. The more recent work of Van Duijn (1983, p. 184) which covers a sample of 160 major innovations shows a similar national distribution of innovation as is reported in Table 5.5. The relevance of this point needs to be emphasised. Given the American dominance of innovation trends the Kondratieff wave needs to be studied in terms of its relevance to this economy. The trends analysed in Chapter 3 suggest that American economic growth has not moved along a long wave. Many other studies have come to a similar conclusion for the pre-1913 period (Bieshaar and Kleinknecht, 1984; Van Ewijk, 1981).

Despite rejecting Mensch's depression trigger idea, Van Duijn still holds to a long-wave periodisation of innovation. However, it is difficult to find such support even within his own data. As was noted above, the dominance of America in the innovation process invalidates many of the long-wave inferences. Moreover, the long-wave periodisation reported by Van Duijn is not distinguished from a shock phasing of innovation. Van Duijn reports the following long-wave innovation flows (1983, p. 182):

1872–92   = 24
1892–1913 = 23
1913–29   = 11
1929–48   = 38

As was noted above, the innovation flow was constant before 1913; the only disturbance arises from the World Wars. Moreover, the differing effects of the First World War from the Second can be understood both in terms of the technological differences between the two wars and the changed world economic leadership structure; in 1913 the world economy was still dominated by Europe while in 1929 the world economy was dominated by America.

Another innovation selection that is relevant to these discussions is Kleinknecht's treatment of Mahdavi's sample of 120 case studies of 'important' innovations.[14] Kleinknecht (1981) classified the Mahdavi sample into three categories:

(i) SI = scientific instrument innovations

(ii) IP = improvement and process innovations

(iii) PI = product innovations

The separation of the category of SI innovations is justified by their origins and purpose; they are primarily developed and used by R and D departments themselves, and can be considered as being directly induced by the needs of research. IP innovations are concerned with more or less radical improvements to existing products or the production processes for existing products. PI innovations cover completely new products and materials; it is the PI innovations that come close to the Mensch and Van Duijn basic innovations. Such a separation between IP and PI innovations can also be justified on economic grounds; IP innovations concern existing products and thus innovation here is based on existing demand, while PI innovations are based on the new products that meet a latent demand.

There are problems with these classifications, for example, capital goods innovations which from the standpoint of their producers are new products but for the final users are process innovations. Such cases were generally classified as IP innovations, according to their final purpose as process innovations. It should also be noted that in using the Mahdavi sample it is necessary to count in ten-year periods since Mahdavi does not allow for a finer periodisation.

Kleinknecht's classifications show that for PI innovations there exists a smaller cumulation with a peak in the 1880s and a larger one with a peak in the 1930s. Testing the null that there is no difference in the number of innovations in different ten-year periods, Kleinknecht postulated that there is a cluster in the downswings of the 1880s and 1930s. A χ^2-test suggests that the null has to be rejected at the 0.001 level of significance for PI innovations in the twentieth century. However, the null cannot be rejected for the PI innovations of the nineteenth century and the IP innovations for both the nineteenth- and twentieth-century phases.

Thus, the only support for a Mensch type hypothesis is found in the case of product innovations during the 1930s. Even in this case the difference between the 1930s and the 1940s is not large; there were fifteen PI innovations in the 1930s and ten in the 1940s. Kleinknecht produces a strong statistical result only by extending his sample to the 1960s, since there were few major PI innovations in the sample beyond 1950.[15] Thus, the cluster seems to be placed in the 1930s and 1940s, not just the 1930s. Clearly such evidenc is compatible with the shock hypothesis rather than the long-wave perspective.

The evidence presented here reinforces the Freeman *et al.* (1982) conclusion that the innovation flow is more random than the work of Mensch, Van Duijn and others suggests. However, in Freeman *et al.* the role of innovation is still seen as causal to long waves. In this perspective long waves are driven by a series of 'New Technology Systems'; thus, despite the more random distribution of basic innovations the Schumpeterian 'swarming effect' is seen to be the force generating a long-wave path:

The bandwagon effect *is* extraordinarily important — in our view it is the main explanation of the upswings in the long waves. (Freeman *et al.*, 1982, p. 67)

However, it is not clear how the New Technology System is *causal* to long waves. Freeman *et al.* outline how technology helped to sustain the postwar boom but this is different from seeking the technological factors that gave rise to long waves. Throughout their discussion technological interrelatedness is related to economic growth itself and, hence, cannot be seen as causal in a one-directional manner. Thus, the Freeman *et al.* framework could be important in explaining a long-wave pattern of growth, but to have effect it requires the existence of long waves.

Conclusions

An examination of the Mensch, Van Duijn and Kleinknecht innovation selections rejects the idea of regular innovation clusters during long-wave depression phases. The evidence also rejects the weaker hypothesis of Van Duijn that innovation flows followed a long-wave path; structural changes in the twentieth century have been confused with long waves. The evidence vindicates the Freeman *et al.* conclusion that the flow of innovation is not responsive to long-wave phases. Their evidence is taken from a sample of 200 major innovations in Britain since 1920. The data studied here is taken from Van Duijn (1981, 1983) and relates to a sample of countries in the world economy for a longer period. Although Freeman *et al.* hold to a more random distribution of innovations over long trend periods they still hold to a long-wave innovation perspective, with the emphasis being placed on the 'swarming effect'. Such an effect would be an important factor only if long waves can be proved to exist. Chapter 3 examined the issue of *existence* for the period 1850–1973 and found no evidence for this growth pattern.

6

The national aspects of Kuznets swings, 1850–1913

With the exception of studies dealing with America (Easterlin, 1968; Kuznets, 1958), the national aspects of long swings have been neglected. Lewis and O'Leary (1955) suggested some time ago that the causation for Kuznets swings is best understood in a national perspective. The evidence presented in this chapter suggests that important national specific aspects have been neglected in long-swing discussions. The problem is particularly serious for understanding the French and German swings since these economies have usually been lumped into a common European core economy in discussions of long swings. Although much attention has been devoted to understanding British long swings most of the emphasis has been placed on international aspects. The idea developed here is that Kuznets swings are a series of episodic events and national growth conditions are essential to understanding these traverses.

Most long-swing studies work with a dynamic income model, assigning a central role to population-sensitive investments. Moreover, the emphasis has been on the Anglo-American economies, with the aim of explaining international migration movements. Kuznets (1958) suggested that internal and international migration responded to development opportunities in the American economy, inducing multiplier-accelerator effects. Abramovitz (1959, 1961) and Easterlin (1968) have offered similar explanations for the pre-1913 era. It is frequently argued that since migrants to America came from such diverse environments (Europe, Canada, Latin America, Asia) they must have been responding to the common stimulus of American economic growth.[1]

Working within the migration perspective, Thomas (1954) attempted to explain migration and aggregate swings in terms of the construct of the Atlantic Economy. In Thomas' early work the Atlantic Economy was taken to consist of Britain and America; in his more recent work it consists of all the core and periphery economies. The high degree of economic integration in the Atlantic Economy implies that the availability of factors of production was a constraint on economic growth within the region. An increase of investment in one region was assumed to impose a decrease of investment in the other region.[2] Since construction activity was greatly influenced by population changes, which, in turn, were influenced by migration movements, migration was the main force generating swings in output and investment. These swings would be inverse for the different parts of the Atlantic Economy.

Description and explanation have been confused in this framework. That exogenous migration movements can generate more aggregate macroeconomy swings is theoretically plausible (Parry-Lewis, 1964). However, exogeneity needs to be justified, as does the monocausal framework. To the extent that migration patterns are influenced by economic considerations, Thomas' (1954) model is misleading; the description of endogenous economic processes has been confused with an explanation of economic change. Moreover, as will be shown later, the emphasis on migration as the *causal* variable has led to a neglect of other important influences on long swings.

Cairncross' (1953) explanation of long swings also neglected important national influences. Cairncross focused his attention on the variation of the sectoral terms of trade between manufactures and agriculture in the world economy.[3] Such a sectoral division was seen to be valid across nations – Britain, France and Germany were seen as industrial economies while much of the rest of the world was taken as the primary producing sector. Investment flows in the international economy were determined by the relative profitability of these two sectors.[4] Migration flows were not an exogenous force on long swings but were merely responding to such underlying economic variations. In Cairncross' framework sectoral terms-of-trade changes implied long-run sectoral disproportionalities in the world economy:

One could expect to find, therefore, that during, or immediately after, a fairly long period in which the terms of trade were relatively unfavourable to Britain there would be heavy investment in the countries supplying her with imports ... On the other hand, when capital goods were expensive and foodstuffs were in over-supply, the continuance of a rapid opening up of agricultural countries would be distinctly surprising. (1953, p. 189)

Cairncross argued that a similar experience is also observed for the other major capital exporters:

Broadly speaking, too, the same sort of changes took place in the terms of trade of France, and, after 1900 at least, of Germany. (1953, p. 190)

Cairncross assumed that the sectoral terms of trade can be proxied by the international terms of trade of Britain, France and Germany. However, with the exception of Britain, such a high degree of international division of labour is not representative of the pre-1913 world economy. In the case of France, Germany and America the international terms-of-trade proxy for sectoral disproportionalities would be wide of the mark, especially in the era of increased tariffs between 1878 and 1913. To test Cairncross' idea fully for these economies the emphasis also needs to be placed on the internal sectoral terms of trade variations. If Cairncross' observations are valid, an inverse sectoral investment path should be observed within national boundaries. This would imply that for economies with a lower degree of international specialisation than Britain, large inverse domestic sectoral swings would give rise to damped aggregate swings. The existence of marked aggregate investment swings in France, Germany and America suggests that Cairncross' causal framework warrants careful re-evaluation. In this chapter the long-swing evidence is re-examined with the aim of illustrating the importance of national specific aspects behind long-swing growth variations.

Investment swings

During the period 1860–1913 British investment followed an irregular si-nusoidal long swing (see Figure 6.1 and Table 6.1). The rate of growth of the capital stock peaked in 1865, 1876 and 1902 and troughed in 1869, 1886 and 1912. The initial variation during the period 1865–76 is more of a Juglar cycle than a complete swing and is best perceived as the high-growth phase of the swing.

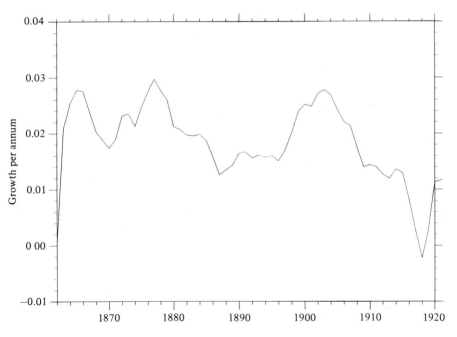

Figure 6.1 Growth of British capital stock. Source: Feinstein, revised capital stock figures, unpublished

Table 6.1 *Peak-to-peak growth phases in British capital stock, 1862–1913 (growth/annum)*

t	$K(\text{£M})$	g_K	Δg_K
1862	2616.9	—	—
1878	3839.3	0.02396	—
1896	5206.4	0.01692	−0.00703
1905	6499.4	0.02465	+0.00773
1913	7323.5	0.01492	−0.00975

g_K = growth of capital stock
Δ = first difference operator

Source: Feinstein, revised capital stock figures, unpublished.

Although the long swing in British investment has been recognised for some time there has been a general failure to relate the investment path of the economy to the long-term output path.[5] In Thomas (1954) domestic investment levels were taken to be above trend in the high-growth phases and below trend in the low-growth phases. Thomas viewed the 1870s and the 1890s as high-growth phases and the 1880s and 1900s as low-growth phases. Such a phasing fits well with Thomas' migration explanation of the swings, but it does not fit with the actual output path of the economy. The *level* of investment in Britain does not have a simple proportional relationship with the rate of growth of output. During the period 1870–1913 investment levels were above trend in the 1870s and 1896–1905. The analysis of British output trends suggested that both 1873–82 and 1899–1907 were downswing phases of growth (see Chapter 3). In fact, for much of the time there exists an inverse relationship between investment levels and the rate of growth of output in British economy.

In a growing economy the rate of addition to investment levels is a more critical variable for understanding trend periods than the levels themselves. Thus, a stress on the turning points of macroeconomic variables is critical to understanding the causality of long swings. In Thomas, maladjustments in the response of investment to changing output and profitability conditions have been mistaken for economic maximising processes. The evidence for Britain suggests that there exists a simultaneous long swing in the trend rate of growth of output and investment, with investment lagging output changes. Thus, from 1876 investment followed the path of output in a downward direction; similarly, investment fell from 1902 following the retardation of output growth from 1899. Hence, despite the level of investment being high in both the 1870s and 1890s, the economic processes in these eras were very different. In the 1870s the economy was adjusting downwards while in the 1890s an upward adjustment was taking place.

Table 6.2 *A sectoral analysis of the peak-to-peak phases in the British capital stock, 1862–1913 (growth/annum)*

	α_i	g_{K_i}	$\alpha_i g_{K_i}$	$\Delta(\alpha_i g_{K_i})$	$\Delta(\alpha_i g_{K_i})/\Delta gK$ (%)
Dwellings					
1862	0.258	—	—	—	—
1878	0.241	0.01987	0.00513	—	—
1896	0.239	0.01626	0.00392	−0.00121	17.0
1905	0.240	0.02498	0.00597	+0.00205	26.6
1913	0.237	0.01353	0.00325	−0.00272	28.0
Gas, electricity and water					
1862	0.0207	—	—	—	
1878	0.0281	0.04292	0.00089	—	
1896	0.0361	0.03095	0.00087	−0.0002	3.1
1905	0.0470	0.05387	0.00195	+0.0011	13.9
1913	0.0498	0.02209	0.00104	−0.0009	9.4
Building and work (*excluding dwellings*)					
1862	0.559	—	—	—	—
1878	0.531	0.02072	0.01160	—	—
1896	0.514	0.01506	0.00800	−0.0036	51.1
1905	0.495	0.02042	0.01049	+0.0025	32.2
1913	0.480	0.01122	0.00555	−0.0049	50.8
Plant, equipment, vehicles and ships					
1862	0.183	—	—	—	—
1878	0.227	0.03765	0.00686	—	—
1896	0.247	0.02170	0.00492	−0.0019	27.5
1905	0.266	0.03265	0.00807	+0.0032	40.7
1913	0.283	0.02273	0.00604	−0.0020	20.9
Agriculture					
1862	0.181	—	—	—	—
1878	0.128	+0.00339	+0.00051	—	—
1896	0.098	−0.00880	−0.00096	−0.00146	20.9
1905	0.072	−0.00399	−0.00032	+0.00064	8.2
1913	0.062	−0.00225	−0.00015	+0.00017	− 1.8

A detailed analysis of the sectoral variations of the British capital stock illustrates the problems of accepting simple monocausal explanations for long swings. Thomas has developed his framework in terms of the dynamic impact of migration on the growth of population-sensitive investments. Dwellings are the clearest component of this type of investment. In addition electricity, gas and water investment is population sensitive. Defining a peak year in the capital stock series as a transition year from above-trend to below-trend growth,[6] I accounted for the peak-to-peak swings in the rate of growth of the

Table 6.3 *Peak-to-peak growth measures and related calculations: French investment, 1846–1913 (growth/annum)*

t	$\bar{g}_{I_t}$	$\hat{\sigma}_{g_{I_t}}$	$\hat{\sigma}_{g_{I_t}}/\bar{g}_{I_t}$	$\Delta\bar{g}_{I_t}$
1846–1856	0.0205	0.1072	5.24	+0.0004
1856–1869	0.0110	0.0445	4.04	−0.0095
1869–1882	0.0296	0.1435	4.85	+0.0186
1882–1891	−0.0159	0.0639	−4.02	−0.0455
1891–1900	0.0213	0.0379	1.78	+0.0372
1900–1907	−0.0053	0.0492	−9.36	−0.0267
1907–1913	0.0626	0.0515	0.96	+0.0679

$\bar{g}_I$ = mean geometric growth rate of investment
$\hat{\sigma}_{g_I}$ = standard deviation of the geometric mean
Δ = first difference operator

Source: Lévy-Leboyer (1978, Table 60, pp. 292–5).

aggregate capital stock in terms of a weighted sectoral analysis. The results (see Table 6.2) suggest that the population-sensitive category accounted for only a small part of the inter-swing variations – accounting for 20.1 per cent of the inter-swing variation during the period 1862–96, 40.5 per cent during the period 1878–1905 and 37 per cent during the period 1896–1913. The evidence does not suggest that population sensitive investments dominated the swings. In particular, the population sensitive category accounted for a very low proportion of the downswing during the period 1878–96. The inadequacy of a monocausal population-sensitive explanation of the investment trends in the British economy is also clear in an examination of the role of the agricultural sector in the swing of 1862–1878–1896. Agriculture accounted for 21 per cent of the downswing during the period 1878–96, suggesting that structural change in the economy was as important as the population-sensitive aspects.

Annual capital stock statistics are not available for the other countries under consideration. However, investment indicators are available and they all suggest the existence of long swings.

Swings in French investment are observed throughout the period 1856–1913 (see Table 6.3). The growth path of investment showed large inter-cycle variations that are statistically significant at the 5 per cent level throughout the period 1856–1913 (see Appendix Table A6.1).[7] The investment swings moved in a similar manner to the swings observed for French commodity production. The pattern of growth was similar for construction and industrial investments. The French evidence further negates the importance of the Atlantic Economy since France was not an integrated member of the Atlantic Economy. The international migration-wave framework that has been used to explain British swings is irrelevant in this case since France was a net receiver of immigrants throughout the pre-1913 period.

Table 6.4 *Peak-to-peak growth measures and related calculations: German net capital formation, 1852–1913 (growth/annum)*

t	$\bar{g}_{I_t}$	$\hat{\sigma}_{g_{I_t}}$	$\hat{\sigma}_{g_{I_t}}/\bar{g}_{I_t}$	$\Delta\bar{g}_{I_t}$
1852–1913	0.0390	0.3458	8.87	—
1852–1856	−0.0200	0.9988	−49.94	—
1856–1863	0.0708	0.4736	6.69	+0.0908
1863–1874	0.0435	0.4317	9.92	−0.0273
1874–1884	−0.0153	0.1510	−9.87	−0.0588
1884–1890	0.0657	0.0807	1.23	+0.0810
1890–1898	0.0620	0.2035	3.28	−0.0038
1898–1907	0.0169	0.1682	9.95	−0.0451
1907–1912	0.0208	0.1658	7.97	+0.0040

See notes to Table 6.3.

Source: Mitchell (1981, pp. 817 and 821).

The long-swing pattern of the German economy, outlined in Chapter 3, is also observed in the investment trends of the economy. Table 6.4 suggests the existence of two complete Kuznets swings throughout the period 1856–1913 with the following phasing:

		Length (in Years)
1856–1874	high growth	18
1874–1884	low growth	10
1884–1898	high growth	14
1898–1912	low growth	14

These swings are statistically significant at the 5 per cent or 10 per cent levels (see Appendix Table A6.2).[8]

American investment data exist on an annual basis only from 1889. As can be seen from Table 6.5 large investment swings are observed throughout the period 1874–1912. The swings are correlated with the output and productivity trends outlined in Chapter 3.

Table 6.5 *Peak-to-peak growth measures: US investment, 1874–1912 (growth/annum)*

t	$\bar{g}_{I_t}$	$\Delta\bar{g}_{I_t}$
1874–1884	+0.05614	—
1884–1892	+0.08273	+0.02659
1892–1899	−0.02053	−0.10326
1899–1906	+0.06374	+0.08427
1906–1912	+0.00433	−0.05941

See notes to Table 6.3.

Source: US Department of Commerce (1978, pp. 186–7).

The evidence presented in this section suggests that the swings outlined in Chapter 3 are also observed in the investment trends of all the countries under consideration. The Kuznets swing was a generalised macroeconomic phenomenon for the leading nations of the world economy.

Profitability long swings

Since investment varied more than other components of aggregate output, the determinants of investment could provide an explanation of the aggregate swings. As a proximate explanation of investment swings in closed economies I will examine profitability trends. This is indeed proximate since, given data availability, the analysis has to be restricted to *ex-post* average profitability, while what would be determining investment decisions would be *ex-ante* marginal profitability expectations.

The absence of a reliable capital stock series for nineteenth century France and America has restricted this section to British and German profitability trends. British non-farm trading profitability is presented in Figure 6.2.[9] Profitability was at an historically high level in 1871 with a rising trend from 1856 to 1871. During the period 1871–1913 profitability fell on trend from 1871 to 1885, rose during the period 1885–99 (with a short sharp interruption during the period 1889–92) and fell again in the Edwardian era. Clearly, with appropriate lags, the profitability trends reproduce the output and investment

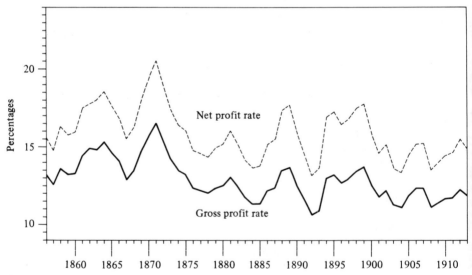

Figure 6.2 British non-farm trading profitability. Source: Feinstein, revised capital stock figures, unpublished

swings of the economy. Thus, to the extent that current profitability influences future investment projects there were forces in the economy implying reduced home investment in the 1870s and early 1880s, rising investment from the mid-1880s until the 1890s and falling investment in the 1900s. Why investment decisions responded to profitability only with long lags is not clear. Investment levels peaked in 1876 and 1903 while profitability peaked in 1871 and 1899. Lags of four to five years are difficult to explain. The problems with the data could, in fact, be explaining such a lagged relationship.[10] The profits data are taken from the income estimate of GDP while the capital stock figures are taken from the expenditure series. As was noted in Chapter 3 these series are out of phase for much of the post-1870 era.

The quinquennial rate of profit calculations given by Hoffmann (1965) for Germany also go some way in helping to account for the growth variations of the German economy (see Figure 6.3). It is interesting that it is the agricultural rate of return that shows the greatest variation and helps to explain the growth phases right up to the early twentieth century. The agricultural rate of profit followed an upward trend from the low levels of the 1850s to the 1860s; a marked fall in the 1870s; increased profitability in the 1880s and 1890s; and a mild swing in profitability in the early twentieth century. The industrial rate of profit followed the same path but with a variation that was under 0.5 per cent for most of the period. What such evidence suggests is a prima-facie case for a need to examine the sectoral relations within national boundaries.

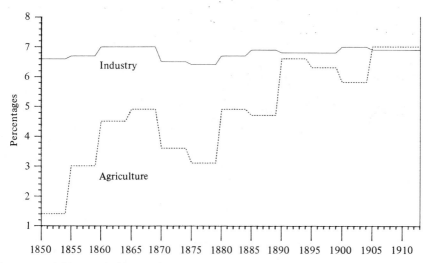

Figure 6.3 Yield to capital in German agriculture and industry. Source: Hoffmann (1965, p. 102)

Sectoral and inter-sectoral aspects

During the pre-1913 period, agricultural growth variations played an important role in the aggregate path of economic growth (Feinstein *et al.*, 1982;
Solomou, 1986a).

In Britain the agricultural sector grew along a long-swing pattern of growth
throughout the period 1855–1913 (see Figure 6.4 and Table 6.6). The low-
growth phases for agricultural production were 1875–81 and 1891–1902. The
inter-swing variations were large, ranging from −2.4 per cent to +2.3 per cent
for output and −2.4 per cent to +2.1 per cent for labour productivity. Both
the downswing phases are statistically significant from the mean-growth path
over the period 1855–1909 at the 5 per cent significance level.[11]

As a way of measuring the impact of the agricultural sector on the
macroeconomy I undertook an economic accounting exercise to determine the
contribution of the agricultural sector to the aggregate output trends. Taking
the reference cycles as those observed for the income estimate of GDP the
relevant calculations are presented in Table 6.7.[12] Clearly the agricultural
sector was unimportant in the step of 1865–73 (see column 5 of Table 6.7). The
sector had a significant impact on the swings during the period 1865–89;
during the 1890s the sector had a significant negative impact on growth but
this was not reflected in the aggregate trends. During the Edwardian period
agriculture had an insignificant effect on the growth path, with a small positive
impact during the period 1899–1907 and a small negative impact during the
period 1907–13.

French agricultural production also followed a marked long-swing pattern

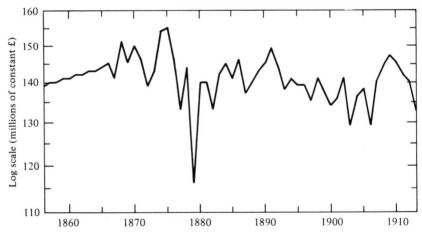

Figure 6.4 British agricultural production in millions of constant (1907) pounds.
Source: Lewis (1978, pp. 260–3)

Table 6.6 *Peak-to-peak growth measures and related calculations: UK agricultural production and labour input*

t	$\bar{g}_a$	$\hat{\sigma}_{g_a}$	$\bar{g}_L$	$\Delta\bar{g}_a$	$\bar{g}_a-\bar{g}_L$	$\Delta(\bar{g}_a-\bar{g}_L)$
1855–1866	+0.00384	0.00367	−0.0103	—	+0.01414	—
1866–1875	+0.00741	0.00465	−0.0101	+0.00357	+0.01751	+0.00337
1875–1881	−0.01700	0.14070	−0.0109	−0.02441	−0.00610	−0.02361
1881–1891	+0.00623	0.04069	−0.0084	+0.02323	+0.01463	+0.02073
1891–1902	−0.00502	0.02992	−0.0081	−0.01125	+0.00308	−0.01155
1902–1909	+0.00595	0.06209	−0.0065	+0.01097	+0.01245	+0.00937

$\bar{g}_a$ = mean geometric growth rate of agricultural output
$\hat{\sigma}_{g_a}$ = standard deviation of the geometric mean
$\bar{g}_L$ = mean geometric growth rate of the agricultural labour force
Δ = first difference operator
$\bar{g}_a-\bar{g}_L$ = growth of labour productivity

Sources: Lewis (1978, pp. 260–3) and Feinstein (1976, Table 60, T131).

Table 6.7 *Growth measures for the agricultural sector over the GDP reference cycle*

t	$\bar{g}_a$	$\Delta\bar{g}_a$	$\alpha_i\bar{g}_a$	$\Delta\alpha_i\bar{g}_a$	$\bar{g}_L$	$\bar{g}_a-\bar{g}_L$
1856–1865	+0.0039	—	+0.0007	—	−0.0096	+0.0135
1865–1873	−0.0009	−0.0048	−0.00014	−0.0008	−0.0104	+0.0095
1873–1882	−0.0081	−0.0072	−0.0011	−0.0010	−0.0101	+0.0020
1882–1889	+0.0104	+0.0185	+0.0011	+0.0022	−0.0081	+0.0185
1889–1899	−0.0043	−0.0147	−0.0003	−0.0014	−0.0083	+0.0040
1899–1907	+0.0027	+0.0070	+0.0002	+0.0005	−0.0046	+0.0073
1907–1913	−0.0086	−0.0113	−0.0006	−0.0008	−0.0015	−0.0071

α_i = share of agricultural sector in GDP (share = column (4)/column (2))

See Table 6.6 for further notes.

Sources: Lewis (1978, pp. 260–3) and Feinstein (1976, Table 60, T131).

of growth during the period 1863–1912, with low-growth phases between the periods 1875–92 and 1899–1912 (see Table 6.8). Given the large weight of the sector in the French economy and the large swings in agricultural production, the sector helped to account for some of the swing phases. In the 1870s the large downswing of agricultural production had a major depressing effect which accounts for the failure of the French economy to recover fully from the Franco-Prussian war, despite a very rapid growth of the industrial sector. During the 1880s the sector had a small beneficial effect on the growth path, which suggests that other factors were more important to the downswing of that period. In the 1890s and the Edwardian period the agricultural sector

Table 6.8 *Peak-to-peak growth measures and related calculations: French agricultural production, c. 1848–1913 (growth/annum)*

(1) t	(2) $\bar{g}_{Y_t}$	(3) $\hat{\sigma}_{g_{Y_t}}$	(4) $\hat{\sigma}_{g_{Y_t}}/\bar{g}_{Y_t}$	(5) $\Delta\bar{g}_{Y_t}$
1848–1858	0.0093	0.0560	6.01	−0.0069
1858–1863	0.0184	0.0630	3.43	+0.0091
1863–1869	0.0122	0.0499	4.09	−0.0062
1869–1875	0.0155	0.0567	3.66	+0.0033
1875–1882	−0.0070	0.0589	−8.45	−0.0225
1882–1894	0.0043	0.0224	5.27	+0.0113
1894–1900	0.0186	0.0497	2.67	+0.0143
1900–1907	0.0021	0.0466	22.16	−0.0165
1907–1913	0.0079	0.0556	7.01	+0.0058

Source: Lévy-Leboyer (1978, Table 60, pp. 292–5).

Table 6.9 *Peak-to-peak growth measures: US agricultural production, 1873–1912 (growth/ annum)*

t	$\bar{g}_{a_t}$	$\Delta\bar{g}_{a_t}$
1873–1880	0.0521	—
1880–1891	0.0223	−0.0298
1891–1898	0.0261	+0.0038
1898–1906	0.0152	−0.0109
1906–1912	0.0131	−0.0021

Source: Potter and Christy (1962).

played an important role in accounting for the upswing of 1892–99 and the downswing of 1899–1907.

The American economy seems to be the exception to the rule. Agricultural growth followed a series of downward steps during the period 1873–1912 (see Table 6.9). Moreover, these steps do not seem to be related to the aggregate swings. Thus, in the American literature the explanation for the aggregate swings has been sought in the variations of the construction and industrial sectors. The European evidence suggests that the agricultural sector was extremely important to the swings before 1913.

As noted earlier, the national inter-sectoral relations also need to be considered when discussing long swings to take into consideration the existence of economies with a lower degree of international specialisation than that of Britain. Cairncross saw the sectoral terms of trade as signalling profitability opportunities in the different sectors. Implicit in Cairncross' framework is the assumption that a steady-state growth path cannot be maintained, since there occurs a sectoral constraint via a disproportionality in the production of manufactures and basic commodities. A slowing-down of the growth path can arise for any of the following reasons:

(a) If growth across sectors is not balanced and growth in the basic sector is lower than the industrial sector.
(b) If the saving propensity of the basic sector is greater than for the manufacturing sector.
(c) If the gestation lags for investment are greater in the basic sector.
(d) In an economy with large amounts of fixed capital any major terms of trade variation across sectors could affect the growth path adversely because the existing sectoral proportionalities are brought into question. Capital and labour immobilities may impose aggregate demand constraints until the economy is restructured to meet the new demands. Not only are resources immobile between sectors but the capital-producing sector has to adjust to meet the new demand patterns implied by a new sectoral income distribution. Thus Kaldor (1976) concluded:

> *any* large change in commodity prices – irrespective of whether it is in favour or against the primary producers – tends to have a dampening effect on industrial activity; it retards industrial growth in both cases, instead of retarding it in the one case and stimulating it in the other. (1976, p. 706)

For America, Potter and Christy (1962) have constructed price series for natural resource commodities since 1870. Price relatives for basic commodities are presented in Figure 6.5. Agricultural relative prices followed a long-swing pattern of adjustment. The following pattern was observed:

1868–1880	falling
1880–1891	rising
1891–1899	falling
1899–1913	rising

The only period when the Cairncross explanation for investment and output swings may be important is during the period 1906–1913, when the sectoral terms of trade moved in favour of the agricultural sector, and industrial output and investment underwent significant retardation. For all other periods the pattern of sectoral terms-of-trade adjustment suggests that relative price variation was demand determined – agricultural relative prices falling with slow-growth phases and rising with high-growth phases. Thus, in the American case, sectoral price variations were more important in creating a debt problem during the downswings than in constraining industrial growth with high relative prices.

The French sectoral terms of trade are presented in Figure 6.6. The similarity of this variable with the French production swings is striking; low-growth phases being associated with adverse sectoral terms of trade for agriculture and high-growth phases being associated with favourable move-

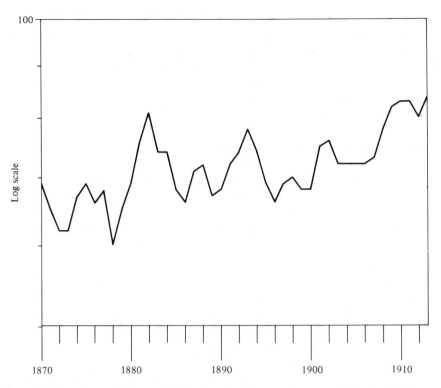

Figure 6.5 American relative agricultural prices. Source: Potter and Christy (1962)

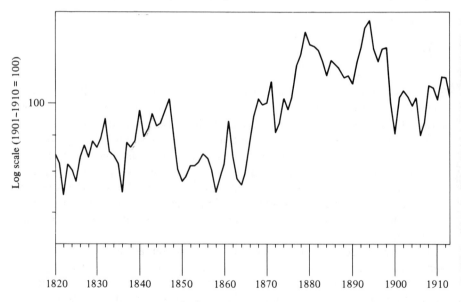

Figure 6.6 French agricultural/industrial price relatives. Source: Annuaire Statistique (1966, pp. 373–4)

Table 6.10 *Growth rates of British export prices and various indices of food and raw materials over peak-to-peak phases for exports (growth/annum)*

t	(1)	(2)	(3)	(4)	(5)
1857–1864	+0.034	+0.0012	−0.0013	+0.0152	−0.0211
1864–1873	−0.005	+0.0035	+0.0103	−0.0048	+0.0217
1873–1880	−0.043	−0.0437	−0.0184	−0.0436	−0.0185
1880–1890	−0.012	−0.0135	−0.0181	−0.0168	−0.0253
1890–1900	+0.004	+0.0135	−0.0449	+0.0119	−0.0056
1900–1907	+0.003	+0.0129	+0.0033	+0.0103	+0.0061
1907–1913	+0.006	+0.0153	+0.0178	+0.0094	+0.0122

(1) = price of exports
(2) = Rousseaux index of industrial raw materials
(3) = Rousseaux index of agricultural produce
(4) = Sauerbeck index of raw material prices
(5) = Sauerbeck index of food prices

Sources: (1) Lewis (1981, Appendix Tables 3 and 4, pp. 38–65);
(2) and (3) Mitchell and Deane (1962, pp. 471–3);
(4) and (5) Mitchell and Deane (1962, pp. 474–5).

ments. Thus, Cairncross' explanation for output and investment swings is also not observed in the case of France. As in the American case, the sectoral terms of trade were demand determined. The variable may contribute to the explanation of long swings in terms of the disproportionality problems discussed above.

In the case of Britain a number of indicators may be used as proxies of the sectoral terms of trade. The most obvious index to use is the international terms of trade, since Britain imported mainly agricultural and raw material products and exported mainly manufactures. However, the increased competition facing Britain after 1870 meant that the composition of her imports consisted of an increasing proportion of finished and semi-finished manufactures. An alternative procedure is to use Sauerbeck's and Rousseaux's indices of food and raw material prices and compare their movement with respect to export prices. The relevant calculations are presented in Tables 6.10 and 6.11. The various indicators show some agreement for the post-1873 period. But during the pre-1873 period there are major differences. In particular, during the period 1864-73 the favourable movement of the international terms of trade is not observed for the other proxies of relative food prices. In the pre-1873 period a large proportion of food was home grown and such differences are to be expected.

The sectoral investment shares provide some support to Cairncross' ideas in the case of British trends. The sectoral terms of trade were an important

Table 6.11 *British terms-of-trade variation and excess of growth of British export prices with respect to various indices of food and raw materials (growth/annum)*

t	TOT	(1)–(2)	(1)–(3)	(1)–(4)	(1)–(5)
1857–1864	+0.026	+0.033	+0.035	+0.019	+0.054
1864–1873	+0.013	−0.009	−0.015	0.000	−0.025
1873–1880	−0.023	0.000	−0.025	0.000	−0.025
1880–1890	+0.009	+0.020	+0.006	+0.005	+0.013
1890–1900	+0.010	−0.010	+0.049	−0.008	+0.009
1900–1907	−0.006	−0.010	0.000	−0.007	−0.003
1907–1913	+0.002	−0.009	−0.012	−0.003	−0.005

Sources: Terms of trade (Mitchell and Deane, 1962, pp. 331–2). For other series see Table 6.10.

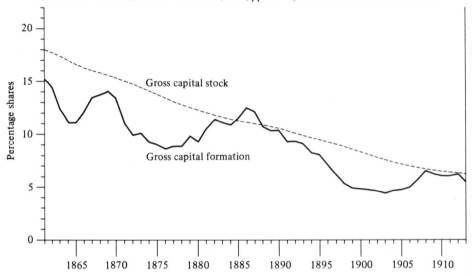

Figure 6.7 Agriculture's share in capital formation and capital stock, 1860–1913. Source: Feinstein (unpublished capital figures)

variable in accounting for variations in the sectoral investment shares. During the period 1873–83, with favourable terms of trade for agricultural commodities, there was increasing investment in the agricultural sector, despite the fact that aggregate domestic investment moved downwards from 1876. In the 1880s and the 1890s the sectoral terms of trade moved against agriculture, and agricultural investment shares followed a long downward path. During the Edwardian era the sectoral terms of trade moved in favour of agriculture, and the share of agricultural investment started rising again (see Figure 6.7).

The evidence presented in this section suggests that agricultural production and the sectoral terms of trade have played an important role in long-swing variations. However, such effects were not uniform across countries. The major differences were dependent on the structure of the economy and the tariff policy being followed. In Britain and France agricultural production grew in a long-swing pattern, while in America agricultural output was not directly linked to the long swings of the economy. In Britain agricultural investment swings were contracyclical to aggregate investment swings, with slow-growing periods being associated with favourable sectoral terms of trade for the agricultural sector. Moreover, in the periods of adverse terms of trade for agriculture the economy was not depressed in an aggregate demand constraint because of the smallness of the agricultural sector. In France the large weight of the agricultural sector in domestic supply, a different tariff policy and a different aggregate long-swing phasing gave rise to very different sectoral terms-of-trade variations. High-growth phases were generally associated with favourable agricultural relative prices while downswing phases were associated with adverse sectoral terms of trade for agriculture. A similar pattern of relative price adjustment was observed in the American economy before 1906. Thus, Cairncross' ideas seem to be more relevant to the British than the French and American economies. However, the terms of trade are an important variable for explaining long swings in all the economies under consideration.

Climatic variations and long swings

Much of the recent climatology literature has emphasised the existence of significant variations in weather-related variables such as temperature and rainfall (Lamb, 1982). The twenty- to twenty-three-year cycle in climate has been discussed extensively in this literature (Lamb, 1977; Manley, 1959). Since in the previous section it was argued that agricultural production swings played an important role in explaining British and French aggregate long swings the relationship between weather and agricultural production needs careful consideration. This relationship is particularly important for the fixed land economies of Europe. In America the relationship between weather, agriculture and the aggregate economy does not seem to be related to long swings because of the extention of the frontier. In an attempt to gain an insight into the impact of weather on the output and productivity swings of fixed land economies, the British case shall be examined in some detail. The existence of sectoral capital and labour figures allows a quantitative examination of the agro-climatic relationship.

Finding a relevant proxy for weather that would capture the effect on agricultural production is not straightforward. Both rainfall and temperature would be critical to weather variations. However, rainfall and temperature variations are not independent of each other and their effect on weather is not additive in any simple way. An index of agricultural drought that relates these two inputs could provide a good proxy of weather variations. Agricultural drought would be determined by:

(i) rainfall,

(ii) evaporation, and

(iii) the timing of the rainfall.

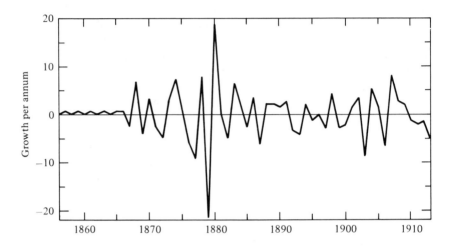

Figure 6.8 The annual geometric growth rate of British agricultural production. Source: Lewis (1978, pp. 160–3)

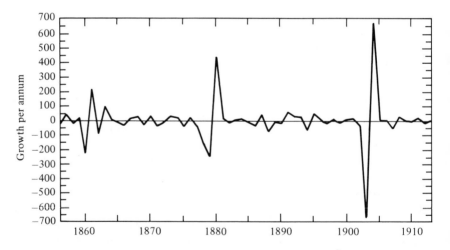

Figure 6.9 The annual geometric growth rate of soil moisture deficits. Source: Wigley and Atkinson (1977, pp. 431–4)

Table 6.12 *Correlations between agricultural
production and mean soil moisture deficits
(growth/annum)*

	r	F-test
1862–1890	0.63	17.9[a]
1891–1909	0.51	5.9[b]
1862–1909	0.48	14.1[a]

[a] Significant at 1 per cent.
[b] Significant at 5 per cent.

Thus, the average soil moisture deficit over the growing season (May–August)
can be used as an index of drought severity. Rodda *et al.* (1976) conclude that
soil moisture deficits provide the best practical drought index. Using homo-
geneous series for precipitation and evaporation data for Kew, Wigley and
Atkinson (1977) have constructed a record of soil moisture deficits back to
1698. This series is employed as a proxy for weather variation for the period
under consideration. Given that the Kew precipitation record is highly correlated ($r = 0.89$) with the south-eastern England precipitation, the results are
representative of south-east England (Wigley and Atkinson, 1977, p. 432).

The statistical methodology employed to analyse the relationship between
weather and agricultural production is that outlined by Wigley (1983) – first, I
seek to identify and, secondly, to quantify the relationship over time.

Correlation analysis is used to identify the relationship between the agro-
climatic variables. As can be seen from Figures 6.8 and 6.9 the growth rates of
agricultural production and soil moisture deficits moved together for much
of the time. The correlation between the growth rates of agricultural production and soil moisture deficits is both high and statistically significant (see
Table 6.12). Moreover, the correlation is higher before 1890 than over the
period 1891–1909, which is compatible with the evidence that the swings in
agricultural production were of a greater amplitude before 1891.

The relationship between weather and agricultural production is also observed over the swing phases of agricultural production growth. Extreme values
for soil moisture deficits are observed in both phases of low agricultural
production (see Table 6.13). In the 1870s the index takes very low mean values,
reflecting both the heavy rainfall of those years and the below average
temperatures. The period 1875–81 was the wettest for the whole era under
consideration. In the 1890s the deficit values rose, reflecting both the high
temperatures and the low rainfall values. For other phases the mean variations
were much lower than those observed for the 1870s and 1890s. Thus, the
weather variable is correlated with the observed agricultural swings.

Finding a correlation between weather variation and agricultural production is not sufficient evidence for the existence of a causal relationship

Table 6.13 *Weather variation over peak-to-peak phases of agricultural production*

t	$\bar{X}$	$\hat{\sigma}$	$\bar{x} - \mu$
Temperatures during growing season[a][b]			
1866–1875	14.361	0.673	+0.2600
1875–1881	13.949	0.780	−0.1524
1881–1891	13.789	0.581	−0.3119
1891–1902	14.224	0.823	+0.1232
1902–1909	13.684	0.650	−0.4173
Rainfall during growing season[c]			
1855–1866	105.490	24.506	+4.2117
1866–1875	91.310	23.720	−9.9700
1875–1881	122.740	29.045	+21.460
1881–1891	104.050	22.589	+2.7655
1891–1902	95.708	17.699	−5.5717
1902–1909	103.130	16.427	+1.8450
Mean soil moisture deficits during growing season[d]			
1855–1866	78.217	29.339	− 1.6973
1866–1875	88.070	17.784	+ 8.1560
1875–1881	61.257	39.169	−18.657
1881–1891	72.655	22.763	− 7.2595
1891–1902	95.792	18.283	+15.878
1902–1909	72.375	31.391	− 7.539

[a] In degrees Celsius.
[b] Growing season May to August inclusive.
[c] Expressed as a percentage of the rainfall for the standard period 1881–1915.
[d] Expressed as an index.
$\bar{x}$ is the average for the specific peak-to-peak phase.
μ is the average for the whole period (1855–1909).
σ is the standard deviation.

Sources: Temperatures from Manley (1974, Table 1); rainfall from Nicholas and Glasspole (1932, Table I); SMDs from Wigley and Atkinson (1977, pp. 432–4).

between these variables. Moreover, in seeking to quantify this relationship the impact of weather needs to be placed in the broader context of the economic determinants of agricultural production. Various correlations between agricultural production and labour and capital inputs are presented in Table 6.14. The only significant correlation observed is that between output growth and labour input growth over the period 1862–1890. The swings of agricultural output and productivity were not the result of variations in factor input growth (see Table 6.15).[13] The same conclusion holds true for variations in total factor input (Feinstein *et al.*, 1982). This conclusion is valid for both growth rates over the peak-to-peak output phases and the first difference in

Table 6.14 *Correlations between agricultural production, labour and capital inputs*

	r_{QK}	F-test	r_{QL}	F-test
1862–1890	−0.17	0.81	0.40	5.06[a]
1891–1909	+0.16	0.47	−0.06	0.07
1862–1909	−0.03	0.05	0.31	4.71[a]

[a] Significant at 5 per cent.
r_{QK} is the correlation of output and capital.
r_{QL} is the correlation of output and labour.

Table 6.15 *Growth of output, labour and gross capital over the peak-to-peak output growth phases for agricultural production*

t	$\bar{g}_a$	$\bar{g}_L$	$\bar{g}_K$	$\Delta\bar{g}_a$	$\Delta\bar{g}_L$	$\Delta\bar{g}_K$
1855–1866	+0.00384	−0.0103	+0.00311	—	—	—
1866–1875	+0.00741	−0.0101	+0.00313	+0.00357	+0.0002	+0.00002
1875–1881	−0.01700	−0.0109	+0.00177	−0.02441	−0.0008	−0.00136
1881–1891	+0.00623	−0.0084	+0.00089	+0.02323	+0.0025	−0.00088
1891–1902	−0.00502	−0.0081	−0.00424	−0.01125	+0.0003	−0.00513
1902–1909	+0.00595	−0.0065	−0.00436	+0.01097	+0.0016	−0.00012

See notes to Table 6.6.
Sources: Lewis (1978, pp. 260–3); Feinstein (1976, Table 60, T131).

growth over such phases. The evidence would suggest that both capital and labour were in surplus and did not affect output variation. Thus, various attempts to relate the impact of weather within a production function framework proved futile since output variations were not related to input variations.[14]

Another possible economic explanation for these swings is that agriculture could have been responding to swings in the aggregate economy, which may have been determined by macroeconomic considerations, or at least non-weather variables. However, the swings in agricultural production were only similar to the aggregate swings over the 1870s and 1880s. During the 1860s and the period 1890–1913 agricultural output swings moved in an inverse pattern to aggregate swings.

Another economic variable that needs to be considered is the pattern of international competition in agricultural commodities (Feinstein et al., 1982; Matthews et al., 1982). Although the degree of international competition seems to be an important variable in accounting for the income and profitability path of the agricultural sector, it does not seem to be the determining factor for the long swings in output and productivity. Although the ratio of the imports of agricultural products to agricultural output rose more rapidly during the 1870s, this does not, in itself, signify the importance of international competition. In particular, during the period 1873–82 the causality for variations in this ratio seem to be running the other way – supply shocks to British agriculture were determining the trends in this ratio. In 1868 Britain still produced 80 per cent of domestic food consumption. The supply shocks of the 1870s implied the need to import increased agricultural commodities. Cheap agricultural commodities were not flooding the British and European markets; the sectoral terms of trade moved in favour of agriculture in the 1870s, as would be expected from a supply shock. Thus, the increased imports of the 1870s were being purchased at a higher relative cost. During the 1880s when the degree of international competition in agricultural commodities increased and the sectoral terms of trade moved against agriculture, the sector witnessed a revival of output and productivity.

Thus, an economic explanation for the swings in agricultural production is inadequate. The impact of climatic change needs to be studied as a possible *causal* explanation. To the extent that weather is a resource for agriculture, weather shocks are expected to influence both output and productivity. Moreover, although man is not a passive force in this framework the pattern of weather variation can be perceived as an unexpected shock on society; contemporaries believed in the constancy of long-term weather conditions (Lamb, 1982). Hence, society was not prepared for the kind of variations discussed here. In addition, man's adjustment to the shock of the 1870s (based on abnormally low soil moisture deficits) was not useful for the shock of the 1890s which was based on abnormally high soil moisture deficits. Technical progress may have lessened the impact of climatic stress over the period 1855–1913 but it was not powerful enough to cancel the impact. Some support for the *lessening* hypothesis is provided by the lower correlations observed for 1891–1909 relative to the pre-1891 era. The evidence for a significant agroclimatic relationship for the US economy in the twentieth century, which can be regarded as the technological leader (Bowden *et al.*, 1981) also means that the agro-climatic relationship needs careful examination for nineteenth-century Britain.

Since a production function cannot be estimated for the late nineteenth century, the impact of weather needs to be analysed as an independent exogenous shock to agricultural production. The general model can be specified as:

$$g_Q = f(g_W) \tag{1}$$

where g_Q is the growth of agricultural output and g_W is the growth of the weather variable. The weather variable cannot be assumed to be linear. Both extremes of weather would have adverse effects on agricultural production. To capture

this it is assumed that these effects will be proxied by a third-order polynomial
— g_W, g_W^2 and g_W^3 will be included as relevant weather variables.[15] These
variables will be assumed to be linear in parameters. Thus, the specific
functional form for (1) can be specified as

$$g_Q = \alpha + \beta g_W + \gamma g_W^2 + \delta g_W^3 + u_t \tag{2}$$

The problem of autocorrelation means that the error term (u_t) cannot be
assumed to be white noise. Hence equation (2) is estimated using an autoregressive model. Given the greater amplitude of the pre-1891 swings, (2) is run
for the whole period (1862–1909) and two sub-periods (1862–90 and 1891–
1909).

The results are presented in Appendix Table A6.3. For the sub-period 1862–
90 this model accounted for 44 per cent of agricultural output variation. Only
the coefficient on the third-order polynomial was significant which suggests a
non-linear relationship. During the sub-period 1891–1909 weather variation
accounted for 39 per cent of the agricultural output variations with the
coefficient on the third-order polynomial being significant at the 10 per cent
level. Moreover, the size of the coefficient fell from 0.00174 during the sub-
period 1862–90 to 0.0011 during the sub-period 1891–1909, which confirms the
reduced impact of weather variation over time. During the whole period 1862–
1909 the weather model accounted for 49 per cent of the variation of
agricultural production with both the first- and third-order coefficients being
highly significant (see Appendix Table A6.3). The magnitude of the climatic
impact reported in this study is similar to that reported in Bowden *et al.*,
(1981, p. 499) for the US in the twentieth century.

Such evidence suggests that the impact of climatic swings was an important
force on the agricultural swings of the British economy throughout the period
1856–1913. The effect of the agricultural sector on the aggregate swings was
very important only during some swing phases, in particular the 1870s and
1880s. Thus, cycles of nature were not the underlying force for the growth
swings of the pre-1913 era. Economic processes acted to filter out many of the
possible cyclical effects of weather variations. However, understanding the
agro-climatic relationship is essential for understanding the swings of the
agricultural sector and some aggregate swings. Such an agro-climatic relationship is not observed in America because of the existence of a moving
territorial frontier. Nevertheless, the British evidence suggests that climatic
variations would be an important variable for understanding the European
long swings, especially since the agricultural sector was far more important in
the other European economies. It should be emphasised that the phasing
outlined here relates only to the British economy. The agroclimatic relationship would be expected to be region specific.

Monetary aspects

Most long-swing studies have been undertaken with an emphasis on the real aspects of growth. Although there has been much discussion on the role of monetary factors in generating price waves, monetary variations have been left out of long-swing studies.[16] However, there is a prima-facie case for seeing monetary variations as being important in helping to account for some long-swing phases.

Because of data availability the focus of this section will be on the monetary aspects of British and American swings. For Britain there are two recently constructed money stock series; one constructed by Bordo (1981) and the other by Friedman and Schwartz (1982). With the exception of the 1880s both series show a similar swing path.[17] The trends observed in the two series are presented in Tables 6.16 and 6.17. The reference peaks are those of the GDP series (compromise estimate), but it is important to stress that using the specific peaks of the series does not alter the phasing.

The American money stock also grew in a long swing (see Table 6.18). The swings in the money stock correlate with the swings in GDP throughout the period 1873–1912.

Friedman and Schwartz (1982) have used the money stock evidence to suggest a causal relationship with the path of real income, based on a modern version of the quantity theory. Their argument is based on American long swings since they did not find significant aggregate long swings for the British economy. The evidence provided in Chapter 3 suggests that output and productivity have also varied along a long swing in the British economy.

To argue for a consistent monetary theory of long swings would require that all the real aspects varying over the swings be the result of monetary variations. For example, both Robertson (1949) and Hayek (1935) develop a monetary theory of the cycle. However, such *pure* theories represent an

Table 6.16 *Growth of Bordo money stock and HPM series over peak-to-peak phases for GDP: Britain (growth/annum)*

t	$\bar{g}_M$	$\hat{\sigma}_{g_M}$	$\bar{g}_{HPM}$	$\bar{\sigma}_{g_{HPM}}$	$\Delta\bar{g}_M$	$\Delta\bar{g}_{HPM}$
1873–1882	0.0037	0.031	0.0133	0.036	—	—
1882–1889	0.0023	0.020	−0.0219	0.025	−0.0014	−0.0352
1889–1899	0.0279	0.021	0.0205	0.038	+0.0256	+0.0424
1899–1907	0.0100	0.016	0.0036	0.023	−0.0179	−0.0169
1907–1913	0.0312	0.012	0.0235	0.017	+0.0212	+0.0199

M = money stock
HPM = high-powered money
Source: Bordo (1981).

Table 6.17 *Growth of Friedman–Schwartz money stock and HPM series over peak-to-peak phases for GDP: Britain (growth/annum)*

t	$\bar{g}_M$	$\hat{\sigma}_{g_M}$	$\bar{g}_{HPM}$	$\hat{\sigma}_{g_{HPM}}$	$\Delta\bar{g}_M$	$\Delta\bar{g}_{HPM}$
1873–1882	0.0041	0.026	0.0020	0.026	—	—
1882–1889	0.0159	0.016	0.0026	0.018	+0.0118	+0.0006
1889–1899	0.0281	0.019	0.0193	0.028	+0.0122	+0.0167
1899–1907	0.0129	0.014	0.0105	0.011	−0.0152	−0.0088
1907–1913	0.0261	0.011	0.0149	0.019	+0.0132	+0.0044

M = money stock
HPM = high-powered money
Source: Friedman and Schwartz (1982, pp. 30–7).

Table 6.18 *Growth of Friedman–Schwartz money stock and HPM series over peak-to-peak phases for GDP: USA (growth/annum)*

t	$\bar{g}_M$	$\hat{\sigma}_{g_M}$	$\bar{g}_{HPM}$	$\hat{\sigma}_{g_{HPM}}$	$\Delta\bar{g}_M$	$\Delta\bar{g}_{HPM}$
1873–1884	0.0498	0.080	0.0384	0.061	—	—
1884–1892	0.0574	0.024	0.0302	0.022	+0.0076	−0.0082
1892–1899	0.0455	0.071	0.0239	0.053	−0.0119	−0.0063
1899–1906	0.0855	0.023	0.0541	0.018	+0.0400	+0.0302
1906–1912	0.0519	0.038	0.0390	0.032	−0.0336	−0.0151

M = money stock
HPM = high-powered money

Source: Friedman and Schwartz (1982, pp. 22–9).

abstraction on reality. A causal framework emphasising real variables is also possible.

The perspective I wish to emphasise is one that sees monetary swings as being generated by the economic system as an organic entity. Friedman and Schwartz are right to emphasise that the monetary aspects of long swings have been neglected, but to then turn a full circle is unfounded. Williamson (1964) and Abramovitz (1973) have argued that monetary swings in America were linked to balance-of-payments conditions and the flows of foreign capital. Such flows were closely related to real conditions in the economy. The exogenous monetary shocks analysed by Friedman and Schwartz do not satisfy the exogeneity assumption. Nevertheless, there were some monetary pressures that can be modelled as exogenous to the long-swing pattern of growth.

Periods of monetary shock have also been periods of aggregate price variations, with significant implications for profitability, investment and output trends. If all price variations were perfectly expected then all real variables

Table 6.19 *Interest, price and* ex-post *real interest variations: Britain*
(growth/annum and levels %)

t	$\bar{r}_1$	$\bar{r}_2$	$\bar{\Pi}$	$\bar{\rho}_1$	$\bar{\rho}_2$
1873–1882	2.938	3.113	−1.678	4.616	4.791
1882–1889	2.650	2.953	−0.919	3.569	3.872
1889–1899	2.232	2.471	0.000	2.232	2.471
1899–1907	3.373	2.754	0.872	2.500	1.882
1907–1913	3.102	3.130	0.887	2.150	2.243

$\bar{r}_1$ = monetary interest on three monthly bills, average for cycle.
$\bar{r}_2$ = monetary interest on consols, average for cycle.
$\bar{\Pi}$ = average price change over cycle, GNP deflator.
$\bar{\rho}_1$ and $\bar{\rho}_2$ = real interest based on $\bar{r}_1$ and $\bar{r}_2$ respectively.

Source: Friedman and Schwartz (1982).

would be left unaffected.[18] However, the variation of prices was not predicted perfectly by agents; this would be particularly true during adjustment periods towards a new price level (such as the 1850s, 1870s and 1890s).

An important link between money, price and investment trends is provided by the variations in the Fisherian real rate of interest over such shocked periods. In Fisher (1933),

$$\rho = r - \pi$$

where, ρ is the real rate of interest, r is the monetary rate of interest and π is the expected price change. In the 1870s, with falling aggregate prices ρ would be expected to rise, unless the market for loanable funds has perfect foresight and adjusts r down by the same proportion as π falls. Hence, in periods of unexpected deflation the real cost of borrowing is expected to increase and vice versa for periods of unexpected inflation.

A direct test for this hypothesis would need a complicated macro-model of the economy. Only a proximate test is attempted by looking at trends in interest rates, prices and *ex-post* real interest rates. The relevant trends for Britain and America are presented in Tables 6.19 and 6.20 respectively.

During the period 1873–82 market interest rates in Britain were remarkably stable, despite deflation averaging 2 per cent per annum. Given the fall in profitability from 1871 and of investment from 1876, a likely cause of high interest rates (and real interest rates) was market rigidity. Average interest rates adjusted downwards in the 1880s when the rate of deflation slowed down markedly, suggesting a degree of market adjustment. However, in the 1890s interest rates continued moving in a downward direction despite the reversal of prices, profitability and investment. Thus, for much of the 1890s market

Table 6.20 *Interest, price and* ex-post *real interest variations: USA*
(growth/annum and levels %)

t	$\bar{r}_1$	$\bar{r}_2$	$\bar{\Pi}$	$\bar{\rho}_1$	$\bar{\rho}_2$
1873–1884	5.316	4.911	−1.688	7.005	6.599
1884–1892	4.930	3.848	−1.487	6.417	5.334
1892–1899	4.397	3.561	−0.359	4.756	3.921
1899–1906	4.761	3.421	+2.085	2.677	1.337
1906–1912	4.745	3.853	+2.229	2.516	1.624

$\bar{r}_1$ = average interest on commercial paper.
$\bar{r}_2$ = average interest on high grade corporate bonds.
$\bar{\Pi}$ = average price change over cycle, GNP deflator.
$\bar{\rho}_1$ and $\bar{\rho}_2$ = real interest based on $\bar{r}_1$ and $\bar{r}_2$ respectively.

rigidity may have generated a Wicksellian cumulative investment process because the market interest rate was below the natural rate.[19] As price trends were perceived to be permanent after some years of inflation, money interest rates adjusted upwards, as did real interest rates. Given the reversal of output, investment and profitability trends in the early twentieth century, the financial adjustment from low interest rates in the 1890s may have overshot.

American money interest rates followed the long-wave path of prices during the period 1873–1913. Nevertheless, the large variation of prices relative to interest rates allows for possible influences during long-swing phases. Both money and real interest rates were high in the cycle of the 1870s. Given that this was a downswing phase in the long swing, there exists some prima-facie evidence that the market failed to adjust interest rates in response to deflationary pressures. Similarly, although interest rates rose during the inflationary period of 1899–1913 the rise was marginal compared to the significant reversal of price trends. Thus, as in the case of Britain, periods of unexpected inflation and deflation had an important influence during some long-swing periods.

Another possible mechanism of influence between money and long swings is through variations in real money balances. To the extent that world prices were being determined by non-monetary factors, differences could occur between monetary and price variation over time, implying large shifts in the growth of real money balances. In Britain real money balances grew very slowly during the Edwardian era relative to the 1873–99 period. During the period 1899–1907 the growth rate of real money balances was practically stagnant. Similarly, in America real money balances grew very slowly during the period 1906–12. Such real money balance change could constrain the growth path with a wealth effect on consumption or via effects on interest rates and investment (Matthews et al., 1982; Pigou, 1943).

Credit, financial crises and long swings

Credit extention and financial crises have played an important role during long swings. This is particularly true for America but is also valid for the other economies. Although domestic financial crises were not of consequence to the British economy after 1866 the international implications of a crisis elsewhere in the world economy had repercussions for the British economy.

Financial crises were not random events but were closely related to the conditions for real growth. Crises generally arose when credit reached levels unwarranted by existing profitability conditions. These profitability problems were not structural in nature, but cyclical – the projects absorbing funds in each long swing were not entirely different. This poses the interesting counterfactual, had credit (both domestic and international) not contracted would marked swings in output and investment be eliminated? Given that the disjunctions between profitability and credit were not structural it is possible that a more planned investment and credit policy would have eliminated many long-swing variations. However, within the institutional frameworks of these economies, financial crisis was the means of correcting market imperfections. A crisis should be seen as a period of readjustment to eliminate the inefficient and speculative projects, in the tradition of Marx, Schumpeter, Hayek and Robertson.

The disjunction between credit expansion and profitability can be explained by a number of factors.

(i) Many projects had long gestation lags. Much of overseas investment was in railways. Although the construction of a single railway may not have entailed a long gestation, the gestation lag that is of relevance is that relating to railway construction and the frontier expansion for productive purposes. This could take some time and was the basis of many nineteenth-century financial crises.

(ii) Expectations relating to investment were formed at a point in time, assuming that the near past will continue for some time, if not indefinitely. Expectations were not formed over complete swings – the swings are in many ways a metaphysical construct that did not concern any one individual.

(iii) As the boom takes hold, speculative investment increases, as outlined by Schumpeter (1939) and Minsky (1964).

(iv) Distance implied a further cost in gathering information about investment projects overseas. It is interesting that as the importance of overseas investment in America declined in the early twentieth century, the severity of monetary contractions during downswing phases was reduced.

Such factors would be expected to vary over space and time.

The extent of financial crises varied across national boundaries. In the USA all late nineteenth-century long-swing booms 'ended' with financial crisis – e.g.

1873, 1893 and 1907 (Kindleberger, 1978b). In Germany the crisis of 1873 was significant. In France the crisis of 1882 associated with *Union Générale* signified the end of a Kuznets' boom in the 1870s. In England the only post-1866 crisis was the Baring crisis of 1890 related to Argentine loans but that was not of any major long-term significance.

The absence of major financial crises in Britain after 1866 raises a number of interesting questions as to the importance of financial crises in generating long swings. The British case illustrates the possibility of a more stable monetary adjustment, partly a reflection of the strength of British financial institutions. Nevertheless, the absence of financial crises did not imply the absence of long swings; although absence of financial crises may help to explain the lower variance of British growth, relative to America. Financial crises overseas certainly affected the mix between home and overseas investment (Stone, 1971) but they did not dominate the trends. The 1873 crisis may have increased the funds available for more marginal domestic investment projects, helping to account for the high domestic investment levels of 1874–76.

The evidence on financial crises suggests that the disjunction between credit and real growth conditions was an important variable in the long swing process but was neither a necessary nor a sufficient condition for long swings. Other variables played an important role in addition to credit. Using Schumpeter's terminology, the financial crisis provides a second approximation to the cycle, but even without the financial crisis there would still exist a cyclical path of economic growth.

Conclusions

In the pre-1913 era the long swing was a generalised growth pattern with national specific characteristics. In Chapter 3 evidence was provided for a long-swing phasing of production and productivity trends for Britain, France, Germany and America. The evidence presented in this chapter suggests that the swings are also observed in investment, profitability, the sectoral terms of trade, agricultural production, climatic variation and the growth of the money stock. Such evidence provides a strong case against a monocausal perspective to long swings; the swings are best seen as being generated by the economic system as an organic entity.

National aspects are essential when seeking to understand the differing long-swing patterns. The simple causality mechanisms of the Atlantic Economy inversities are misleading. The Atlantic Economy perspective has neglected important aspects that help our understanding of British long swings and is totally misleading when used to explain European swings.

The evidence presented so far suggests that the swings were episodic rather than endogenous. Moreover, they were not the result of s systematic exogenous variable. Migration swings have already been ruled out in this respect. Climatic swings can also be ruled out. Climatic variations are important in explaining the long swings of agricultural production and productivity, but structural change in the economy filtered out many of the cycle-generating effects of climatic change. The irregular periodicity of the swings also adds support to the episodic perspective. Moreover, the sectors accounting for many of the swings were very different over time.

Nevertheless, although the swings were a series of episodic events, the structure of the various economies is important to understanding the adjustment process. Even if the initial cause of a long swing was a series of episodic events, over time the adjustment response to the shock must have generated more complicated causal processes.

Statistical appendix

Table A6.1 *Significance tests for differences in long-swing and long-wave phases: French investment, 1846–1913* ('t' values in parenthesis)

Results of regressing $g_{I_t} = \alpha + dZ_t + \varepsilon_t$, $\varepsilon_t \sim N(0, \sigma_\varepsilon^2)$
or $g_{I_t} = \alpha + dZ_t + u_t$, $u_t = \rho_1 u_{t-1} + \varepsilon_t$
or $g_{I_t} = \alpha + dZ_t + u'_t$, $u'_t = \rho_1 u_{t-1} + \rho_2 u_{t-2} + \varepsilon_t$
                          $Z_t = (1 \ 0)$

(1) t	(2) $\hat{\alpha}$	(3) $\hat{d}$	(4) $\hat{\rho}_1$	(5) $\hat{\rho}_2$	(6) $Z_t = 1$ for t
Long-swing phases					
1846–1869	0.010072	0.016388	0.55326	− 0.2854	1846–1856
	(0.42)	(0.45)	(2.77)	−(1.43)	
1856–1882	0.035804	− 0.031226	− 0.10193	− 0.4295	1856–1869
	(1.98)	−(1.98)[a]	−(0.58)	−(2.43)	
1869–1891	− 0.018472	+ 0.058931	− 0.32152	− 0.4271	1869–1882
	−(0.88)	(2.13)[a]	−(1.67)	−(2.22)	
1882–1900	0.023656	− 0.041622	0.42110	− 0.3959	1882–1891
	(1.46)	−(1.79)[a]	(1.96)	(1.83)	
1891–1907	− 0.005981	0.035530	0.46387		1891–1900
	−(0.26)	(1.19)[b]	(2.20)		
1900–1913	0.05291	− 0.05478			1900–1907
	(2.23)	−(1.67)[a]			
Long-wave phases					
1846–1900	0.0036429	0.017163	0.19986	− 0.28499	1846–1882
	(0.19)	(0.74)	(1.53)	−(2.19)	
1856–1900	0.003836	0.016012	0.03272	− 0.33105	1856–1882
	(0.25)	(0.80)	(0.23)	− 2.33	
1882–1913	0.017212	− 0.010045	0.03531		1882–1900
	(0.81)	−(0.37)	(2.10)		

[a] Significant at 5 per cent.
[b] Significant at 10 per cent.

Table A.62 *Significance tests for differences in long-swing and long-wave phases: German net capital formation, 1852–1913 ('t' values in parenthesis)*

Results of regressing $gI_t = \alpha + d_1 Z_1 + d_2 Z_2 + u_t,\ u_t = \rho_1 u_{t-1} + \varepsilon_t$
$Z_t = (0\ 1)$

t	$\hat{\alpha}$	$\hat{d}_1$	$\hat{d}_2$	$\hat{\rho}_1$	$Z = 1$ for t
Long swings					
1856–1912	0.0761	− 0.0832	− 0.0553	− 0.5505	1874–1884
	(2.7)	− (1.4)[a]	− (1.2)[a]	− (4.98)	and
					1898–1912
Long-wave phases					
1856–1890	0.021355	0.03833		− 0.60189	1856–1874
	(0.53)	(0.68)		− (4.39)	
1874–1912	0.034176	−0.01906			1874–1890
	(1.02)	(0.37)			

[a] Significant at 0.1 level.

Table A6.3 *Regression results for explaining the growth path of agricultural production ('t' values in parenthesis)*

Results of regressing:
$g_{Q_t} = \alpha + \beta g_{W_t} + \gamma g^2_{W_t} + \delta g^3_{W_t} + u^t$
g_{Q_t} = agricultural output growth
g_{W_t} = weather growth

1862–1890			
$\hat{\alpha}$	−0.003526	− (0.51)	$R^2 = 0.46$
$\hat{\beta}$	Insignificant		$\bar{R}^2 = 0.44$
$\hat{\gamma}$	Insignificant		
$\hat{\delta}$	0.001742	(3.00)	
$\hat{\rho}_1$	−0.42180	− (2.51)	
$\hat{\rho}_2$	Insignificant		
1891–1909			
$\hat{\alpha}$	0.00053	(0.11)	$R^2 = 0.45$
$\hat{\beta}$	−0.042083	− (1.55)	$\bar{R}^2 = 0.39$
$\hat{\gamma}$	Insignificant		
$\hat{\delta}$	0.00110	(1.81)	
$\hat{\rho}_1$	−0.34289	− (1.58)	
$\hat{\rho}_2$	−0.32614	− (1.50)	
1862–1909			
$\hat{\alpha}$	0.001367	(0.43)	$R^2 = 0.51$
$\hat{\beta}$	0.037708	(3.92)	$\bar{R}^2 = 0.49$
$\hat{\gamma}$	Insignificant		
$\hat{\delta}$	−0.00069	− (2.65)	
$\hat{\rho}_1$	−0.65686	− (4.80)	
$\hat{\rho}_2$	−0.31667	− (2.31)	

Sources: Agricultural production from Lewis (1978, pp. 260–3); weather index from Wigley and Atkinson (1977, pp. 432–4).

7

The international aspects of Kuznets swings, 1850–1913

This chapter represents an extension of the causal processes generating long swings. Since all the countries under consideration were open economies, an international perspective is essential for understanding long swings.

A major problem in much of the existing literature is a failure to distinguish between descriptive models of international capital flows and causal models. Thomas (1954) has emphasised the inversity between home and overseas investment in the British economy within a causal perspective. At the other extreme Lewis and O'Leary (1955) argue that the inversity of British home and overseas investment was a coincidence and was not observed for the other major capital exporters. The present chapter argues that an inverse pattern between home and overseas investment is observed for *all* the major capital exporters but the causal processes generating such a pattern are not easy to determine. By providing more evidence on the French and German cases it is possible to break away from the Anglo-American centred explanations that have been postulated so far.

Long swings in overseas investment

Major long-swing downswings in the domestic economy will generate an inverse overseas investment path as long as two conditions are satisfied:
 (i) free international capital movement, and
 (ii) non-synchronisation in the profitability potential of different regions of the world economy.

Both conditions were satisfied in the pre-1913 era. Similarly, a causal mechanism running from the pull of overseas profitability conditions on a fixed domestic savings ratio will also give rise to an inversity between home and overseas investment.[1]

The causality for the pre-1913 home and overseas investment inversities is complicated. The national aspects of long swings, discussed in the previous chapter, suggest that a causal link running from domestic downswings to overseas investment is highly plausible. Moreover, the large flexibility of the savings ratio of the pre-1913 era suggests that the pull explanation of downswings in the domestic economy is unfounded (Edelstein, 1982, p. 172).

Overseas investment showed wide annual variability. To minimise the possibility of generating statistical artefacts, the measures reported here are the mean levels $(\bar{L}_F)$ of overseas investment over identified long swings.[2] Where an irregular sinusoidal swing path exists, as in the case of Britain, the question of the existence of long swings does not arise. The first difference of the mean level will be used as a proxy of long-swing variations.[3]

Long swings in British overseas investment are observable in the un-transformed data (see Figure 7.1).[4] The period 1872–1913 witnessed two complete swings in overseas investment. The downswing of the 1870s was short, only lasting over the period 1872–7. Thus, the mean level of overseas investment during the two Juglars 1865–73 and 1873–82 was only marginally different; Imlah's series showing the 1870s as being slightly lower and Simon's series as slightly higher (see Table 7.1).

In seeking to relate the overseas investment path to domestic output and

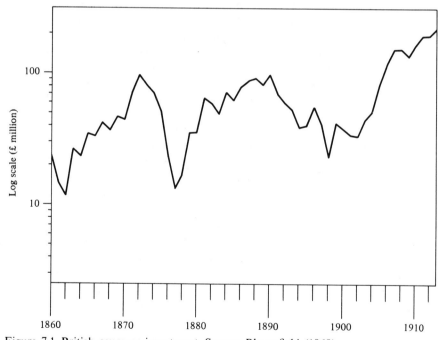

Figure 7.1 British overseas investment. Source: Bloomfield (1968)

Table 7.1 *British overseas investment over peak-to-peak phases* (million £/annum)

t	$\bar{L}_{F1}$	$\hat{\sigma}_{L_{F1}}$	$\Delta \bar{L}_{F1}$	$\bar{L}_{F2}$	$\hat{\sigma}_{L_{F2}}$	$\Delta \bar{L}_{F2}$
1865–1873	54.22	23.4	—	50.33	26.7	—
1873–1882	45.22	23.8	−8.99	53.15	24.7	+2.82
1882–1890	75.56	16.5	+30.33	89.11	31.2	+35.96
1890–1899	52.24	20.8	−23.32	65.17	23.7	−23.94
1899–1907	66.34	42.9	+14.10	86.76	26.4	+21.59
1907–1913	175.71	31.2	+100.37	176.14	34.9	+89.38

$\bar{L}_{F1}$ = mean level/annum from Imlah's balance-of-payments data.
$\bar{L}_{F2}$ = mean level/annum from Simon's portfolio creations data.
$\hat{\sigma}$ = standard deviation of mean.
Sources: Imlah (1958) and Simon (1968).

investment swings it is important to note the different phasing between output and investment swings. Thus, the output downswing of the 1870s was initially associated with a fall in overseas investment and then a rapid increase from 1877. Similarly the upswing in overseas investment during the 1880s was associated with a revival of output growth and investment from 1886. Thomas' (1973) emphasis on *levels* of domestic and overseas investment is misleading. After 1860 the British economy witnessed a long-run multiplier-accelerator mechanism, with output trends taking the lead by two or three years (Matthews *et al.*, 1982). In this perspective output and investment swings can be related in a consistent framework. The low level of overseas investment in the 1870s was not due to prosperity in Britain, resulting in the withdrawal of funds from the world economy, but was the result of a high degree of synchronisation in the world depression of the 1870s. Britain did try to find new outlets for its capital in Africa, Australia and the Empire but these regions could not absorb the high levels of potential overseas investment existing in the early 1870s. Financial crises in America and Argentina in 1873 led to a collapse of investment in these regions.

The French overseas investment data are taken from the work of White (1933) covering both direct and indirect estimates. The series indicate an upward trend throughout the period 1882–1912; thus, long swings in the French context are observed as variations in the rate of change, not in the level of overseas investment. Although France was a net capital exporter it was also a capital importer. Since the gross capital exports (total foreign investment by French citizens) and the net capital exports (gross minus foreign investment by other countries into France) show the same trends, only the net trends are reported.

The swings in overseas and domestic investment are presented in Figure 7.2. The swings are even clearer in Figure 7.3 which shows the rate of growth of

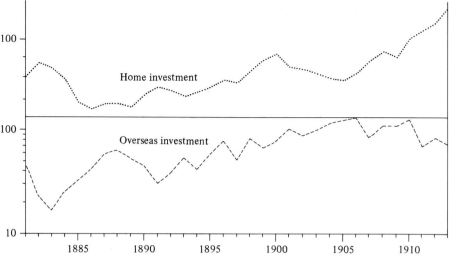

Figure 7.2 French home and overseas investment (constant prices). Sources: White (1933) and Lévy-Leboyer (1978)

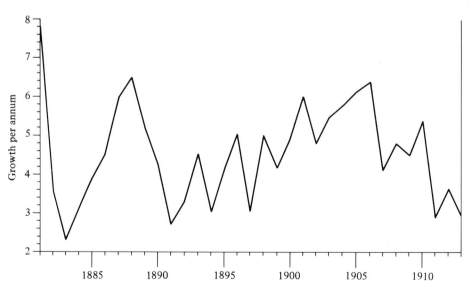

Figure 7.3 Growth of the French overseas 'net' capital stock. Source: White (1933, p. 121)

Table 7.2 *French overseas investment over peak-to-peak output phases* (*million francs/annum*)

t	$\bar{L}_{F1}$	$\hat{\sigma}_{L_{F1}}$	$\Delta_{L_{F1}}$	$\bar{L}_{F2}$	$\hat{\sigma}_{L_{F2}}$	$\Delta\bar{L}_{F2}$
1882–1892	499.55	178.14	—	400.64	335.44	—
1892–1899	687.50	171.44	+187.95	776.12	316.06	+375.50
1899–1907	1281.70	305.04	+594.20	1290.30	273.20	+514.18
1907–1913	1395.00	271.79	+113.30	1383.50	515.63	+93.20

$\bar{L}_{F1}$ = level/annum from White's 'net' portfolio data.
$\bar{L}_{F2}$ = level/annum from White's balance-of-payments data.
Source: White (1933).

the net overseas capital stock. The period 1883–8 witnessed a rising growth rate of the overseas capital stock. This remained high until 1889. The 1890s witnessed a low and trendless growth rate while 1899–1913 witnessed another complete swing with rising growth during the period 1899–1906 and falling growth during the period 1906–13. Taking the reference swings as those observed for domestic output and investment, trend swings in overseas investment are observed throughout the period 1882–1913 (see Table 7.2).[5]

Much confusion exists in the analysis of French foreign investment. The confusions seem to arise because the French swings differ from the British pattern. Both Cameron (1961) and Kindleberger (1964) have argued that French capital exports correlate with high rates of domestic growth. The evidence presented here suggests that the largest increases in foreign investment are observed during the slow-growth phases, although the level of overseas investment increased in both slow- and high-growing eras. Bloomfield (1968) concluded that French capital exports did not follow a long swing. This chapter suggests that long swings are observed with a minimal of data transformations. The swings are very different from the level variations observed in the British economy, but there is no reason to use the British case as a model of long-swing variations. Falkus (1979) explains the increased French foreign investment into Russia after 1890 in terms of stagnation in France in the 1890s. This is clearly an invalid explanation of the trends; the path of overseas investment to any one region need not determine or reflect the aggregate growth performance of the capital exporting country. Russia was indeed an important and a growing recipient of French capital during the 1890s; its share of French capital exports increased from 17 per cent in 1890 to 25 per cent in 1900. Nevertheless, the increased capital exports to Russia did not result in rapid capital exports in the aggregate. The 1890s were a high-growth phase for the French economy and a period of *decelerating* capital exports.

Long swings in French overseas investment are observed throughout the period 1882–1913.[6] The different nature of French swings is to be expected.

Table 7.3 *German overseas investment over peak-to-peak output phases (million marks/annum)*

t	$\bar{L}_{\mathrm{F1}}$	$\bar{\sigma}_{L_{\mathrm{F1}}}$	$\Delta\bar{L}_{\mathrm{F1}}$
1884–1893	518.8	147.0	—
1893–1900	396.5	181.6	−122.3
1900–1907	573.0	165.7	+176.5
1907–1913	977.6	594.3	+404.6

$\bar{L}_{\mathrm{F1}}$ = level/annum from Bloomfield's balance-of-payments data.
Source: Bloomfield (1968, pp. 42–46).

First, France was a relatively backward economy when compared to Britain during this period. Secondly, the international distribution of French investment was European centred,[7] and the European economies were facing very different production conditions from the frontier economies that Britain was investing in. Finally, financial crises in the capital receiving countries did not affect French overseas investment to the same extent as Britain.

A long swing in overseas investment is also observed for Germany; a downward trend during the period 1886–1900 was followed by a rising trend during the period 1900–13 (see Table 7.3).[8] The swings in German overseas investment are observed most clearly as ratios of income and home investment (see Figures 7.4 and 7.5).

Bloomfield (1968) found evidence for the existence of long-run fluctuations, but not of the long-swing type. A five-year moving average generated peaks in 1886, 1902 and 1913. The large variation in the German series makes the five-year moving average difficult to interpret. The evidence presented here suggests that overseas investment followed a downward trend during the period 1886–1900 and an irregular upward trend during the early twentieth century. Thus, the variation of overseas investment was inverse to home investment (see Chapter 6). Lewis and O'Leary (1955, p. 142) suggested that German

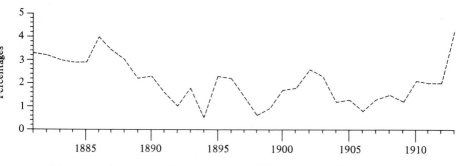

Figure 7.4 Share of overseas investment to NDP. Sources: Mitchell (1981) and Bloomfield (1968)

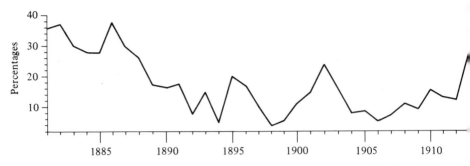

Figure 7.5 Share of overseas to domestic investment. Sources: Mitchell (1981) and Bloomfield (1968)

capital exports moved in a procyclical manner with domestic investment:

the periods of heaviest capital exports coincided with the periods of heaviest home investment if the building cycle is a good guide.

This was clearly not the case. The periods of high overseas investment were the periods of downswing in domestic investment, such as the 1870s and the Edwardian era.

Thus, the inverse home–overseas investment path was a generalised pattern for all the major capital exporters. However, such evidence has little to say on the causal processes generating this pattern. The widely differing national swing variations suggests a causal framework that is dependent on specific national growth conditions with allowance for possible influences from the international economy.

The international terms of trade and long swings

In this section Cairncross' (1953) sectoral terms-of-trade hypothesis is examined at the international economy level of analysis. Cairncross was using the terms of trade as a relative profitability proxy. However, when using such unit-value price indices, care must be taken to derive a relevant price relative. Given that at any one time capital exporters were interested in specific regions of the world economy, the relevant relative price structure needs to be specific to capital exporters and capital importers.

In this study two international terms of trade indicators are analysed:
(a) $\text{TOT}(1) = P_x/P_M$

$\text{TOT}(1) =$ net barter terms of trade

$P_X =$ unit price of exports, measured f.o.b.

$P_M =$ unit price of imports, measured c.i.f.

This is the index used by Cairncross to test the relative profitability idea of international investment flows. However, since the TOT(1) variations are not

Table 7.4 *British TOT(1) data over peak-to-peak phases (1913 = 100)*

t	P_{X_1}	P_{X_2}	P_{M_1}	P_{M_2}	TOT(1)A	TOT(1)B
1872	123	129	123	123	100	105
1881	94	103	106	106	88	97
1889	86	94	89	89	96	106
1899	80	83	79	79	101	105
1907	93	92	94	94	99	98
1913	100	100	100	100	100	100

P_{X_1} = unit value credits on merchandise.
P_{X_2} = unit value credits on current account.
P_{M_1} = unit value debits on merchandise.
P_{M_2} = unit value debits on current account.
$A = P_{X_1}/P_{M_1}$
$B = P_{X_2}/P_{M_2}$
Source: Kindleberger (1956, Ch. 2).

specifically related to the price structure of capital importers the index will provide a bad proxy for the type of international investment observed in the pre-1913 era, which was region or country specific. This variable is used here only for the purpose of making some comparisons with Cairncross' (1953) study.

(b) $TOT(2) = P_{X_i}/P_{X_j}$

$TOT(2)$ = a regional price relative

P_X = price of exports (f.o.b.)

i, j = countries or regions of the world economy

The advantage of this index is that it is disaggregated enough to be able to deal with the pattern of pre-1913 overseas investment. Moreover, since prices are treated f.o.b. for both regions the problem of shipping costs can be removed.

The British TOT(1) index followed a long-swing path during the period 1872–1913 (see Table 7.4). The British net barter terms of trade moved adversely in the 1870s, favourably in the 1880s and 1890s and adversely again in the Edwardian period. The explanatory power of the British TOT(1) index has already been examined in some detail by Cairncross (1953) and Kindleberger (1956). Only during the period 1890–1913 can the TOT(1) index help explain the path of capital exports, and even in this period the variation was small. Thus, Kindleberger (1956) concluded that the TOT(1) index cannot explain the pattern of British overseas investment during the period 1870–1913. However, the discussion of Cairncross' ideas should not end here. As noted above, the TOT(1) index is a bad proxy of the profitability considerations that Cairncross was trying to measure. The TOT(2) indicators provide a more relevant variable. Such indicators are presented in Table 7.5.

Table 7.5 *British TOT(2) trends over peak-to-peak phases for British exports: levels and growth rates (growth/annum; levels in parenthesis)*

t	USA	NW Europe	Other Europe	Temperate countries	Tropical countries	World
1855	(132.2)	(84.4)	(102.2)	(125.5)	(122.6)	(103.6)
1860	−0.032	+0.001	−0.012	−0.003	−0.029	−0.010
1866	−0.075	+0.044	+0.043	+0.033	+0.037	−0.013
1872	+0.085	−0.001	−0.016	−0.022	−0.016	+0.035
1881	−0.019	−0.019	−0.016	−0.028	−0.017	−0.015
1889	+0.008	−0.001	+0.005	+0.004	0.000	+0.002
1899	+0.012	−0.001	+0.008	+0.003	+0.005	+0.002
1907	−0.014	+0.011	−0.007	−0.009	+0.001	+0.001
1913	−0.002	+0.002	+0.005	0.000	−0.004	0.000
1913	(100)	(100)	(100)	(100)	(100)	(100)

Source: Lewis (1981, Appendix Tables 3 and 4).

The pattern of price variation observed in Table 7.5 shows clearly the inadequacy of the TOT(1) proxy. During the period 1866–72 a markedly favourable movement in the British TOT(1) index was due to the effect of variation in the Anglo-American price relatives. The TOT(2) indicators for NW Europe, other Europe, temperature countries and tropical countries were all adverse for Britain. This adverse TOT(2) pattern continued during the 1870s. Although overseas investment fell significantly during the period 1872–7, the role of financial crises in the capital importing countries needs to be added as an important explanatory variable. During the 1880s, although the TOT(2) indicators were generally in Britain's favour, the magnitude of the gains were marginal compared to the losses of the late 1860s and 1870s. Thus, the profitability signal existing for most of the 1870s persisted into the 1880s. During the period 1890–1913 the TOT(2) indicators moved in a similar manner to the TOT(1) indicator but showed far greater variation. Thus, the TOT(2) indices suggest that Cairncross' explanation of overseas investment in terms of relative profitability signals is a valid perspective, especially when financial crises are allowed to have an impact on the allocation of overseas investment.

The French international terms of trade are presented in Table 7.6. The series is the official valuations series reported in White (1933) and Kindleberger (1956). It is quite clear that this series is not related to the long swings in overseas investment outlined earlier. During the period 1883–99 the variation of the series was extremely low. However, the weakness of the official valuations series made White favour the market quotations series.

Although the market quotations series runs for a shorter period and is of an unweighted nature (Kindleberger, 1955, p. 328) the variation of the series is

Table 7.6 *French TOT(1) data over peak-to-peak phases for exports* (*1913 = 100*)

t	P_{X_1}	P_{X_2}	P_{M_1}	P_{M_2}	TOT(1)A	TOT(1)B
1872	131	127	125	124	105	102
1883	107	106	95	95	113	112
1890	101	99	91	91	111	109
1899	92	89	83	83	111	107
1907	100	99	90	90	111	111
1913	100	100	100	100	100	100

P_{X_1} = unit value credits on merchandise.
P_{X_2} = unit value credits on current account.
P_{M_1} = unit value debits on merchandise.
P_{M_2} = unit value debits on current account.
$A = P_{X_1}/P_{M_1}$
$B = P_{X_2}/P_{M_2}$
Source: Kindleberger (1956, Ch. 2).

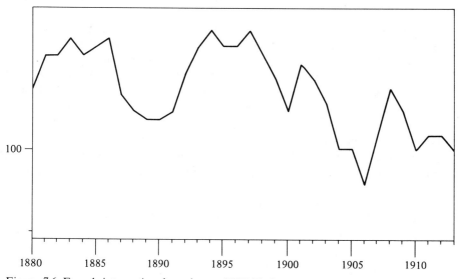

Figure 7.6 French international net barter TOT(1). Source: White (1933, p. 252)

more relevant to long-swing discussions. The pattern observed (see Figure 7.6) can be summarized as:

    1880s unfavourable
    1890s favourable
    1899–1907 unfavourable
    1907–13 favourable

Periods of unfavourable variations were correlated with increased overseas

Table 7.7 *NW Europe's TOT(2) trends over peak-to-peak phases for exports: levels and growth rates (growth/annum; levels in parenthesis)*

t	USA	Other Europe	Temperate countries	Tropical countries	World
1853	(156.6)	(121.1)	(148.7)	(145.3)	(122.7)
1860	−0.033	−0.0122	−0.004	−0.0301	−0.0109
1866	−0.120	−0.0011	−0.011	−0.0066	−0.0192
1872	+0.086	−0.0138	−0.021	−0.0147	−0.0001
1883	0.000	+0.0075	−0.011	−0.0022	+0.0035
1890	+0.001	−0.0015	+0.008	+0.0016	+0.0001
1899	+0.013	+0.0106	+0.005	+0.0103	+0.0070
1907	−0.024	−0.0172	−0.019	−0.0095	−0.0134
1913	−0.005	−0.0070	−0.002	−0.0066	−0.0024
1913	(100)	(100)	(100)	(100)	(100)

Source: Lewis (1981, Appendix Tables 3 and 4).

investment flows and periods of favourable variations with reduced overseas investment.

The TOT(2) variations of NW Europe also help explain the overseas investment path of the French economy (see Table 7.7). Given that the trading and capital export links of France were focused on periphery Europe, the TOT(2) index with respect to 'other Europe' would be the most relevant economic indicator. This index showed a mild adverse movement in the 1880s, a favourable movement in the 1890s, a large adverse variation during the period 1899–1907 and a mild adverse variation during the period 1907–13. This pattern clearly helps to explain the path of French overseas investment. The adverse terms of trade of NW Europe with respect to temperate and tropical countries in the early twentieth century also created an investment opportunity in such regions, as both the French and German portfolios became more geographically diversified.[9]

The German terms of trade (see Table 7.8) witnessed a large unfavourable variation during the 1870s. The series was little changed in the 1880s and 1890s and moved adversely again in the Edwardian period. Since the German capital export figures only go back to the early 1880s it is difficult to test the role of the terms of trade in explaining the overseas investment path. A relationship can be observed if the starting point of the capital export series is regarded as representative of the capital exports during the 1870s. As can be seen from Figures 7.4 and 7.5 the share of overseas investment was extremely high before 1886. The share of overseas investment as a proportion of domestic investment ranged between 28 per cent and 38 per cent between 1881 and 1886 and fell on trend throughout the period 1886–98. During the Edwardian period the trend started rising again. Thus, adverse fluctuations in the terms of trade were associated with large capital exports.

Table 7.8 *German TOT(1) data over peak-to-peak phases for exports* (*1913 = 100*)

t	P_{X_1}	P_{X_2}	P_{M_1}	P_{M_2}	TOT(1)A	TOT(1)B
1872	182	175	125	125	146	140
1883	115	113	104	104	111	109
1890	101	99	93	93	109	107
1899	91	89	84	84	108	106
1907	98	97	96	96	102	101
1913	100	100	100	100	100	100

P_{X_1} = unit value credits on merchandise.
P_{X_2} = unit value credits on current account.
P_{M_1} = unit value debits on merchandise.
P_{M_2} = unit value debits on current account.
$A = P_{X_1}/P_{M_1}$
$B = P_{X_2}/P_{M_2}$
Source: Kindleberger (1956, Ch. 2).

Table 7.9 *Difference between non-domestic and domestic realised rates of return: selected periods (geometric means)*

Share class	1870–1876	1877–1886	1887–1896	1897–1909	1910–1913
(1) Equity	−4.60	+6.08	−3.59	+8.62	−5.27
(2) Debentures	+1.93	+2.28	+0.24	+2.42	+0.06
(3) Total	−1.02	+2.69	−1.19	+3.85	−1.81

Source: Edelstein (1976).

In contrast to much of the literature the evidence presented here suggests that there is a relationship between the relative price structure of different parts of the world economy and international capital flows. Cairncross obtained a bad fit with the international terms of trade because unit-value relative prices are too aggregated to explain the region-specific pattern of overseas investment before 1913. To the extent that the terms of trade is proxying a relative profitability variation this would be the expected result; the overseas investment of Britain, France and Germany was undertaken by individuals seeking a relatively favourable return to their money capital. In the case of Britain the relative profitability idea can be tested more directly using Edelstein's (1976) sample of 566 first- and second-class equity preference and debenture stocks covering 1870–1913. Given that the data does not represent a full spectrum of portfolio investments, any inference about the level of returns refers only to the covered spectrum. However, the timing and direction of the pattern of relative returns is likely to be captured by this sample of first- and second-class returns, as long as wealth holders owned assets of best and worst returns and allocated funds according to return and risk considerations. The pattern of relative returns followed a marked long swing (see Table 7.9) with the following phasing:

1870–6	home profitability dominated
1877–86	overseas profitability dominated
1887–96	home profitability dominated
1897–1909	overseas profitability dominated
1909–13	home profitability dominated

This inverse pattern of home and overseas rates of return is highly correlated with the allocation between home and overseas investment.

The evidence examined suggests that swings in home and overseas investment were accompanied by relative profitability variations. The latter are observed in the changes of the relative price structure of capital exporters and capital importers and in the more direct relative rates-of-return evidence for Britain. However, the terms-of-trade variable cannot be viewed as an exogenous determinant of long swings. In a world-economy perspective such terms-of-trade variations would be endogenous. Thus, at best this evidence provides only a proximate explanation of long swings in overseas investment. To understand the underlying causal mechanism for long swings the terms-of-trade patterns need to be explained. The national aspects discussed in the previous chapter provide a part of the explanation. In the following section the focus is on the international determinants of relative price and profitability variations.

The international determinants of relative profitability variations

Some of the national specific aspects of profitability variations have already been discussed in the previous chapter. The pattern of growth in the world economy also contributes to a more complete explanation of relative profitability and relative price variations. As an illustration I shall consider the adverse terms of trade facing industrial countries during the period 1899–1913.

In Chapter 3 it was argued that *circa* 1890 the growth path of the world economy accelerated. This stepping-up of economic growth is observed both for world industrial production and world GDP. However, this acceleration is not observed in world agricultural production (Lewis, 1978).

Assuming a fairly stable relationship between the raw material and final product input–output relationship then the non-balanced growth path of the agricultural and industrial sectors during the period 1890–1913 explains why the sectoral terms of trade moved against industrial sectors.[10] Although technical progress resulted in a more efficient use of raw materials, the available evidence does not suggest a structural change in the efficiency of utilizing raw materials after 1890 (Saunders, 1952).

Thus, the pattern of growth in the world economy after 1890 implied an inverse profitability potential in the industrial and agricultural sectors of the world economy.[11] Given that these sectors were increasingly placed in different nations, the profitability variation implied international movements of resources. The adverse sectoral terms of trade depressed industrial profitability via a number of mechanisms.

(i) The increased cost of raw materials increased input costs.

(ii) The adverse terms of trade constrained real wage growth. The problems of adjusting from a rising real-wage traverse to a stagnating real-wage traverse imposed growth problems on many industrial nations.

(iii) The favourable profitability of agricultural producers attracted large flows of migrants which depressed the profitability of population-sensitive investments in the industrial nations.

(iv) To the extent that there existed autonomous domestic factors generating depressed swings in industrial nations (such as overinvestment in the 1890s) the adverse terms of trade had a cumulative effect.

The adjustment processes imposed by high growth in the world industrial production during the period 1890–1913 imposed a growth constraint on many industrial nations during the early twentieth century.

The profitability potential of the agricultural economies was financed by the relatively depressed European economies – Britain and Germany over the whole Edwardian period and France during the period 1900–7.[12]

The pattern of economic growth which has been outlined emphasises the important links between the long-run growth path of the world economy and the long swings in the national economies. Past literature has sought to explain long swings independently of any longer-run phenomena (Abramovitz, 1961; Easterlin, 1968; Thomas, 1973). Such perspectives miss out important interrelatedness of economic processes.

Monetarists have viewed the terms of trade as a dependent variable (Viner, 1924). The evidence of significant non-balanced capacity variations in the world economy raises strong doubts against this perspective. Structural changes in the world economy provided the basis for many monetary variations.

Conclusions

The long swings discussed in Chapters 3 and 6 had clear international aspects. Long swings are observed not only for domestic output, productivity and investment but also for international investment flows. Inverse long swings between home and overseas investment were observed in all the major capital exporters – Britain, France and Germany. Although the French and German long swings are trend variation swings rather than level swings, such differences are to be expected given the differing economic structures across national boundaries.

The variation of overseas investment correlates with changes in the terms of trade for all the major capital exporters. This suggests that the swings were profitability induced swings. To the extent that more direct relative profitability evidence exists, it suggests that this was the case. Clearly this relationship between overseas investment and the terms of trade is only a proximate explanation of the investment swings. In a world economy perspective the terms of trade are an endogenous variable. However, as was illustrated above, much of the terms-of-trade variation was due to structural changes in the world economy. The national specific aspects of long swings, outlined in the previous chapter, would also contribute to an explanation of the terms-of-trade variations. The international variations were the result of simultaneous domestic influences and structural changes in the world economy.

8

A long-term perspective of interwar economic growth

The pre-1913 world economy grew along a non-steady and non-balanced growth trajectory. Kuznets swings were a generalised growth pattern for the four national economies under consideration. Although the world economy did not grow along a Kondratieff wave, there is evidence of a long-run G-wave growth path (see Chapter 3). In France and America a long-swing pattern of growth is also observed for the interwar years. Given the critical role of America in the performance of the world economy during this period, a long-swing perspective of the 1930s depression warrants further study. Moreover, understanding the long-swing aspects of growth will help to situate the initial conditions of national growth trajectories.

Long-term economic growth trends

The interwar years are generally grouped together as an era of retarded economic growth. This is a view that is shared by Bieshaar and Kleinknecht (1984), Van Duijn (1983), Svennilson (1952) and Maddison (1982). The argument of this chapter is that such a perspective hinders our understanding of the interwar years by hiding significant differences between the growth paths of the 1920s and 1930s.

As can be seen from Table 8.1, with a few major exceptions, much of the world economy recovered successfully from the First World War growth shock. The significant exceptions were Germany and Britain.[1] The world economy, as measured by Maddison's sample of sixteen capitalist countries, grew at 2.7 per cent per annum during the period 1872–1913 and only 2.2 per cent per annum during the period 1913–29. However, if Britain and Germany are excluded the world growth rate rises to 2.6 per cent over the latter period. Moreover, the severity of the 1930s depression was clearly not due to the existence of a major long-term depression in Britain and Germany – both economies saw an acceleration of their long-term growth paths in the 1930s.

Table 8.1 *The long-term growth performance of the world economy, 1872–1937 (growth/annum)*

	1872–1913	1913–1929	1929–1937	1913–1937
Australia	0.0334	0.0130	0.0193	0.0151
Austria	0.0227	0.0031	−0.0182	−0.0040
Belgium	0.0203	0.0142	0.0025	0.0103
Canada	0.0375	0.0242	−0.0037	0.0149
Denmark	0.0268	0.0266	0.0218	0.0250
France	0.0160	0.0144	−0.0051	0.0079
Germany	0.0285	0.0120	0.0300	0.0178
Italy	0.0151	0.0166	0.0142	0.0158
Japan	0.0245	0.0364	0.0237	0.0321
Norway	0.0211	0.0288	0.0308	0.0295
Sweden	0.0271	0.0280	0.0220	0.0260
UK	0.0180	0.0070	0.0196	0.0112
USA	0.0403	0.0310	−0.0016	0.0198
World[a]	0.0269	0.0219	0.0085	0.0174

[a] The weighted sum of Maddison's sixteen capitalist countries.
Source: Maddison (1982).

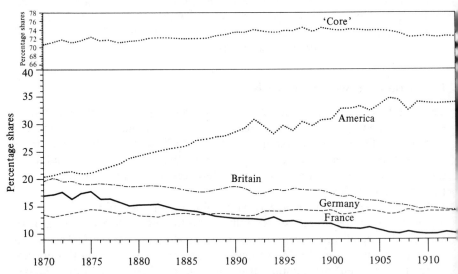

Figure 8.1 Shares of 'world' GDP. Source: Maddison (1982)

Such evidence conflicts with the idea of the interwar as an era that was progressively moving into severe depression. Not only had much of the world economy made a successful adjustment to the war shock but the countries facing severe problems in the 1920s were not the same as those of the 1930s.

The G-wave growth trajectory of the world economy is also important for understanding the world depression of the 1930s. The G-wave gave rise to significant leadership changes in the world economy of the pre-1913 era. As can be seen from Figure 8.1, during the period 1870–1913 the American share of world production increased significantly while the British and French shares declined. The First World War accelerated such tendencies so that by 1929 America was the dominant country in the world economy. Such economic domination increased the fragility of the world economy. The long-term perspective put forward here supports Kindleberger's (1973) interpretation of the 1930s depression as being caused by an absence of leadership.

In 1929 the degree of dominance of the world growth path by a single country was unprecedented by pre-1913 trends. Hence, the world economy became more prone to national (i.e. American) growth shocks. The nearest comparison to the position of America in 1929 was the position of Britain in 1873, when the swings of the world economy between 1856 and 1882 followed the pattern of growth observed in the British economy. After 1882 such a dominance was not observed and the world growth path followed a very different trajectory from Britain. Given the structure of the interwar world economy, an outline of the long-swing aspects of the American economy is warranted.

Long swings

The long-swing evidence presented in Chapters 3, 6 and 7 suggests that the 1930s depression was unprecedented only in terms of its severity. Depressions with similar characteristics were observed on previous occasions. In particular, the 1930s downswing in the American economy falls in a class of similar downswings during the periods 1873–84, 1892–9 and 1906–12.[2] In arguing the case that the long swing is relevant for understanding the interwar growth path, the emphasis is placed on the American long swings and the changing role of America in the structure of the world economy. In Britain and Germany the long-swing pattern of growth was not observed for the post-1913 period. While in the 1890s a major downswing in the American economy was filtered out of aggregate world trends by rapid growth in other economies, during the period 1906–12 the downswing of the US economy had a major depressing effect on the world economy and during the 1930s America imposed the major constraint on the world.

Although the First World War had important effects on the American economy, the structure of the economy was not transformed by it. In fact, given the episodic nature of pre-1913 long swings, the war acted as a major shock sustaining the long-swing pattern of growth. Both in the American economy and the world economy of the 1920s the growth path showed the characteristics of a catching-up cum reconstruction cycle resulting from the war years (Jánossy, 1971).

The long-swing pattern of the interwar years showed signs of both continuity and change. The war acted to synchronise the growth paths of many parts of the world economy as reconstruction cycles coincided. On the whole during the period 1913–29 the world economy was quite successful in recovering to the pre-1913 growth path. The dominant exceptions were Britain and Germany, and even in these cases a marked upswing had started during the period 1924–9. The world economy as a whole sustained very rapid growth rates during the period 1924–9. Kuczynski's index of world industrial production grew at 6 per cent per annum and the GDP of Maddison's sixteen capitalist countries grew at 3.6 per cent per annum. Such rapid growth rates were historically unprecedented. The previous peak in Maddison's world GDP trends was reached during the period 1899–1907 at a rate of 3.1 per cent per annum and the previous peak in Kuczynski's world industrial production index was reached in the 1890s with a growth rate of 4.6 per cent per annum.

Thus, the degree of synchronisation in the world economy was high in the postwar reconstruction cycle of 1924–9. The coincidence of such a rapid growth path, together with the dominant position of America in world production, took away a major inbuilt stabilizer of the world economy which had existed in the pre-1913 era. Inversities of economic growth were the rule in the pre-1913 period and this tended to dampen the swings of the world economy in the aggregate.[3] The absence of such an inbuilt stabilizer in the structure of the interwar world economy implied the possibility of swings with a greater amplitude than those observed for the pre-1913 era. Moreover, the dominant weight of America implied that the world economy was increasingly dependent on the growth performance of one country.

It should be stressed that the synchronisation and the American domination of the world economy were not necessarily adverse. The evidence merely points to the *possibility* of severe world crises. Given the structure of the American economy with a large primary producing sector and extensive credit financing for both primary producers and consumers, the economy was prone to severe destabilizing shocks.

The high degree of synchronisation of the world economy during the period 1924–9 also gave rise to a pattern of overseas investment flows that were markedly different from the pre-1913 era. The characteristic pattern of overseas investment by the leading capital exporters before 1913 showed long-term inversities between home and overseas investment. Such a pattern had its foundation in the non-synchronisation of economic growth across nations, partly due to the existence of a scale of relative backwardness and partly due to the random long-swing variations across national boundaries. In contrast, during the period 1924–9 capital exporters were investing both at home and overseas. To explain these differences Kindleberger (1973) has emphasised the leadership qualities of Britain before 1913 in following an inverse home–overseas investment pattern and American failure to lead by following a pro-cyclical overseas investment pattern. However, the evidence suggests that the different pattern was due to a difference in the structure of the world economy. In both the British and American cases the flow of funds was based on individual decision making. A further destabilising factor was that the flow of funds in the 1920s was increasingly based on political considerations. While before 1913 the capital flows were mainly from industrial economies towards primary producers, after the war the flows across industrial economies were of increasing importance. In particular, Germany took most of the world's capital resources in the 1920s as a way of overcoming the potential transfer problem imposed by reparations.[4]

Thus, the long swing continued to operate as an important force in the interwar American economy and the new economic structure of the world economy provides an explanation for the increased amplitude of the American and world depressions of the 1930s. Temin (1976, p. 52) has dismissed the relevance of the Kuznets swing for understanding the 1930s depression because of the greater amplitude of the 1930s downswing and the implausible way in which the First World War shock could generate a depression a decade later. The argument presented here suggests that the Kuznets swing operated in a changed world economy and the new conditions help our understanding of the world depression.

The emphasis in this section has been placed on the American long swings in a changing world economy. In general, the long-term performance of various economies is also important in understanding the differential national responses to the world depression of the 1930s. In France, like America, the growth path of the 1920s represented rapid growth, catching up on the losses of the war years. In Britain and Germany the long-term growth performance of the period 1913–29 was poor compared to that of 1872–1913. The slow growth era of 1899–1913 continued over the period 1913–29. Thus, the initial growth conditions of France and America in 1929 were very different from those of Britain and Germany; this may contribute to an understanding of why Britain and Germany recovered successfully in the 1930s while France and America stagnated. For nations experiencing a strong upswing in the 1920s the build-up of excess capacity must have imposed significant constraints on recovery in the 1930s.

Inter-sectoral relationships

Even in the interwar years, the size of the agricultural sector was such as to warrant a careful examination of the inter-sectoral aspects of growth variations. In America agriculture still accounted for 15.2 per cent of GDP in

1919, employed 25 per cent of the population and provided most of the domestic food consumption. In France agriculture accounted for 22 per cent of GDP in 1938, employed 33 per cent of the occupied males and provided 80 per cent of domestic food consumption. Britain seems to be the exception amongst industrial economies with an agricultural sector that only accounted for approximately 6 per cent of GDP in the interwar years. In a world-economy perspective the importance of the agricultural sector is even more striking. Three-fifths of world trade was in foodstuffs and raw materials (Aldcroft, 1977).

In much of the literature on the interwar world depression, agriculture has been given an autonomous influence on the origins of the depression since there is some evidence for overproduction of primary commodities from the 1920s (Timoshenko, 1933; Kindleberger, 1973). For example, in Timoshenko's (1933) work the overproduction of the 1920s played a critical role via balance-of-payments disequilibria. As the incomes of primary producers fell, they lowered their demand for manufactured products which depressed the industrial sectors of the world economy.

The main pieces of evidence that have been drawn to argue the case for an autonomous primary producers problem in the 1920s are the increase in stocks of primary commodities and the adverse sectoral terms-of-trade movements for primary producers. However, the idea that the sectoral terms of trade moved against primary producers in the 1920s is not well founded. The Potter and Christy (1962) price indicators for America suggest that relative agricultural prices were high and rising for most of the 1920s. The trend increase of agricultural relative prices during the period 1899–1913 continued over the period 1913–19. During the period 1919–23 the terms of trade moved against agriculture but during the period 1923–9 the trend was in favour of agriculture. By 1929 the level reached the peak of 1919 again. Thus, the American sectoral terms-of-trade movements suggest a continuation of the pre-1913 long-swing pattern when high-growth periods were associated with favourable terms-of-trade movements for agriculture. The problems of American agriculture in the 1920s were related to the debt problems resulting from the short and sharp relative price changes of 1920–1, not with overproduction.

The existing literature has relied extensively on the British international terms of trade for drawing inferences about the movement of world sectoral prices. However, the British terms of trade do not seem to be representative of the rest of the world, being the product of policy variables rather than real forces in the world economy. The British terms of trade rose from a level of 100 in 1913 to over 140 in 1921. Throughout the interwar they remained in the range of 118 to 150, falling from 1921 to 1929 and rising between 1929 and 1933.

The 40 per cent increase between 1913 and 1921 is not so easy to understand, especially since both France and Germany started the 1920s with a terms-of-trade level lower than 1913 (Kindleberger, 1956). The reason for this cannot be found in an overvalued pound–dollar ratio since in 1920 the pound had a low dollar value. However, the pound may have been overvalued relative to the unstable European currencies, since Britain was in a favoured position to provide the goods for the restocking booms of 1919–20. Thus, the British pattern of relative international prices seems to have been peculiar rather than representative of industrial economies.

Given the peculiar pattern of the British terms of trade, the international terms of trade between manufactures and tropical crops (Lewis, 1978, pp. 283–4) is of interest. The index started off in 1920 with a level of relative prices for manufactures slightly lower than 1913, showing that the British pattern was exceptional. The steep rise in industrial relative prices between 1920 and 1921 was followed by an equally steep decline between 1921 and 1924. During the period 1924–9 the variation in relative prices was small, ranging between 100 and 104. Since the level of this index was 100 in 1913, following a period of favourable movement towards primary producers during the period 1899–1913, the primary sector's relative prices were high for most of the 1920s. Moreover, this stability in the aggregate relative prices for primary commodities needs to be broken up into two components. Food and raw material price relatives are expected to behave differently.[5] The slower population growth rates and changes in diets implied an adverse effect on the relative prices of many food products. However, the rapid growth of the world economy during the period 1924–9 implied a large demand for raw materials. Although the data available are not refined enough to pick up these effects, they are clearly reflected in the production trends for food and raw materials. During the period 1913–29 food production increased by 18 per cent while raw material production grew by 60 per cent.

The evidence for an excess building of stocks of primary commodities in the 1920s is also not well founded. The stocks of primary commodities, as shown by the index numbers produced by the League of Nations, increased considerably during the period 1925–9 (Kindleberger, 1973). No doubt speculation in commodities was part of the explanation. However, in an era of expanding consumption the stocks of convenience held by merchants and manufacturers would tend to increase. Rowe (1965) has calculated that allowing for increased consumption, only three commodities faced serious problems in the 1920s – sugar, wheat and coffee. The ratio of stocks to absorption seems to have declined for tin, petroleum, meat and dairy, wool, flax, jute, rye, oats and maize.

The evidence for an autonomous primary production problem in the 1920s which helps us to understand the severity and causality of the 1930s depression is weak. No doubt some commodities and the countries specialising in those commodities suffered. However, neither the terms-of-trade evidence nor the stocks evidence points to an aggregate overproduction problem. Fleisig (1972) has also shown that Timoshenko's (1933) balance-of-payments mechanism for the transmission of the primary producers' problem to the world economy is unfounded. During the 1925–9 period the value of primary exports rose from $9,900 million to $10,200 million giving primary producers additional reserves to purchase industrial commodities.

In stating the case against a primary production problem in the 1920s I am not proposing that the inter-sectoral relations were not critical to understanding the dynamics of depression in the 1930s. The inter-sectoral relations were important in constraining economic growth in two major ways. Firstly, the indebtedness of primary producers, both in America and the world economy was critical to the origins of banking and financial crises. Secondly, the large terms-of-trade variation in favour of manufactures acted to constrain aggregate demand by bringing into question the structural relations within nations and the world economy. If relative price changes are viewed only in terms of their distribution effects, the losses of one group would be the gains of another and any aggregate impacts would depend only on differences in marginal propensities to consume. However, a large terms-of-trade variation also implies a restructuring of the capital goods sector before the new pattern of demand can be satisfied. The gains of industrial sectors would not be used to purchase agricultural machinery and implements. During the 1899–1929 period the share of agricultural equipment was increasing in world trade but during the 1930s this rising trend was reversed (Tyszynski, 1951). Over a thirty-year period the capital-goods sector had developed to meet a particular demand structure – once the demand pattern changed in the 1930s a restructuring process had to take place. Thus, Kaldor (1976) concluded:

any large change in commodity prices – irrespective of whether it is in favour or against the primary producers – tends to have a dampening effect on industrial activity; it retards industrial growth in both cases, instead of retarding it in the one case and stimulating it in the other. (1976, p. 706)

The importance of the inter-sectoral relations is clearly observed in the different national experiences between Britain, France and America during the 1930s. In Britain the smallness of the agricultural sector implied that the large terms-of-trade variation of 1929–33 provided a large windfall income gain to domestic aggregate demand without major structural disproportionality problems. However, in America and France the income gain of the industrial sector was the income loss of the primary producing sector. Thus, the terms-of-trade gains of these economies were also the terms-of-trade losses of large domestic agricultural sectors; not only were the windfall gains of these economies small but they also faced structural adjustment problems given the large size of their agricultural sectors. This partly explains why Britain recovered more successfully than either France or America in the 1930s.

Debt problems and financial crises

The role of credit and financial crises in generating cycles of economic growth has been recognised by many economists. Schumpeter (1939) recognised this in his four-phase schema for cyclical processes; the overextension of credit was assigned a central role in moving the economy into depression. Hicks (1974) also makes this distinction in his two-phase schema for the 1930s depression; the monetary depression from 1930 to 1933 had its origins in an overextension of credit in the 1920s leading to the banking crises of the early 1930s.

Financial crises have been viewed both as exogenous events and endogenous processes to the economic system. Schumpeter (1939) saw the 1931 banking crisis in Germany as an exogenous event. Friedman and Schwartz (1982) viewed the American banking failures of the early 1930s as an historical accident. At the other end of the spectrum Minsky (1964) has argued the case for viewing financial crises as an endogenous result of the fragility of the capitalist system, a fragility developed during the boom period:

The hypothesis is that the financial panic which is present during deep depressions and absent during mild depressions is not a random exogenous affair; rather it is endogenous to the economy. The financial panic is made possible by the the the changes in the financial structure that take place during the long swing expansion. (1964, p. 325).

Whether financial crises are seen as exogenous events or endogenous processes does not affect the general conclusion that the severity of the 1929–33 downswing can be partly understood in terms of the presence or absence of this variable. Financial crises in America and Germany made the amplitude of the depression significantly greater in these countries than for Britain and France. Nevertheless, since the major concern of this chapter is with the origins of the 1930s depression, the idea of an endogenous financial crisis requires further study.

Minsky (1964, 1982) has postulated that the development of financial fragility is an aspect of the boom. An increasing financial fragility is observed in a rise in the debt-to-income ratio, a rise in the price of stock market assets and a decrease in ultimate liquidity.

Some support for Minsky's ideas can be found in the financial trends of the American economy. As can be seen from Table 8.2 the household liabilities-to-income ratio and common stock prices increased rapidly while ultimate liquidity either declined or grew very slowly. McClam (1982) has also argued that there is some evidence for demand-determined variations in the money stock during the interwar period. Breaking up the income velocity of money

Table 8.2 *Growth of financial variables in American economy* (*percentage growth/annum*)

	1922–29	1929–33	1933–39
GNP	5.0	−14.4	8.4
Household equity ownership	13.9	−19.8	4.2
Household Debts			
Total	12.7	−8.5	0.4
Mortgages	11.7	−5.1	1.1
Consumer	11.6	−15.8	14.3
Household disposable income	4.7	−13.9	7.5

Source: Minsky (1984, p. 272).

into two components, a credit velocity of money and an income velocity of total credit:

$$Y/M = (TC/M) \times (Y/TC)$$

where Y is income, M is money stock and TC is total credit. During the period 1920–41 the income velocity of total credit followed a positive relationship with variations in the rate of growth of money itself ($R^2 = 0.55$). Thus, variations in the stock of money were being determined by the same factors influencing credit demand. During the postwar period a relationship between the two variables is insignificant.

Two other aspects of financial fragility should also be noted. During the period 1920–9 the ratio of private-to-public debt in the US rose to unprecedented magnitudes. The 1929 level was historically high for the whole period 1920–80 (McClam, 1982, p. 275). Similarly, the debt-to-income ratio of the private sector was on an historically high level in 1929, the highest observed for the whole period 1880–1980 (Goldsmith, 1984).

However, the evidence is not all in favour of an endogenous financial long swing. Friedman (1982, p. 96) has shown that the real debt-to-income ratio did not see a rising trend in the 1920s – the upward movement in the ratio took place during the period 1920–1 with the large fall in prices. Employing an international perspective there are even more important criticisms to be levelled against Minsky's instability hypothesis. The debt-to-income ratio followed a diverse movement that was not correlated with financial crises. For example, in Germany the ratio fell from 2.15 in 1913 to 1.02 in 1929 and yet the economy proved prone to a major banking crisis in 1931. In contrast the British ratio rose from 1.55 to 2.76 during the same benchmark years without a major domestic banking crisis (Goldsmith, 1984, p. 288).

The evidence suggests that one model cannot explain all the financial crises of the interwar years. For example, Minsky's model offers little for understanding the German banking crisis. Germany was both economically back-ward and politically unstable. James (1984, 1985) has shown that banking collapse can be explained in terms of the consequences and weaknesses in the sphere of public finance. Even for America the idea of a financial long swing is unfounded. The American economy was financially fragile in 1929 but this was only partly linked to the boom itself (Friedman, 1982). Thus, the increased debt-to-income ratio observed by Goldsmith (1984) for the benchmark years 1913 and 1929 seems to take place during the war and immediate postwar years.

However, whatever the reasons, the American economy was in a financially fragile situation in 1929. Since America played such a critical role in the transmission of depression to the world economy, the American debt problem of the 1930s should figure centrally in an explanation of the severity and length of the depression.

The level of indebtedness in America in 1929 gave rise to a Fisherian debt-deflation crisis (Fisher, 1933). The liquidation of debt between 1929 and 1933 led to a rapid fall in prices and a large increase in the real debt burden. Such monetary aspects could help to explain the real contraction of the American economy via a number of transmission mechanisms. First, the life-cycle consumption framework would see the $100 billion (1958) drop in household net worth as an important constraint on consumption between 1929 and 1932. If a distinction is made between the consumers' holding of financial assets and the effect from his holding of liabilities, as is done in Mishkin's (1978) 'liquidity hypothesis' on the assumption of imperfect capital markets for tangible consumer goods, the large fall in consumer durables demand and housing demand can be better understood.

Population-sensitive investments

Population-sensitive investment has been emphasised in all long-swing dis-cussions. In America, of the seven major business contractions since the civil war three were major depressions (1873–8, 1892–4 and 1929–32) and each coincided with a major downturn of building (Hickman, 1974). In Britain the role of population-sensitive investments in explaining investment swings before 1913 has been emphasised (Thomas, 1973). Similarly, the delayed housing boom of the 1930s has been seen as an important explanation of the peculiarities of British interwar growth. Lévy-Leboyer (1978) has shown that in France the twenty-year investment cycle dominated growth variations with peaks in 1826, 1846, 1869, 1882, 1900, 1913 and 1930.

Such evidence raises the question of whether there was an independent building cycle which set the basic pattern of long swings or whether building cycles themselves were part of the aggregate long swings. An independent building cycle could result from either exogenous driving forces or structural factors in the housing sector.

The idea of an independent building cycle has received some support in the literature. Derksen (1940) argued the case for an endogenous building cycle in the American economy. Bolch and Pilgrim (1973) argued that the level of residential construction was the most important determinant of American national income. In fact they concluded that the *exogenous* fall in residential construction produced a fall in income almost as large as the actual fall. In Forresters' System Dynamics National Model of the American economy a Kuznets construction cycle results from the structural relations of the economic system (Forrester, 1977).

The idea of an independent building cycle causing the major contractions of history is not well founded. The only reason Derksen derived a building cycle out of his model is due to the lag structure he employed which, as Hickman (1974) has argued is highly unrealistic. The Kuznets building swings outlined in the System Dynamics National Model are simulated swings based on structural relations of the postwar period. Moreover, their amplitude is mild compared to the actual historical swings. Even the building swings of the pre-1913 era were not induced by autonomous cycles of population-related variables but were the result of demographic–economic interactions (Easterlin, 1966). Bolch and Pilgrim (1973) only derived their result by assuming that the residential construction variable is exogenously determined. A more refined econometric model by Hickman (1974) which assumed that the rate of family formation is both the product of economic and demographic variables gives the result that most of the decline in construction during the 1930s was due to economic variables not exogenous demographic variables.

The economic–demographic interactions were an important factor in explaining the length and severity of the 1930s depression. However, the only exogenous impact is observed in the effects of the Immigration Act of 1924 which retarded the growth of the weighted rate of population increase between 1925 and 1934.

Similar economic–demographic interactions help us to understand the pattern of growth in the French economy. Although natural population increased to a peak in the ten years centred on 1926, the peak was not of such a large magnitude as to explain the upswing of the 1920s on purely demographic trends (Lévy-Leboyer, 1978). More important was the fact that the boom of the 1920s attracted a large flow of migrants. During the period 1921–31 France attracted 235,500 migrants per annum. The inflation and rent freeze delayed the peak of building activity until after 1929; 604,000 dwellings were built during the period 1929–32. Thus, the French boom was sustained until much later than in other countries. Moreover, the overcapacity of building accumulated during the 1920s, and especially 1929–32, explains the stagnation of construction in the 1930s.

In Britain the situation was very different. A backlog of building demand was accumulated during the First World War. Moreover, a wave of postwar marriages added to housing demand. By 1923 the estimated shortage was 800,000 houses (Parry-Lewis, 1965). Rent controls prevented the necessary building boom in the 1920s. Rent controls were introduced for working-class tenants in 1915 and by the early 1920s were being applied to 98 per cent of rented houses. These controls were generally abolished by the early 1930s setting the basis for a housing boom to meet the demand for rented accommodation built up in the 1920s. The overbuilding observed in France and America was not apparent in Britain. The housing boom in the British economy is an important factor in accounting for the marked revival of British growth during the 1930s.

Conclusions

The interwar world economy was characterised by both continuity and change. The interaction of the American long swing in a changing world economy can explain both the greater amplitude of the 1930s depression in America and the occurrence of a deep depression in the world economy. The structural changes emphasised are:
  (i) the increased dependence of the world economy on America;
 (ii) the greater synchronisation of world economic growth in the cycle of 1924–9; and
(iii) the ending of the long-term inversities between home and overseas investment by the major capital exporters.
Thus, within the new structure for the world economy the American non-steady growth path had entirely different implications when compared to the pre-1913 era.

An examination of the possibility of an autonomous primary producer's problem in the 1920s, as an explanation of the origins of the 1929 depression, failed to find such an influence. Nevertheless, the large sectoral terms of trade variations of 1929–33 acted as a major constraint on world growth once the depression started.

A similar examination of Minsky's financial instability hypothesis also failed to find strong evidence for a cyclical path for financial variables. Nevertheless, the level of indebtedness in 1929 was extremely high and may help to explain the severity and length of the American depression.

The interaction of economic and demographic variables was an important factor in accounting for the inter-country differences in economic growth. The overcapacity of the American and French construction sectors was absent in Britain.

The evidence presented in this chapter reinforces the view expressed in earlier chapters that the swings observed in various economies are the result of episodic events rather than true cycles. The increased amplitude of the American interwar swings can only be understood in the light of the structural changes taking place in the world economy.

9

Some conclusions on the postwar boom, 1950–1973

The postwar boom of 1950–73 appears to fall in the time band of a Kondratieff wave upswing; however, the evidence presented in the previous chapters suggests that the Kondratieff wave is noted by its absence before 1950. Hence, the postwar boom needs to be understood in unique historical terms. The major influence behind the long-run growth variations of the world economy before 1950 arose from the combined effects of an underlying catching-up growth process and the impact of shocks. The 1950–73 rapid growth era can also be understood as a catching-up wave under different initial conditions from the high-growth path of the world economy during the period 1890–1929.

The technological gap

The factors accounting for the existence of rapidly growing economies at different stages of world economic development have been discussed extensively in the historical growth literature. Some of the more important aspects are as follows.

(i) Late developers have the advantage of flexible labour supplies (Kaldor, 1966: Kindleberger, 1967).

(ii) If the cost of moving from a lower to a higher technology is an increasing function of the level of technology, then the rate of development will slow down as the country develops. Countries with a lower level of technology will have a greater potential for growth since the transition costs of moving from one technology to another are lower (Ames and Rosenberg, 1971).

(iii) If institutions adapt themselves to a given technology the late developers may have an advantage over the early developers in that there are fewer institutional constraints on late developers to adopt new technology (Kindleberger, 1978a; Olson, 1982). Moreover, the late developers, by the fact of their 'relative backwardness', will adopt institutions that favour rapid economic growth (Gershenkron, 1962).

(v) The existence of a technological gap will favour the growth path of the late developers. The 'relatively backward' nations not only have a pool of technical knowledge to utilise, but they can also avoid the mistakes of the leading economies (Abramovitz, 1979; Gomulka, 1971).

The focus of this section is on the role of the technological gap in explaining the postwar boom.

The existence of a technological gap generates a wave in productivity growth. Gomulka (1971) has observed a hat-shaped relationship between productivity growth and the size of the technological gap; both high and low levels of technological gap would imply low-productivity growth, while the middle-range gap would be associated with high-productivity growth. Hence, as long as countries have the capacity to borrow technology their productivity growth would be fast in the initial stages when the technological gap is wide, but as the gap is closed there is a tendency for retardation.

The size of the technological gap is usually proxied by comparing the labour productivity levels of various countries with that of the leading innovator. This exercise is undertaken on the assumption that there is a relationship between the productivity level and the technological level. Such an assumption would be valid if there is free exchange of technical and scientific information, if productivity differences are due to technological and not resource differences and if the productivity differences are large. Since borrowing technology is not without cost, the potential for increasing productivity through borrowed technology is constrained long before the technological gap tends to zero.

The productivity level calculations currently available originate from the Gilbert (1958) comparisons with uniform 1955 price weights. Denison (1967) and Maddison (1967) have derived figures for other dates by extrapolating from this earlier study. Although the recent data of Kravis *et al.* (1978) are an improvement on these studies, their results for Britain, France and Germany do not change the relatives to any significant extent.

Abramovitz (1979) has derived figures for the productivity relatives of eight European economies, Japan and Canada in 1950 using the work of Denison and Maddison. His figures are also extrapolated back to 1913 and forward to 1970 (see Table 9.1). Abramovitz's calculations show that the ten-country relative productivity level averaged around 60 per cent of the American level in 1913 with a wide variance. Between 1913 and 1950 the productivity relative fell by 20 per cent, mainly due to the beneficial effect of the World Wars on American economic growth. The level rose from 48 per cent to 70 per cent of that of America between 1950 and 1970. Moreover, the variance of the sample declined asymptotically, suggesting that the less productive the country in 1950 the more rapid was the productivity rise. In the case of Britain, France

Table 9.1 *Output per worker in 1965 dollars measured at US relative prices for a sample of ten countries (US = 100) (variances in parenthesis)*

	1913	1950	1955	1960	1965	1970
Relative for ten countries	62.2 (0.096)	48.4 (0.096)	50.8 (0.078)	57.0 (0.053)	60.1 (0.029)	69.8 (0.019)

Source: Abramovitz (1979).

and Germany alone, the relative productivity level averaged 65 per cent of that of America in 1913, fell to 49 per cent in 1950 and rose to 75 per cent in 1973.

The technological gap of 1950 helps to explain some of the peculiarities of the postwar boom. As was noted in Chapter 3, the growth path of all the European economies was historically unprecedented during the period 1950–73 while American economic growth was not exceptional. The different initial conditions of Europe and America provide an explanation for this pattern of development.

Nevertheless, the technological gap theories cannot provide a complete explanation of the boom. Both France and Germany surpassed the 1913 relative productivity level by the early 1960s. Britain is the exception since a productivity gap remained significant into the early 1970s. More direct evidence on the balance of trade in technology also raises further doubts as to the importance of the technological gap for explaining the later stages of the boom. Both France and Britain were innovating economies. Although France had a deficit on its balance of trade in technology during the period 1950–73, this was minimal during the 1965–73 period when the economy showed signs of accelerating growth. Britain in fact had a small surplus on its balance of trade in technology throughout the period 1950–73. Only Germany had a large trade deficit in technology.[1]

The technological gap was not the only technological factor helping to explain the long boom. Although the idea of regular innovation clusters was rejected (see Chapter 5), there is extensive evidence to suggest that the postwar era gave rise to a 'New Technology System', based on the technical and social interrelatedness of families of innovations and the many follow-up innovations made during the diffusion period (Freeman *et al.*, 1982).[2] Thus, the favourable technological conditions gave rise to a long era of self-feeding technical progress which was able to sustain itself for longer than the actual technological gap.

Other factors accounting for the postwar boom

The technological gap has little to say on the later stages of the postwar boom. In this section the focus is on the role of flexible labour supplies, flexible and cheap raw material supplies and stable international leadership as explanatory variables for the long boom.

The initial growth conditions of 1950 provided a potential for rapid catching-up growth. The actual catching-up observed required flexible labour supplies for the innovating and high productivity manufacturing sectors. Flexible labour supplies for the manufacturing sector have been emphasised by Kaldor (1966) and Kindleberger (1967). In Britain, with less than 10 per cent of the labour force in agriculture, the service sector formed the dominant source of surplus labour. However, there are greater limits to the amount of labour that can be drawn out of the service sector, since income elasticities for services tend to be high in comparison to agricultural products. The decline in the share of British manufacturing employment between 1955 and 1973 could thus be viewed as the result of labour shortages for manufacturing. Alternatively, it could also be argued that the demand from manufacturing was low, giving rise to a classic identification problem. In contrast, the large shares of the agricultural labour force in France and Germany created a more flexible labour supply for the manufacturing sector.

Flexible labour supplies were directly favourable to growth, since in 1950 the productivity levels in the agricultural and tertiary sectors were much lower than for the manufacturing sector. Thus, the re-allocation of labour towards the manufacturing sector gave rise to a beneficial structural effect on productivity and output growth. Such employment shifts, however, were only of small quantitative importance to the increase in productivity and output growth.

In seeking to relate flexible labour supplies to the actual productivity growth path, much of the recent historical growth literature has emphasised the importance of what has come to be known as Verdoorn's law. In this perspective the rate of growth of productivity in manufacturing is not given exogenously but is dependent on the rate of growth of manufacturing output. In addition, the rate of growth of manufacturing output is an important factor in determining the rate of growth of productivity in the non-manufacturing sector. The relationship is usually specified as:

$$g_p = a_0 + a_1 g_Q \qquad a_1 > 0$$

where g_p is the growth of labour productivity in manufacturing and g_Q is the growth of output in manufacturing. Thus, flexible labour supplies serve the function of allowing the manufacturing growth path to expand which gives rise to a cumulative process of economic growth.

Much econometric work has been undertaken to test this relationship. Since output may not be an independent variable, employment growth is usually used as a proxy for output growth. In general, most studies have raised strong doubts as to the significance of the relationship. Rowthorn (1975) has shown

Table 9.2 *Growth in the net barter terms of trade between primary products and manufactures since 1950* (1960 = 100) (*growth/annum*)

t	1(a)	1(b)	2	3	4	5	6
1950–1970	−0.015	−0.015	−0.023	−0.014	−0.012	—	−0.019
1950–1955	−0.015	−0.016	−0.009	−0.011	−0.005	—	−0.018
1955–1960	−0.020	−0.020	−0.051	−0.045	−0.049	—	−0.049
1960–1965	−0.011	−0.010	−0.012	−0.012	+0.008	−0.010	−0.002
1965–1970	−0.014	−0.013	−0.018	−0.014	−0.002	+0.006	−0.008

1(a) is the United Nations index (1913 = 100).
1(b) is the United Nations index (1960 = 100).
2, 3, 4 and 5 are derived from World Bank indices. These indices are of market quoted prices of primary commodities of specific grades, weighted by their shares in the exports of developing countries in the years 1967–9 for columns 2 and 3, 1974–6 for column 4 and 1975 for column 5. The indices relating to manufactures are unit value indices pertaining to total manufactured exports (columns 2 and 3) or to manufactures exported to developing countries from developed market economies (column 4). Thirty-five primary commodities are included in column 2; columns 3 and 4 exclude petroleum.
6 is UNCTAD index of market quoted prices.
Source: Spraos (1980).

that significance depends on the inclusion of Japan in the cross-sectional samples. Stoneman (1979) tested the relationship for British time series during the period 1800–1970 and found it to be insignificant. Chatterji and Wickens (1980) also found that Verdoorn's law does not hold in the long run. Of all the major recent studies only Cornwall (1979) has provided some support for a Verdoorn relationship.

Hence, the rapid economic growth of the postwar era was permitted by flexible labour supply. However, the growth of manufacturing employment does not explain rapid economic growth in a Verdoorn law perspective. Flexible labour supplies were a necessary but not a sufficient condition for rapid economic growth.

In the light of the importance of the increase in the relative price of energy and other raw materials after 1973, and in the importance of sectoral terms of trade variations before 1950, this variable deserves careful consideration as an explanatory factor for the length of the postwar boom.

The sectoral terms of trade moved against primary commodities during the period 1950–73 (see Table 9.2). In contrast to the pre-1950 era when the terms of trade generally moved in favour of primary commodities during high-growth periods, throughout the period 1950–73 the terms of trade moved in favour of the manufacturing sector. Thus, the kind of constraints on economic growth noted for the Edwardian era were completely absent in the postwar era. The relative price of petroleum declined even faster than other primary

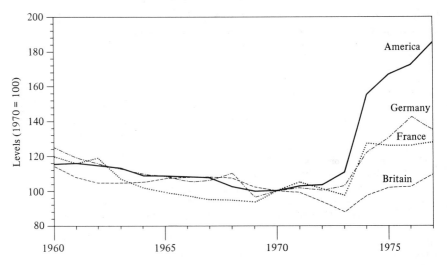

Figure 9.1 Relative energy prices. Source: Rasche and Tatom (1981, p. 35)

commodities (see column 2 of Table 9.2). The trends for the relative price of energy, including domestically produced energy are presented in Figure 9.1. The relative price of energy fell significantly during the period 1960–73. The fall was most marked in Britain during the 1967–73 period. However, France, Germany and America also saw a major fall during this period. Since the decline of relative input prices was fairly smooth this did not induce any major restructuring of the capital goods industries (Nordhaus, 1974).

The role of hegemonic political and economic leadership is also of critical importance as a stabilizing influence. The Second World War gave rise to a continuation of the pre-1929 trends of American domination of the world economy. The favourable effect of the Second World War on American economic growth meant that in 1945 the world economy was dominated by America. During the interwar period, although America was increasing its importance in the world economy, a stable domination was absent. The basic problem in 1945 was the need to find a system which ensured that the level of monetary liquidity in the exchange system was not restricted by the level of the physical volume of gold available. America's economic strength meant that Bretton Woods provided a monetary system which could secure both the goals of rapid reconstruction and monetary flexibility. The flexibility was found in the gold exchange standard which established the convertibility of the US dollar into gold. The US was able to prevent the gold standard system from being accepted at the Bretton Woods conference by its power to render gold inoperative for international exchange. The US had the power to dictate the price of gold since it had control of 78 per cent of western gold reserves at the end of the war (Innes, 1981).

Thus, after the war the 'normalcy' of the gold standard was not sought, and free trade was a high priority. Interwar debts were replaced with aid, avoiding the debt triangles of the 1920s. American economic leadership gave the world economy a stable and flexible monetary system for the expansion of international transactions. This made possible an unprecedented expansion of world trade with favourable growth implications.

Conclusions

The postwar boom was founded on transitory variables – the technological gap, flexible labour supplies, flexible and cheap raw material supplies and the dominant leadership position of America in 1950. Such a clustering of favourable growth factors in 1950 made possible the most rapid and longest high-growth phase in modern economic history.

The basis of the boom was the existence of a technological gap. However, even with the closing of the gap in the early 1960s the boom was able to feed on flexible labour supplies and cheap raw materials. Growth expectations could also be important in sustaining the boom. However, in a period of full employment, real factors will determine the growth path of the economy in the long run. Given that many of the causal variables behind the postwar boom were transitory, there may have existed a tendency towards underutilisation which was counterbalanced by high growth expectations.

With time there would have been problems in adjusting to a lower growth trajectory; however, the problems were not major before 1973. Assuming that the technological gap was an important force in the postwar boom then the long-run productivity growth rate would have been in the region of 2 per cent of the labour productivity growth path of America during the period 1950–73. However, even in the late 1960s the productivity growth of France, Germany and Britain was much higher than America, suggesting that the technological gap was still large, as in the case of Britain, or that the European economies were pushing the technological frontier to the right.

Those who point to the profitability trends before 1973 as a sign that the events of the post-1973 era can be predicted from the nature of the boom have been misled (Mandel, 1980, 1981). The profitability trends reflect the pre-1973 growth path and do not point to major problems necessarily arising in 1973. Hill's (1979) profit-rate calculations for Britain, Germany and America are presented in Figure 9.2. The British and German rates show significant downward trends over the period 1955–73. In both cases the profit-share variation accounts for a larger part of the fall than the capital–output ratio. The American rate does not have a significant trend, falling during the period 1955–8, rising during the period 1958–66 and falling again for the period 1966–73. The American swings in profitability are clearer in the capital–output ratio but are also observed in the profit share.

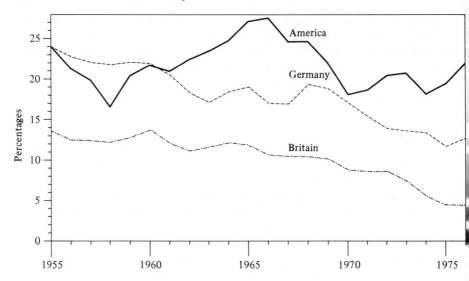

Figure 9.2 Gross profit rates manufacturing. Source: Hill (1979, Table 6.1)

The profitability trends are compatible with the emphasis on the technological gap as an explanation of the boom. However, despite the falling profitability, the growth path of the 1960s was on an historically high trend.
Falling profitability in the 1950s and 1960s did not signify a major growth
crisis in 1973. The idea that the post-1973 growth problems can be predicted
from the pre-1973 profitability trends is an example of *post hoc ergo propter
hoc* reasoning. As in 1929 the world growth path was shocked into depression.

10

Conclusions

The evidence presented in this study rejects a Kondratieff wave phasing of post-1850 economic growth. The coincidence of the postwar boom falling within the Kondratieff time band is an exceptional event. The case against Kondratieff waves is based on an examination of production, productivity, investment, absolute prices, relative prices and innovation trends. The strongest case against the Kondratieff wave phasing of economic growth is to be found in an examination of the production and investment trends of Britain, France, Germany and America. In all these countries significant growth variations have been shorter than the Kondratieff periodicity.

In much of the recent long-wave literature it is widely believed that the strongest evidence for this pattern of growth is provided by trends in the world economy. This study has shown that although the world economy witnessed major long-run discontinuities in growth, these do not belong to a long-wave pattern or a long-wave explanatory framework. The period 1850–1913 witnessed accelerating growth due to unique changes in the structure of the world economy. Allowing for the break in growth during the war years, the accelerating path lasted over the period 1850–1929. I used the phrase 'shocked Gerschenkronian catching-up waves' (G-waves) to describe the observed world growth path after 1850, since relative backwardness and differential growth rates across nations figure centrally in my account of the world growth path. G-waves are historical waves of irregular length and amplitude. The world economy has not grown along a steady and balanced path but has moved along a number of episodic traverses due to the effects of the World Wars and changes in the international economic structure. Certainly the observed G-waves do not fall in the Kondratieff wave periodicity.

The strong case against a Kondratieff wave periodisation of production trends is supported from an analysis of price and innovation trends. Regular innovation clusters, capable of generating a long-wave growth process have not been observed in the nineteenth and twentieth centuries. The aggregate trends suggest the existence of episodic disturbances rather than waves. Moreover, the national distribution of innovations suggest that innovation clusters cannot be used to explain Kondratieff waves in economic growth since America, as the dominant innovator, did not follow such a growth path.

This study has also argued against the idea of a Kondratieff wave in prices. Thus the production and price data are seen to be complementary. A popular critique of the long-wave framework is that the waves are price waves, due to monetary disturbances, without any real dimensions. Such a dichotomy between real and monetary variables is not justified, either empirically or theoretically. Major displacements of the price level have occurred which can only be understood by bringing together the evidence on Kuznets swings, G-waves, monetary variations, wars, policies and structural changes in the price, cost, productivity relationship. Such an interaction of variables acted to generate a series of shocked square waves in the price level. The Kondratieff wave pattern of wholesale prices during the period 1873–1913 is not part of a generalised price long wave. Wholesale prices behaved differently from GDP deflators and the trends in wholesale prices were not determined by a uniform causal process throughout the period 1873–1913. In the twentieth century an inflationary bias has been the dominant feature of prices.

Kuznets swings are found to be more generalised than has previously been recognised. The swings are best viewed as episodic events rather than cycles of growth and they are a pattern of growth limited to specific historical eras. In Germany and Britain, Kuznets swings are a pre-1913 phenomenon, while in France and America there is some evidence that the swing pattern continued into the interwar period. Previous literature has discussed Kuznets swings in terms of the American economy and has failed to recognise the evidence for aggregate swings in the European economies.

The long swings discussed in this study are both aggregate and sectoral phenomena. Long swings are observed in aggregate output, productivity, investment, profitability, migration, the money supply, climatic variation, agricultural production and construction. Such evidence raises strong doubts as to the validity of the simple monocausal frameworks that have been developed for analysing long swings. The only consistent explanatory framework is one that emphasises the interrelatedness of variables.

The absence of long swings in the performance of the world economy and the evidence of differing national long-swing patterns suggest that, for much of the time, national specific aspects are essential when seeking to understand the various swing patterns across countries. The simple causality mechanisms of the Atlantic economy inversities are highly misleading, neglecting many relevant aspects with respect to British long swings and failing to provide any framework for understanding European swings. National growth swings are found to be related to a large number of economic variables; moreover, these did not operate uniformly over time but varied with each long-swing phase. Thus there is no cycle as such, beyond the fact that a series of shocks were operating sequentially on a given economic structure. Hence the swings were episodic rather than endogenous. Moreover, they were not the result of a systematic exogenous variable; for example, climatic variations are important in explaining the long swings of agricultural production but structural change in the economy filtered out many of the cycle-generating effects of climatic change. The absence of long swings at the world economy level does not mean that the swings did not have international influences and determinants. This study has shown that swings in domestic activities are reflected as inverse swings in overseas investment for Britain, France and Germany. The British swings were the most marked since they were observed as variations in levels; the French and German swings were only observed as variations in rates of growth. The swings had international repercussions and were only partly determined by conditions in the world economy. Thus during the period 1899–1913 one reason for the adverse terms of trade facing European industrial economies was the structural change taking place at the level of world industrial production and world agricultural production.

One important conclusion that I wish to draw is that economic growth has not been steady. In rejecting the relevance of the Kondratieff wave for national economies and the world economy I do not wish to create the impression that growth was steady in the long run. The world economy has seen major long-run variation throughout the period 1856–1973 – the process is described with the phrase 'G-waves' to distinguish the actual growth path from the postulated Kondratieff wave path. Such G-waves were extremely irregular and were generated by factors which have not been discussed by the Kondratieff wave literature, such as differential growth across countries and the degree of 'relative backwardness' in the world economy. Moreover, the various cyclical paths were interlinked; the G-wave growth path created conditions which helped to move the sectoral terms of trade against industrial sectors during the period 1899–1913, providing a degree of synchronisation across industrial economies with falling investment and real wages. It should be emphasised that since a degree of relative backwardness still exists in the world economy this is a sufficient condition for the G-wave growth path continuing into the future once rapid economic growth is resumed.

Notes

1 Perspectives on long-term economic growth variations

1 Kondratieff waves and Kuznets swings are distinguished by, *inter alia*, the length of the growth variation. The Kondratieff wave is also referred to as the long wave and the Kuznets swing as the long swing.

2 Balanced growth is taken to be the Solow–Samuelson (1953) definition:

> By balanced growth (or decay) we mean a state of affairs in which the output of each commodity increases (or decreases) by a constant percentage per unit of time, the mutual proportions in which commodities are produced remaining constant (1953, p. 412).

3 Natural growth refers to the sum of population and technological growth.

4 The Juglar cycle represents a growth variation that is taken to have a length of nine to eleven years. Its origins are to be found in the work of Juglar (1862).

5 How a low price level induces greater savings is not analysed by Kondratieff. Without considering the elasticity of price expectations it is difficult to see how he arrived at this conclusion. His framework assumed that a low price level redistributes income away from debtors towards creditors with a high marginal propensity to save.

6 An analysis of how credit expansion has an upper limit in a gold standard era would have greatly aided the validity of Kondratieff's framework.

7 Innovation in Schumpeter covers (i) new goods or a new quality of a good, (ii) new methods of production, (iii) the opening up of new markets, (iv) new sources of supply of raw materials, and (v) new organisation for an industry.

8 The Kitchin cycle refers to an inventory cyclical variation of between two to three years (Kitchin, 1923).

2 Statistical methodology

1 The length of the resulting cycle in Slutsky can be calculated from the simple formula,

$$\cos\frac{2\Pi}{L} = r_1$$

where L is the length of the cycle and r_1 is the first-order serial correlation of the terms in the sinusoid. The formula holds only where the second differences of the series in question are inversely proportional to the ordinate at that point, i.e. it is a sinusoid in the limit.

3 Production trends in the world economy

1 The compromise estimate is constructed as a linear average of the income, expenditure and output estimates of GDP.

2 For a more detailed outline of the statistical significance results see Solomou (1983, Ch. 3). Matthews et al. (1982) note that a difference of 0.4 per cent in the annual growth rate, compounded over a forty-year period, would make a difference of 17 per cent in the level in the final year and is thus an economically significant magnitude. However, separating the issues of economic significance and statistical significance is difficult. Only if a difference of 0.4 per cent exists with some degree of certainty can we proceed to discuss its economic relevance. Such a conclusion cannot be made.

3 The growth path during the period 1899–1913 was significantly lower than the mean growth path during the period 1856–1913 at the 10 per cent significance level (see Appendix Table A3.2).

4 The t-statistic for a significant difference between the periods 1856–73 and 1873–99 is only -0.05 (see Table A3.1).

5 The t-statistics on the significance of inter-cycle variations between the periods 1857–1866–1874–1890–1899–1913 were all insignificant, ranging between $+0.08$ and $+0.33$ (see Appendix Table A3.3).

6 For example, in the case of services, accounting for one-third of total output in 1907, the volume of output is based on linear interpolations. The manufacturing index is measured by the consumption of raw materials unadjusted for changes in stocks (Feinstein et al., 1982). It should be stressed that not all the observed linearity in output growth is due to this factor. The inverse growth swings of some important sectors was also critical. In particular during the period 1873–1913 the agricultural sector's growth swings moved inversely to those of the construction sector.

7 The t-statistic on the significance of inter-cycle variations ranged between $+0.37$ and $+0.52$ (see Appendix Table A3.4).

8 Both the 1873–82 and 1899–1913 downswing phases were significant from the mean growth path during the period 1856–1913 at the 5 per cent significance level (see Appendix Table A3.5).

9 The t-statistic for a difference between the periods 1899–1913 and 1873–82 is only -0.23; the t-statistic for a difference between periods 1865–82 and 1882–1913 is -0.29.

10 Fuller (1970) pointed out that the GDP data before 1913 were subject to large errors and should only be used to analyse growth over longer periods than a year. The discrepancies for growth phases such as the 1880s and the 1890s suggest that the various measures are inadequate even for longer phases.

11 Significant at the 5 per cent level (see Appendix Table A3.6).

12 Not significant at the 10 per cent level.

13 Significant at the 5 per cent level.

14 Both the slow growth periods, 1884–91 and 1899–1913, were significant at the 5 per cent level.

15 The t-statistic for a difference between periods 1871–91 and 1891–1913 is only -0.55.

16 Two reasons can be given for this constancy. Firstly, the TFI series is dominated by the variation of labour input which shows a fairly constant exponential growth between 1856 and 1913. Secondly, the contribution of labour and capital inputs to the TFI series are inversely correlated ($r = -0.8$ for 1882–1906 and $r = -0.5$ for 1856–1913).

17 The swings are significant at the 1 per cent level.

18 The t-statistic for a difference between periods 1873–81 and 1899–1913 is only -0.14.

19 Significant at the 5 per cent level.

20 The postwar growth rate was significantly higher than the rates for 1856–73 and 1873–1913 at the 5 per cent and 1 per cent levels respectively.

21 In a recent paper Greasley (1986) he argued that the major errors in the GDP series are to be found in the income estimate. Service incomes were not adequately represented and coalmining was given a large weight compared to its 4 per cent share of GDP. Correcting for some of these errors and omissions he concludes that British economic growth during the period 1856–1913 followed a number of swings rather than a climacteric after 1899.

22 The growth path of 1857–74 is not distinguished from that of 1874–90 at either the 5 per cent or 10 per cent significance levels.

23 Another point of criticism of Hoffmann's work has been developed by Holtfrerich (1983). Since Hoffmann uses the price and value added structure of 1913 there are biases in his indices the further back we go. Using a variable weighting structure Holtfrerich calculated a magnitude for the biases involved. As expected, the divergences are greatest during the period 1850–73 and diminish over time. However, the new calculations do not suggest that Hoffmann's trend periods are affected; in fact the amplitude of the downswing during the period 1874–84 is higher in the revised Holtfrerich data.

24 See Appendix Table A3.7 for some statistical tests of a long-wave and long-swing periodisation of French commodity production.

25 This difference is significant at the 10 per cent level (see Appendix Tables A3.12 and A3.13).

26 The idea of an accelerating growth path over the period 1856–1913 is also reinforced by the fact that the trend for world industrial production is best approximated by a second-order polynomial, with both the first- and second-order coefficients being highly significant (Solomou, 1986b).

27 In mathematical terms, the world growth rate is defined as the weighted sum of the growth of the parts, i.e.

$$g_{w_t} = \sum_{i=1}^{n} g_{i_t} \alpha_{i_t}$$

where g_{w_t} is the world growth rate, g_{i_t} is the growth rate of national parts and α_{i_t} is the share of national parts, which are a function of relative growth rates. Over time the high g_i will also increase the corresponding α_i and hence, g_{w_i} tends to increase. This is, of course, an abstraction on reality since the growth paths of the national parts do not follow a steady-state trend and the degree of synchronisation in the world economy is not constant over time.

28 The sixteen include Australia, Austria, Belgium, Canada, Denmark, Finland, France, Germany, Italy, Japan, The Netherlands, Norway, Sweden, Switzerland, United Kingdom and United States.

29 The inter-period differences in growth between periods 1872–90 and 1890–1913 are significant at the 5 per cent level.

30 Similar calculations were undertaken employing the share averages of the cycle of 1872–82 as the weights. The results are similar to those employing 1870 weights.

4 Price trends

1 In Wicksell (1898) the elasticity of price expectations is implicitly assumed to be unity, representing a major simplifying assumption. In practice this elasticity could take on a wide range of values and could also vary over time.

2 The increased rate of gold production from the late 1840s caused silver to appreciate rapidly and disappear from specie circulation in the core economies (Martin, 1977).

3 Between 1848 and 1857, in addition to the Crimean War and the Indian Mutiny, Britain engaged in three more military undertakings: the Kaffir War (1948–53), the war with Persia (1856–7) and the Second China War (1856–60).

4 The mechanism by which a monetary expansion leads to an inflationary process need not be seen in terms of the simple identity of the Quantity Theory formula. A Keynesian approach to the role of money can be found in the work of Cairnes (1873) and Hughes (1960).

5 The Latin Monetary Union consisted of France, Belgium, Switzerland and Italy.

5 Innovation clusters and Kondratieff waves

1 The concept of the product life cycle was developed in the early work of Kuznets (1930) and Burns (1934). It is an interesting paradox that although both these authors showed an interest in long waves they did not employ the concept of the product life cycle as an aid to rationalising a long-wave growth path. The reason seems to be that both held to different innovation ideas from Schumpeter's cluster thesis. An aggregate product life cycle for the economy was not perceived as reasonable.

2 Julius Wolff was a German economist of the early twentieth century. For an outline of Wolff's ideas see Kuznets (1930, Ch. 2).

3 The product life-cycle framework postulates that diminishing returns would be observed in particular sectors/products, but as long as new inventive opportunities exist there is no reason why old firms should not move to more profitable activities – thus, innovation here also involves a change of product. Obviously there are lags in such adjustments but they will not necessarily generate a long-wave growth

pattern, since there is no a priori reason to expect a cluster of product cycles.

4 Rosenberg and Frischtak (1983) have pointed out that psychological and technological factors may operate to prevent major *substitute* technologies from developing but the same arguments cannot apply to *complementary* technologies. In this respect they argue that purely technologically induced long waves are unlikely.

5 Thus, in 1910 the British Secretary of State for war could argue that 'we do not consider that aeroplanes will be of any possible use for war purposes' (Jewkes *et al.*, 1969, p. 174).

6 The nature of the unknown population raises both methodological and conceptual problems. Indeed, the Schumpeterian methodology of seeing innovation as a unique point could be criticised, arguing with Usher (1971) that it is continuous changes that characterise innovation changes.

7 For example, in the second edition Jewkes *et al.* point out that they omitted the computer from the first edition because they did not realise how important it would be.

8 The concern of Jewkes *et al.* with twentieth century invention means that the aeroplane does not appear in their lists whereas rockets and helicopters do.

9 For a review of the recent literature on this theme see Kamien and Schwartz (1975).

10 Defence requirements seem to have been the original spur to the expansion of Research and Development (R and D) sectors. In Britain there was a rapid increase in R and D expenditure from about 1935, when the existence of the German Luftwaffe was publicly acknowledged. British R and D expenditure rose from 0.1 per cent of GNP in 1928 to 0.25 per cent in 1938 and 1 per cent in 1958.

11 See Siegel (1956) for an outline of the runs test.

12 Mensch argues that the runs test results show that *regular* cluster phases are significant. However, a sample of three clusters clearly falls in small sample categories and is compatible with 'random' patterns. A more relevant test would be to ask which specific clusters are, in fact, historically significant as a first step in determining a non-random pattern.

13 For n_1 and $n_2 \leq 20$ there exist runs test tables giving a random range for r. In the case of $n_1 \geq 1$ and $n_2 < 1$ the range is $9 < r < 21$; since $r = 21$ this cluster stands out as significant. For $n_1 \geq 2$ and $n_2 < 2$ the random range is $9 < r < 20$. According to this definition the sample (period B in Table 5.2) is random. For runs tables see Siegel (1956, pp. 252–3).

14 Kleinknecht (1981); the reference to Mahdavi, K.B. is to, *Technological Innovation*, (Stockholm, 1972).

15 Moreover, if the SI classification is not separated out the bunching of PI innovations in the 1930s does not stand out (Freeman *et al.*, 1982, p. 50).

6 The national aspects of Kuznets swings, 1850–1913

1 An important exception is Williamson (1964). Williamson has emphasised that in some periods American pull conditions were more dominant than conditions in Britain, while in others the opposite was true.

2 This assumes that the savings ratio was inflexible. In fact, the British savings ratio varied between 10 per cent and 17 per cent between 1850 and 1914 (Edelstein, 1982, p. 12).

3 It is important to note a subtle difference between Thomas' and Cairncross' monocausal frameworks; while Thomas' migration variable is taken to be a classic exogenous variable, Cairncross' terms of trade is meant to proxy a dynamic equilibrating variable and, thus, cannot be seen to be purely exogenous.

4 Terms-of-trade variations would proxy relative profitability only if it is assumed that production in both sectors is subject to constant returns to scale.

5 The failure to note the existence of long swings in aggregate production is the result of using the 'compromise' or 'output' estimates of GDP. The accepted view is that the inversities between swings in home investment and exports produced damped and insignificant swings in the aggregate trends (Ford, 1968). Chapter 3 has shown that long swings are an aggregate phenomenon.

6 The peak years are 1862, 1878, 1896, 1905 and 1913.

7 Table A6.1 also reports the results of some tests relating to the long-wave periodisation. It is clear that French investment did not follow a long wave path during the period 1856–1913. A unit root test on the stationarity of French investment suggests that this condition is satisfied at the 10 per cent significance level.

8 Table A6.2 also reports some results relating to the long-wave periodisation of German investment. There is no evidence for a long-wave phasing of the 1850–1913 period. A unit root test on German investment suggests that the series is stationary at the the 10 per cent significance level.

9 The data was kindly provided by John Odling-Smee; the information regarding its derivation can be found in Matthews *et al.* (1982, Ch. 6).

10 From 1888 annual profits figures can be derived from Stamp (1916) but there are major problems in deriving annual series before that.

11 The agricultural production series was found to be stationary. The $\hat{\tau}_\tau$ unit root test for the period 1855–1913 was equal to -3.64, significant at the 5 per cent level.

12 Feinstein *et al.* (1982) undertake a similar exercise using the 'output' estimate of GDP. However, since this series does not follow a long-swing path this exercise is not meaningful since the denominator is zero. The comparison proposed here is not ideal since the errors of different series may differ. Nevertheless, as long as the income estimate is a valid measure of GDP trends, this comparison will help us to determine the bounds of agriculture's contribution to the aggregate swings.

13 Land input variations were minor for most of this period, particularly during the period 1885–1913. An important omission, however, is the failure to consider fertiliser inputs in the production relationship. An annual series is not available for the period; O'jala (1952, p. 213) reports a value series for only a few benchmark years.

14 A number of attempts were made to estimate a three-stage least squares system of equations for output, capital and labour growth rates but the system was persistently underidentified.

15 The choice of a third-order polynomial was based on empirical tests; the fourth and fifth powers proved insignificant.

16 The exceptions are Williamson (1964), Abramovitz (1973) and Friedman and Schwartz (1982).

17 The differences in the two series for the 1880s can be accounted for by a different consideration of bank amalgamations in this period.

18 This assumes wage and price flexibility.
19 The Wicksellian cumulative process may have been important over short periods. The evidence does not support Hughes' (1968) assertion that the Wicksellian cumulative process is valid for long periods.

7 The international aspects of Kuznets swings, 1850–1913

1 The idea that the savings ratio was fixed for the British economy is unfounded empirically (Edelstein, 1982, p. 172).
2 The peak-to-peak dates chosen are those relating to the Juglar cycles. Since the Juglar cycle is being used as a proxy for long-swing phases there is no danger of averaging out the long-swing variations.
3 $\bar{L}_F$ is calculated by including both peak years in the average for the cycle. The calculations are similar if the average is taken over non-autocorrelated periods.
4 This conclusion follows from Imlah (1958) and Simon (1968). Recently, Platt (1980) has suggested that the British overseas investment figures are overestimates. The major problem arises from 'partials' (loans issued simultaneously in London and other international markets). Thus, despite the conformity of the direct and indirect measures for overseas investment he suggested the possibility that both series may be wrong. It should be noted that, since the basic problem is how to deal with partials adequately, the long swing in the various capital exporters, because of its non-synchronised nature, has significant implications for deriving adequate national capital export figures. Deflating the monetary capital export series does not yield any significant differences in the swing pattern. The price indices used were the price of tradables and the GDP deflator.
5 Deflating the French overseas investment figures does not yield any significant differences in trends. The price indices used were those for wholesale, retail and tradables.
6 The results presented here accord with Lewis and O'Leary (1955) who also find an inverse home and overseas investment path for the French economy during the period 1880–1913.
7 In 1900 71 per cent of French foreign investment flowed to Europe (Feis, 1961, p. 51).
8 The same trends are observed for 'real' German capital exports. The monetary values have been deflated by wholesale prices, the GNP deflator and tradable prices.
9 While Europe absorbed 71 per cent of French overseas investment in 1900, the ratio fell to 61 per cent in 1914 (Feis, 1961, p. 51).
10 The British case suggests an adverse movement of the sectoral terms of trade with respect to raw materials beginning in the 1890s.
11 The non-balanced growth path between industry and agriculture was noted by Phelps-Brown and Ozga (1955). They suggested that the variable inducing the change was increased industrial capacity in the world economy. Beenstock (1983, Ch. 3 and 6) has analysed this type of growth traverse in terms of a 'transition theory', entailing new industrialisers competing with the old and adversely affecting the terms of trade of industry. Historically, he argues that the late nineteenth-

century British 'Great Depression' can be understood in such terms. The evidence suggests that a better application of the theory would be to explain the retardation of industrial Europe during the Edwardian era.

12 The relative position of the three major capital exporters changed significantly during the period 1900–13. While in 1901–5 the relative shares of Britain, France and Germany were 37.3 per cent, 39.3 per cent and 23.4 per cent respectively, by 1910–13 they were 66.4 per cent, 13.7 per cent and 21.7 per cent (Bloomfield, 1968, p. 47).

8 A long-term perspective of interwar economic growth

1 As can be seen from Table 8.1 Austria was also an exception. Although the American and Canadian long-term growth rates retarded by about 1 per cent per annum during the period 1913–29 compared to the pre-1913 era, this should not be viewed as signalling growth problems in these economies. The closing of the territorial frontier imposed constraints on the potential output of both economies. The long-term comparisons of productivity were more favourable to the 1913–29 period.

2 All these cycles had the characteristic of a major depression followed by a mild recovery. As noted in Chapter 3, although the Romer revisions of the American GDP figures suggest a much less variable series before 1913, the long-swing behaviour of the economy is not affected.

3 Hence, the marked long swings of national economies were not observed for the world economy during the period 1872–1913. As was noted in Chapter 3 the world growth rate followed a series of upward steps during the period 1872–1907. However, as early as the 1907–13 cycle the retardation of the American economy was reflected as a world economy retardation, despite more rapid growth in industrial Europe.

4 The Dawes plan provided Germany with large loans to meet the reparation payments. The flow of capital into Germany was of such a magnitude that a transfer problem did not actually arise in the 1920s (Fleisig, 1976; Haberler, 1976).

5 The British evidence suggests that the terms of trade of food and raw materials followed different trends for much of the pre-1913 period. During the 1870s the terms of trade were adverse with respect to food and favourable with respect to raw materials. In the 1890s the opposite was the case.

9 Some conclusions on the post-war boom, 1950–1973

1 See Japanese Science and Technology Agency, *Kagaku Gijutsu Hakusho* (White paper on Science and Technology), 1980, p. 162.

2 Such a pattern has been well documented for synthetic materials and electronics (Freeman *et al.*, 1982).

Bibliography

ABBREVIATIONS:

A.E.R.	*American Economic Review*
E.D.C.C.	*Economic Development and Cultural Change*
Ec.H.R.	*Economic History Review*
E.J.	*Economic Journal*
J.P.E.	*Journal of Political Economy*
N.B.E.R.	*National Bureau of Economic Research*
O.E.C.D.	*Organisation for Economic Co-operation and Development*
O.E.P.	*Oxford Economic Papers*
Q.J.E.	*Quarterly Journal of Economics*
R.E.S.	*Review of Economic Statistics*

Abramovitz, M. 1951. 'Economics of Growth'. In B.F. Haley, (ed.), *A Survey of Contemporary Economics*, Illinois, pp. 132–78.

Abramovitz, M. 1956. 'Resource and Output Trends in the United States', *A.E.R.*, Papers and Proceedings, pp. 5–23.

Abramovitz, M. 1958. 'Long Swings in U.S. Economic Growth'. In *N.B.E.R. Thirty Eighth Annual Report*, New York, pp. 47–56.

Abramovitz, M. 1959. 'Historical and Comparative Rates of Production, Productivity and Prices'. Statement in U.S. Congress. Joint Economic Committee, *Employment, Growth and Price Levels, Hearings* (86th Congress), Pt.II, Washington, pp. 411–66.

Abramovitz, M. 1961. 'The Nature and Significance of Kuznets Cycles', *E.D.C.C.*, IX, 3, pp. 225–49.

Abramovitz, M. 1968. 'The Passing of the Kuznets Cycle', *Economica*, XXXV, pp. 349–67.

Abramovitz, M. 1973. 'The Monetary Side of Long Swings in U.S. Economic Growth', Memorandum No. 146, Center for Research in Economic Growth, Stanford University.

Abramovitz, M. 1979. 'Rapid Growth Potential and its Realization; the Experience of Capitalist Economies in the Postwar Period'. In E. Malinvaud (ed.), *Economic Growth and Resources*, Vol. 1, London.

Adelman, I. 1965. 'Long Cycles – Fact or Artifact?', *A.E.R.*, LV, 3, pp. 444–63.

Adelman, I. and Adelman, F.L. 1959. 'The Dynamic Properties of the Klein–Goldberger Model', *Econometrica*, 27, 4, pp. 596–625.

Aftalion, A. 1913. *Les crises générales et periodique de surproduction*, Paris.

Aldcroft, D.H. 1974. 'McCloskey on Victorian Growth: A Comment', *Ec.H.R.*, XXVII, 2, pp. 271–4.

Aldcroft, D.H. 1977. *From Versailles to Wall Street, 1919–1929*, London.

Aldcroft, D.H. and Fearon, P. (eds.) 1972. *British Economic Fluctuations, 1790–1939*, London.

Ames, E. and Rosenberg, N. 1971. 'Changing Technological Leadership and Industrial Growth'. In N. Rosenberg (ed.), *The Economics of Technological Change*, London.

Annuaire Statistique De La France, 1966. Résumé Rétrospectif, Paris.

Ashworth, W. 1977. 'Typologies and Evidence: Has 19th Century Europe a Guide to Economic Growth?', *Ec.H.R.*, XXX, 1, pp. 140–58.

Bairoch, P. 1973. 'European Foreign Trade in the XIX Century: The Development of the Value and Volume of Exports (Preliminary Results)', *Journal of European Economic History*, 2, 1, pp. 5–36.

Bairoch, P. 1975. *The Economic Development of the Third World since 1900*, London.

Bairoch, P. 1976. 'Europe's Gross National Product: 1800–1975', *Journal of European Economic History*, 5, 2, pp. 273–340.

Bambrick, S. 1970. 'Australia's Long Run Terms of Trade', *E.D.C.C.*, 19, 1, pp. 1–5.

Bandera, V.N., Glazier, I.A. and Berner, R.B. 1975. 'Terms of Trade between Italy and the United Kingdom, 1815–1913', *Journal of European Economic History*, 4, 1, pp. 5–48.

Barnett, H.J. 1979. 'Scarcity and Growth Revisited'. In V.K. Smith, (ed.), *Scarcity and Growth Reconsidered*, Baltimore and London.

Barnett, H.J. and Morse, C. 1963. *Scarcity and Growth: The Economics of Natural Resource Availability*, Baltimore.

Beenstock, M. 1983. *The World Economy in Transition*, London.

Berend, I.T. and Ranki, G. 1980. 'Foreign Trade and the Industrialization of the European Periphery in the XIXth century', *Journal of European Economic History*, 9, 3, pp. 539–84.

Bieshaar, H. and Kleinknecht, A. 1984. 'Kondratieff Long Waves in Aggregate Output? An Econometric Test', *Konjunkturpolitik*, 30 pp. 279–303.

Bird, R.C., Desai, M.J., Enzler, J.J. and Taubman, P.J. 1965. '"Kuznets Cycles" in Growth Rates: The Meaning', *International Economic Review*, 6, 2, pp. 229–39.

Bloomfield, A.I. 1968. *Pattern of Fluctuation in International Investment Before 1914*, Princeton Studies in International Finance, No. 21, Princeton.

Bolch, B.W. and Pilgrim, J.D. 1973. 'A Reappraisal of Some Factors Associated with Fluctuations in the United States in the Interwar period', *Southern Economic Journal*, XXXIX, 3, pp. 327–44.

Bordo, M.D. 1975. 'John E. Cairnes on the Effects of the Australian gold discoveries, 1851–1873: an Early Application of the Methodology of Positive Economics', *History of Political Economy*, 7, 3, pp. 337–59.

Bordo, M.D. 1977. 'The Income Effects of the Sources of New Money: A Comparison of the United States and The United Kingdom, 1870–1913', *Explorations in Economic History*, 14, pp. 20–43.

Bordo, M.D. 1981. 'The U.K. Money Supply, 1870–1914'. In P. Uselding, (ed.), *Research in Economic History*, Vol. 6, London.

Bowden, M.J, Kates, R.W., Kay, P.A., Riebsome, W.E., Warrick, R.A., Johnson, D.L., Gould, H.A. and Weiner, D. 1981. 'The Effect of Climatic Fluctuations of Human Populations: Two Hypotheses'. In T.M.L. Wigley, M. Ingram and G. Farmer (eds.), *Climate and History*, Cambridge.

Box, G.E.P. and Jenkins, G.M. 1976. *Times Series Analysis*, San Fransisco.

Burns, A.F. 1934. *Production Trends in the U.S. since 1870*, N.B.E.R.

Burns, A.F. 1944. 'Frickey on the Decomposition of Time Series', *R.E.S.*, XXVII, 3, pp. 136–47.

Burns, A.F. and Mitchell, W.C. 1946. *Measuring Business Cycles*, N.B.E.R.

Buse, A. and Lim, L. 1977. 'Cubic Splines as a Special Case of Restricted Least Squares', *J.A.S.A.*, 72, pp. 64–8.

Cairncross, A.K. 1953. *Home and Foreign Investment, 1870–1913: Studies in Capital Accumulation*, Cambridge.

Cairnes, J.E. 1873. 'Essay Towards a Solution of the Gold Question', *Essays in Political Economy*, London, pp. 52–108.

Cameron, R. 1961. *France and the Economic Development of Europe, 1800–1914*, Princeton.

Carre, J.J., Dubois, P. and Malinvaud, E. 1976. *French Economic Growth*, Oxford.

Chatfield, C. 1980. *The Analysis of Time Series*, London and New York.

Chatterji, M. and Wickens, M.R. 1980. 'Verdoorn's Law – The Externalities Hypothesis and Economic Growth in the U.K.'. In D. Currie, R. Nobay and D. Peel (eds.), *Macroeconomic Analysis: Essays in Macroeconomics and Econometrics*, London.

Chatterji, M. and Wickens, M.R. 1982. 'Productivity, Factor Transfers and Economic Growth in the U.K.', *Economica*, 49, 193, pp. 21–38.

Church, R.A. 1975. *The Great Victorian Boom 1850–1873*, London.

Clark, J., Freeman, C. and Soete, L. 1981. 'Long Waves, Inventions, and Innovations', *Futures*, 13, 4, pp. 308–22.

Clarke, H. 1847. 'Physical Economy – a Preliminary Inquiry into the Physical Laws Governing the Periods of Famine and Panics', *Railway Register*, London.

Collins, M. 1983. 'Long Term Growth of the English Banking Sector and Money Stock, 1844–80', *Ec.H.R.* XXXVI, 3, pp. 374–94.

Coombs, R.W. 1981. 'Innovation, Automation, and the Long Wave Theory', *Futures*, 13, 5, pp. 360–70.

Cooper, R.N. and Lawrence, R.Z. 1975. 'The 1972–1975 Commodity Boom', *Brookings Papers*, 3, pp. 671–715.

Coppock, D. 1961. 'The Causes of the Great Depression, 1873–1896', *Manchester School*, XXIX, pp. 205–32.

Cornwall, J. 1972. *Growth and Stability in a Mature Economy*, London.

Cornwall, J. 1979. *Modern Capitalism: Its Growth and Transformation*, London.

Cottrell, P.L. 1975. *British Overseas Investment in the Nineteenth Century*, London.

Crafts, N.F.R. 1979. 'Victorian Britain Did Fail', *Ec.H.R.*, XXXII, 4, pp.533–7.

Crafts N.F.R. 1983. 'British Economic Growth, 1700–1831: A Review of the Evidence', *Ec.H.R.*, 36, pp. 177–99.

Cripps, T.F. and Tarling, R.J. 1973. *Growth in Advanced Capitalist Economies, 1950–1970*, Cambridge.

Crouzet, F. 1970. 'An Annual Index of French Industrial Production in the 19th Century'. In R. Cameron, (ed.), *Essays in French Economic History*, Illinois, pp. 245–79.

Crouzet, F. 1974. 'French Economic Growth in the Nineteenth Century Reconsidered', *History*, 59, 196, pp. 167–79.

Day, R.B. 1976, 'The Theory of Long Waves: Kondratiev, Trotsky, Mandel', *New Left Review*, 99, pp. 67–82.

Day, R.B. 1981. *The 'Crisis' and the 'Crash': Soviet Studies of the West*, London.

Deane, P. and Cole, W.A. 1967. *British Economic Growth 1688–1959: Trends and Structure*, Cambridge.

Dearman, J.B. 1974. 'World Commodity Price', *Economic Trends*, 247, pp. VI–XII.

Delbeke, J. 1981. 'Recent Long-Wave Theories: A Critical Survey', *Futures*, 13, 4, pp. 246–57.

Denison, E.F. 1967. *Why Growth Rates Differ*, Washington.

Derksen, J.B.D. 1940. 'Long Cycles in Residential Building: An Explanation', *Econometrica*, 8, pp. 97–116.

De Wolff, S. 1924. 'Prosperitäts – und Depressionsperioden'. In O. Jensen (ed.), *Der lebendige Marxismus: Festgabe zum 70 Geburtstage von Karl Kautsky*, Jena.

Dickey, D.A. and Fuller, W.A. 1981. 'Likelihood Ratio Statistics for Autoregressive Time Series with a Unit Root', *Econometrica*, 49, pp. 1057–72.

Dowling, J. and Poulson, B.W. 1974. 'Long Swings in the U.S. Economy: A Spectral Analysis of 19th and 20th Century data', *Southern Economic Journal*, 40, 3, pp. 473–80.

Dupriez, L.H. 1978. '1974 A Downturn of the Long Wave?', *Banca Nazionale Del Lavoro Quarterly Review*, 126, pp. 199–210.

Easterlin, R.A. 1966. 'Economic-Demographic Interactions and Long Swings in Economic Growth', *A.E.R.*, LVI, 5, pp. 1063–104.

Easterlin, R. 1968. *Population, Labor Force and Long Swings in Economic Growth: The American Experience*, New York.

Edelstein, M. 1976. 'Realized Rates of Return on U.K. Home and Overseas Portfolio Investment in the Age of High Imperialism', *Explorations in Economic History*, 13, pp. 283–329.

Edelstein, M. 1977. 'U.K. Savings in the Age of High Imperialism and After', *A.E.R.*, Papers and Proceedings, 61, 1, pp. 288–94.

Edelstein, M. 1982. *Overseas Investment in the Age of High Imperialism*, London.

Eichengreen, B.J. 1981. 'Asset Markets and Investment Fluctuations in Late Victorian Britain', *Harvard Institute of Economic Research, Discussion Paper*, No. 834.

Eichengreen, B.J. 1982. 'The Proximate Determinants of Domestic Investment in Victorian Britain', *Journal of Economic History*, XLII, 1, pp. 87–96.

Eklund, K. 1980. 'Long Waves in the Development of Capitalism', *Kyklos*, 33, 3, pp. 383–419.

Enoch, C.A. and Panic, M. 1981. 'Commodity Prices in the 1970s', *Bank of England Quarterly Bulletin*, 1, 21, pp. 42–53.

Epstein, R.C. 1929. *Industrial Profits in the U.S.*, (N.B.E.R., New York).

Evans, G.B.A. and Savin, N.E. 1981. 'Testing Unit Roots 1', *Econometrica*, 49, pp. 753–79.

Falkus, M. 1979. 'Aspects of Foreign Investment in Tsarist Russia', *Journal of European Economic History*, 8, 1, pp. 5–36.

Feinstein, C.H. 1972. *National Income Expenditure and Output of the United Kingdom, 1855–1965*, Cambridge.

Feinstein, C.H. 1976. *Statistical Tables of National Income, Expenditure and Output of the U.K., 1856–1965*, Cambridge.

Feinstein, C.H., Matthews, R.C.O. and Odling-Smee, J. 1982. 'The Timing of the Climacteric and its Sectoral Incidence in the U.K. 1873–1913'. In C.P. Kindleberger and C. di Tella (eds.), *Economics in The Long View: Essays in Honour of W.W. Rostow*, Vol. 3, London and Basingstoke.

Feis, H. 1961. *Europe: The World's Banker 1870–1914*, New York.

Fellner, W. 1956. *Trends and Cycles in Economic Activity: An Introduction to Problems of Economic Growth*, New York.

Fels, R. 1956. 'The Long Wave Depression, 1873–1897', *The Review of Economics and Statistics*, XXXI, 1, pp. 69–73.

Fisher, I. 1933. 'The Debt-deflation Theory of Great Depressions', *Econometrica*, 1, pp. 337–57.

Fleisig, H. 1972. 'The United States and the Non-European Periphery During the Early Years of the Depression'. In H. Van Der Wee (ed.), *The Great Depression Revisited*, The Hague.

Fleisig, H. 1976. 'War-related Debts and the Great Depression', *A.E.R.*, Papers and Proceedings, 66, 2, pp. 52–8.

Floud, R. and McCloskey, D.N. (eds.) 1981. *The Economic History of Britain Since 1700*, Vols. 1 and 2, Cambridge.

Ford, A.G. 1968. 'Overseas Lending and Internal Fluctuations, 1870–1914'. In A.R. Hall (ed), *The Export of Capital From Britain 1870–1914*, London.

Ford, A.G. 1974. 'British Investment in Argentina and Long Swings, 1880–1914'. In R. Floud (ed.), *Essays in Quantitative Economic History*, Oxford.

Forrester, J.W. 1977. 'Growth Cycles', *De Economist*, 125, 4, pp. 525–43.

Forrester, J.W. 1978. 'Changing Economic Patterns', *Technology Review*, 80, 8, pp. 3–9.

Forrester, J.W. 1981. 'Innovation and Economic Change', *Futures*, 13, 4, pp. 323–31.

Freeman, C. 1979. 'The Kondratiev Long Waves, Technical Change and Unemployment', O.E.C.D., Discussion Paper (March). Also in *Structural Determinants of Employment and Unemployment*, Vol II, O.E.C.D., pp. 181–96.

Freeman, C. 1981. *Technical Innovation and Long Waves in World Economic Development*, Special Issues of *Futures*, 13, 4, and 13, 5.

Freeman, C., Clark, J. and Soete, J. 1982. *Unemployment and Technical Innovation: A Study of Long Waves and Economic Development*, London.

Fremdling, R. 1977. 'Railroads and German Economic Growth: A Leading Sector Analysis with a Comparison of the U.S. and G.B.', *Journal Economic History*, XXXVII, 3, pp. 583–604.

Fried, E.R. and Schultze, C.L. (eds.) 1975. *Higher oil Prices and the World Economy*, Washington.

Friedman, B.M. (ed.) 1982. *The Changing Roles of Debt and Equity in Financing U.S. Capital Formation*, Chicago and London.

Friedman, M. and Schwartz, A.J. 1982. *Monetary Trends in the U.S. and the U.K.*, Chicago and London.

Friedman, P. 1978. 'An Econometric Model of National Income, Commercial Policy and the Level of International Trade: The Open Economies of Europe, 1924–1938', *Journal of Economic History*, XXXVIII, 1, pp. 148–80.

Frisch, R. 1933. 'Propagation Problems and Impulse Problems in Dynamic Economics', *Essays in Honor of Gustav Cassel*, London.

Fuller, M.F. 1970. 'Some tests on the Comparability of Historical Series of National Accounts Estimates', *Bulletin of the Oxford University Institute of Economics and Statistics*, 32, pp. 219–29.

Fuller, W.A. 1976. *Introduction to Statistical Time Series*, New York.

Gallman, R.E. 1966. 'G.N.P. in the U.S.-1909', *Output, Employment and Productivity in the U.S. after 1800, Studies in Income and Wealth*, Vol. 30, N.B.E.R., pp. 3–24.

Garvy, G. 1943. 'Kondratieff's Theory of Long Waves', *R.E.S.*, XXV, 4, pp. 203–19.

George, P.J. and Oksanen, E.H. 1973–74. 'Saturation in the Automobile Market in the Late Twenties: Some Further Results', *Explorations in Economic History*, II, 1, pp. 73–85.

Gerschenkron, A. 1962. *Economic Backwardness in Historical Perspective*, New York and London.

Giersch, H. 1979. 'Aspects of Growth, Structural Change and Employment – A Schumpeterian perspective', *Weltwirtschaftliches Archiv*, 115, 4, pp. 629–52.

Gilbert, M. 1958. *Comparative National Products and Price Levels*, Paris.

Goldsmith, R.W. 1984. 'The Stability of the Ratio of Nonfinancial Debt to Income', *Banca Nationale Del Lavoro Quarterly Review*, 150, pp. 285–305.

Gomulka, S. 1971. *Inventive Activity, Diffusion and the Stages of Economic Growth*, Aarhus.

Good, D.F. 1974. 'Stagnation and Take Off in Austria, 1873–1913', *Ec.H.R.*, XXVII, 1, pp. 72–87.

Good, D.F. 1978. 'The Great Depression and Austrian Growth after 1873', *Ec.H.R.*, XXXI, 2, pp. 290–4.

Gordon, D.M. 1978. 'Up and Down the Long Roller Coaster', *U.S. Capitalism in Crisis*, New York, Union for Radical Political Economics.

Gordon, D.M. 1980. 'Stages of Accumulation and Long Economic Cycles'. In T.K. Hopkins and I. Wallerstein (eds.), *Processes in the World System*, Beverly Hills.

Gordon, R.A. 1974. *Economic Instability and Growth: The American Record*, New York.

Graham, A.K. and Senge, M. 1980. 'A Long Wave Hypothesis of Innovation', *Technological Forecasting and Social Change*, 17, 4, pp. 283–311.

Granger, C.W. and Hatanaka, M. 1964. *Spectral Analysis of Economic Time Series*, Princeton.

Greasley, D. 1986. 'British Economic Growth: The Paradox of the 1880's and the Timing of the Climacteric', *Explorations in Economic History*, 23, 4.

Habakkuk, H.J. 1968. 'Fluctuations in House Building in Britain and the U.S. in the 19th century'. In A.R. Hall (ed.) *The Export of Capital From Britain, 1870–1914*, London.

Haberler, G. 1976. 'The World Economy, Money and the Great Depression, 1919–1939', American Enterprise Institute for Public Policy Research, Washington D.C.

Hahn, F.H. and Matthews, R.C.O. 1965. 'The Theory of Economic Growth: A Survey'. In AEA-RES, *Surveys of Economic Theory*, Vol. II, London.

Harkness, J.P. 1968. 'A Spectral-Analytic Test of the Long Swing Hypothesis in Canada', *Review of Economics and Statistics*, L, pp. 429–36.

Harley, C.K. 1977. 'The Interest Rate and Prices in Britain, 1873–1913: A Study of the Gibson Paradox', *Explorations in Economic History*, 14, 1, pp. 69–89.

Harley, C.K. 1980. 'Transportation, the World Wheat Trade, and the Kuznets Cycle, 1850–1913', *Explorations in Economic History*, 17, pp. 218–50.

Harley, C.K. 1982. 'British Industrialisation Before 1841: Evidence of Slower Growth During the Industrial Revolution', *Journal of Economic History*, 42, pp. 267–89.

Hart, P.E. (ed.) 1968. *Studies in Profit, Business Saving and Investment in the U.K., 1920–1962*, Vol. II, London.

Hartman, R.S. and Wheeler, D.R. 1979. 'Schumpeterian Waves of Innovation and Infrastructure Development in Great Britain and the U.S.: The Kondratieff Cycle Revisited'. In P. Uselding (ed.), *Research in Economic History*, 4, pp. 37–85.

Hatanaka, M. and Howrey, E.P. 1966. 'On the Long Swing Hypothesis', Princeton University Econometric Research Program Research Paper, No. 15, Princeton.

Hawke, G.R. 1970. *Railways and Economic Growth in England and Wales, 1840–1870*, London.

Hayek, F.A. 1935. *Prices and Production*, London.

Helphand, A. 1901. *Die Handelskrise und die Gewerkshaften, Munich.*

Hendry, D.F. and Ericsson, N. 1983. 'Assertion Without Empirical Basis: An Econometric Appraisal of Friedman and Schwartz' *Monetary Trends in ... The United Kingdom*', Bank of England Panel Paper No. 22.

Hickman, B.G. 1963. 'Postwar Growth in the U.S. in the Light of the Long Swing Hypothesis', *A.E.R.*, LIII, 2, Papers and Proceedings, pp. 490–507.

Hickman, B.G. 1974. 'What Became of the Building Cycle?'. In P. David and M. Reder, (eds.), *Nations and Households in Economic Growth: Essays in Honor of Moses Abramovitz*, New York and London.

Hicks, J.R. 1965. *Capital and Growth*, Oxford.

Hicks, J.R. 1974. 'Real and Monetary Factors in Economic Fluctuations', *Scottish Journal of Political Economy*, XXI, 3, pp. 205–14.

Hill, T.P. 1979. *Profits and Rates of Return*, O.E.C.D.

Hoffmann, W.G. 1955. *British Industry*, Oxford.

Hoffmann, W.G. 1958. *The Growth of Industrial Economies*, Manchester.

Hoffmann, W.G. 1965, *Das Wachstum der Deutschen Wirtschaft seit der Mitte Das 19 Jahrhunderts*, Berlin.

Holtfrerich, C.L. 1983. 'The Growth of Net Domestic Product in German 1850–1913'. In R. Fremdling and P.K. O'Brien, (eds.), *Productivity in the Economies of Europe*, Stuttgart.

Howrey, E.P. 1968. 'A Spectrum Analysis of the Long Swing hypothesis', *International Economic Review*, 9, pp. 228–52.

Huffman, W.E. and Lothian, J.R. 1980. 'Money in the U.K., 1833–1880', *Journal of Money, Credit and Banking*, XII, 2, Pt. 1

Hughes, J.R.T. 1960. *Fluctuation in Trade, Industry and Finance*, London.

Hughes, J.R.T. 1968. 'Wicksell on the Facts: Prices and Interest Rates, 1844–1914'. In J.N. Wolfe, (ed.), *Value, Capital and Growth: Papers in Honour of Sir John Hicks*, Edinburgh.

Imlah, A.H. 1958. *Economic Elements in the Pax Britannica*, Cambridge.

Innes, D. 1981. 'Capitalism and Gold', *Capital and Class*, 14, pp. 5–35.

Isard, W. 1942. 'A Neglected Cycle: The Transport-Building Cycle', *R.E.S.*, XXIV, 4, pp. 149–158.

James, H. 1984. 'The Causes of the German Banking Crisis of 1931', *Ec. H.R.* XXXVII, 1.

James, H. 1985, *The Reichsbank and Public Finance in Germany, 1924–33*, Frankfurt.

Jánossy, F. 1971. *The End of the Economic Miracle*, New York.

Jenks, L.H. 1971. *The Migration of British Capital to 1875*, London.

Jewkes, J., Sawers, D. and Stillerman, R. 1969. *The Sources of Invention*, London.

Juglar, C. 1862. *Des crises commerciales et leur retour périodique en France, en Angleterre et aux Etats Unis*, Paris.

Kaldor, N. 1966. *Causes of the Slow Rate of Economic Growth in the United Kingdom*, Cambridge.

Kaldor, N. 1976. 'Inflation and Recession in The World Economy', *E.J.*, 86, pp. 703–14.

Kaldor, N. 1977. 'Capitalism and Industrial Development: some lessons from Britain's experience', *Cambridge Journal of Economics*, 1, 2, pp. 193–204.

Kalecki, M. 1968. 'Trend and Business Cycles Reconsidered', *E.J.*, LXXVIII, pp. 263–76.

Kamien, M.I. and Schwartz, N.L. 1975. 'Market Structure and Innovation: A Survey', *Journal of Economic Literature*, XIII, 1, pp. 1–37.

Kendrick, J.W. 1977. *Understanding Productivity: An Introduction to the Dynamics of Productivity Change*, Baltimore and London.

Kennedy, W.P. 1982. 'Economic Growth and Structural Change in the United Kingdom, 1870–1914', *Journal of Economic History*, XLII, 1, pp. 105–14.

Keynes, J.M. 1936. *The General Theory of Employment, Interest and Money*, Vol.VII of *The Collected Writings of John Maynard Keynes*, 1973, London and Basingstoke.

Kindleberger, C.P. 1955. 'Industrial Europe's Terms of Trade on Current Account, 1870–1953', *E.J.*, LXV, 257, pp. 19–35.

Kindleberger, C.P. 1956. *The Terms of Trade: A European case study*, New York and London.

Kindleberger, C.P. 1964. *Economic Growth in France and Britain, 1851–1950*, Cambridge, Mass. and London.

Kindleberger, C.P. 1967. *Europe's Postwar Growth: The Role Of Labour Supply*, Cambridge, Mass.

Kindleberger, C.P. 1973. *The World in Depression*, London.

Kindleberger, C.P. 1978a. 'The Aging Economy', The Bernhard Harms Lecture, *Weltwirtschaftliches Archiv*, 114, 3, pp. 407–21.

Kindleberger, C.P. 1978b. *Manias, Panics and Crashes*, London.

Kindleberger, C.P. 1982. 'British Financial Reconstruction, 1815–22 and 1918–25'. In C.P. Kindleberger and C. di Tella (eds.), *Economics in The Long View: Essays in Honour of W.W. Rostow*, Vol. 2, London and Basingstoke.

Kitchin, J. 1923. 'Cycles and Trends in Economic Factors', *R.E.S.*, V, 1, pp. 10–16.

Kitchin, J. 1930. Report to Gold Delegation of the Financial Committee of the League of Nations, Geneva.

Kleinknecht, A. 1981. 'Observations on the Schumpeterian Swarming of Innovations', *Futures*, 13, 4, pp. 293–307.

Klolz, B.P. 1973. 'Oscillatory Growth in Three Nations', *Journal of American Statistical Association*, 68, 343, pp. 562–7.

Klolz, B.P. and Neal, L. 1973. 'Spectral and Cross Spectral Analysis of the Long Swing Hypothesis', *Review of Economics and Statistics*, LV, pp. 291–8.

Kondratieff, N.D. 1922. *Mirovoe khozyaistvo i ego kon'iunktury vo vrema i posle voiny*, Volgada.

Kondratieff, N.D. 1924. 'On the Notion of Economic Statics, Dynamics, and Fluctuations', *Sotsialisticheskoe Khoziaistvo*, No. 2, pp. 349–82. An abridged English translation appears as 'The Static and Dynamic View of Economics'. *Q.J.E.*, XXXIX. 4, 1925, pp. 575–83.

Kondratieff, N.D. 1979. 'The Major Economic Cycles', translation, *Review*, II, 4, pp. 519–62. First published (1925) as *Voprosy kon'iunktury*, I, pp. 28–79. An abridged English translation (1935) appears as 'The Long Waves in Economic Life', *R.E.S.*, XVII, 6, pp. 105–15.

Kondratieff, N.D. and Oparin, D.I. 1928. *Bol'shie tsikly kon'yunktury*, Moscow. An English translation appears as *The Long Wave Cycle*, New York: Richard and Snyder, 1984.

Kravis, I.B., Kenessey, Z., Heston, A. and Summers, R. 1978. *International Comparisons of Real Product and Purchasing Power*, Baltimore.

Kuczynski, Th. 1978. 'Spectral Analysis and Cluster Analysis as Mathematical Methods for the Periodisation of Historical Processes – A Comparison of Results Based on Data about the Development of Production and Innovation in the History of Capitalism. Kondratieff Cycles – Appearance or Reality?', Paper for Seventh International Economic History Congress, Edinburgh.

Kuczynski, Th. 1980. 'Have There been Differences Between the Growth Rates in Different Periods of the Capitalist World Economy since 1850? An Application of Cluster Analysis in Time Series Analysis'. In J.M. Clubb and E.K. Scheuch (eds.), *Historical Social Research of Historical and Process-Produced Data*, Stuttgart.

Kuznets, S.S. 1930. *Secular Movements in Production and Prices: Their Nature and their Bearing upon Cyclical Fluctuations*, Cambridge Mass.

Kuznets, S.S. 1940. 'Schumpeter's Business Cycles', *A.E.R.*, XXX, 2, pp. 257–71.

Kuznets, S.S. 1952. 'Long Term Changes in the National Income of the U.S.A. since 1870'. In S. Kuznets (ed.) *Income and Wealth of the U.S.*, Cambridge.

Kuznets, S.S. 1958. 'Long Swings in the Growth of Population and in Related Economic Variables', *Proceedings of the American Philosophical Society*, 102, 1, pp. 25–52.

Lamb, H.H. 1977. *Climate: Present, Past and the Future*, Vol. 2, London.

Lamb, H.H. 1982. *Climate, History and the Modern World*, London.

Lange, O. 1944a. Book Review of J.A. Schumpeter's *Business Cycles*, *R.E.S.*, XXIII, 3, pp. 190–3.

Lange, O. 1944b. *Price Flexibility and Employment*, Bloomington, Ind.

League of Nations. 1945. *Industrialisation and Foreign Trade*.

Lenoir, M. 1913. *Etudes sur la formation et le mouvement des prix*, Paris.

Lévy-Leboyer, M. 1978. 'Capital Investment and Economic Growth in France'. In P. Mathias and M.M. Postan (eds.), *The Cambridge Economic History of Europe* Vol. 7, Cambridge.

Lewis, W.A. 1949. *Economic Survey*, London.

Lewis, W.A. 1952. 'World Production, Prices and Trade', *Manchester School*, XX, 2, pp. 105–38.

Lewis, W.A. 1978. *Growth and Fluctuations 1870–1913*, London.

Lewis, W.A. 1980a. 'Rising Prices: 1899–1913 and 1950–1979', *Scandinavian Journal of Economics*, 82, 4, pp. 425–36.

Lewis, W.A. 1980b. 'The Slowing Down in the Engine of Growth', *A.E.R.*, 4, 70, pp. 555–64.

Lewis, W.A. 1981. 'The Rate of Growth of World Trade, 1830–1973'. In S. Grassmann and E. Lundberg (eds.), *The World Economic Order*, London.

Lewis, W.A. and O'Leary, P.J. 1955. 'Secular Swings in Production and Trade, 1870–1913', *Manchester School*, XXIII, 2, pp. 113–52.

Lipsey, R.E. 1963. *Price and Quantity Trends in the Foreign Trade of the U.S.*, N.B.E.R., Princeton, N.J.

Lowe, A. 1976. *The Path of Economic Growth*, Cambridge.

Lundberg, E. 1968. *Instability and Economic Growth*, New Haven.

Maddison, A. 1962. 'Growth and Fluctuation in the World Economy, 1870–1960', *Banca Nazionale del Lavoro Quarterly Review*, 61, pp. 127–95.

Maddison, A. 1967. 'Comparative Productivity Levels in the Developed Countries', *Banca, Nazionale Del Lavoro Quarterly Review*, 83, pp. 295–315.

Maddison, A. 1979. 'Long Run Dynamics of Productivity Growth', *Banca Nazionale Del Lavoro Quarterly Review*, 128, pp. 3–44.

Maddison, A. 1980. 'Phases of Capital Development'. In R.C.O. Matthews (ed.), *Economic Growth and Resources: Vol. 2, Trends and Factors*, London.

Maddison, A. 1982. *Phases of Capitalist Development*, Oxford and New York.

Mandel, E. 1975. *Late Capitalism*, London.

Mandel, E. 1980. *Long Waves of Capitalist Development: The Marxist Interpretation*, Cambridge.

Mandel, E. 1981. 'Explaining Long Waves of Capitalist Development', *Futures*, 13, 4, pp. 332–8.

Manley, G. 1959. 'Temperature Trends in England, 1698–1957', *Archiv für Meteorologie Geophysik und Bioklimat*, IX, pp. 413–33.

Marley, G. 1974, 'Central England Temperatures: Monthly Means 1659 to 1973', *Quarterly Journal of the Royal Meteorological Society*, 100, pp. 389–405.

Mann, H.B. and Wald, A. 1943. 'On the Statistical Treatment of Linear Stochastic Difference Equations', *Econometrica*, 11, pp. 173–200.

Marchetti, C. 1979. 'Energy Systems – The Broader Context', *Technological Forecasting and Social Change*, 14, pp. 191–203.

Martin, D.A. 1977. 'The Impact of Mid-Nineteenth Century Gold Depreciation Upon Western Monetary Standards', *Journal of European Economic History*, 6, 3, pp. 641–58.

Mathias, P. and Postan, M.M. (eds.) 1978. *The Cambridge Economic History of Europe*, VII, I, Cambridge.

Matthews, R.C.O. 1959. *The Business Cycle*, Cambridge.

Matthews, R.C.O. 1974. 'Some Aspects of Postwar Growth in the British Economy in Relation to Historical Experience'. In R. Floud (ed.), *Essays in Quantitative Economic History*, Oxford.

Matthews, R.C.O. (ed.) 1980. *Economic Growth and Resources Vol. 2; Trends and Factors*, London.

Matthews, R.C.O., Feinstein, C. and Odling-Smee, J. 1982. *British Economic Growth*, Oxford.

Mayer, T. 1978. 'Money and the Great Depression: A Critique of Professor Temin's Thesis', *Explorations in Economic History*, 15, pp. 127–45.

McClam, W.D. 1982. 'Financial Fragility and Instability: Monetary Authorities as Borrowers and Lenders of Last Resort'. In C.P. Kindleberger and J.P. Laffargue (eds.), *Financial Crises*, Cambridge.

McCloskey, D.N. 1970. 'Did Victorian Britain Fail?', *Ec. H.R.*, XXIII, pp. 446–59.

McCloskey, D.N. 1974. 'Victorian Growth: A Rejoinder', *Ec.H.R.*, XXVII, 2, pp. 275–7.

McCloskey, D.N. 1979. 'No it Did Not: A Reply to Crafts', *Ec.H.R.*, XXXII, 4, pp. 538–41.

Mensch, G. 1979. *Stalemate in Technology: Innovations Overcome the Depression*, Cambridge, Mass.

Mensch, G., Coutinho, C. and Kaasch, K. 1981. 'Changing Capital Values and the Propensity to Innovate', *Futures*, 13, 4, pp. 276–92.

Metz, R. and Spree, R. 1981. 'Kuznets-Zyklen im Wachstum der deutschen Wirtschaft während des 19. und fruhen 20. Jahrhunderts'. In D. Petzina and G. van Roon (eds.), *Konjunktur, Krise, Gesellschaft*, Stuttgart.

Minsky, H.P. 1964. 'Longer Waves in Financial Relations: Financial Factors in the More Severe Depressions', *A.E.R.*, Papers and Proceedings, LIV, 3, pp. 324–35.

Minsky, H.P. 1978. 'The Financial Instability Hypothesis: A Restatement', *Thames Papers in Political Economy*, London.

Minsky, H.P. 1982. 'The Financial-instability Hypothesis: Capitalist Processes and the Behaviour of the Economy'. In C.P. Kindleberger and J.P. Laffargue (eds.), *Financial Crises*, Cambridge.

Minsky, H.P. 1984. 'Banking and Industry Between the Two Wars: The United States', *Journal of European Economic History*, 13, 2, pp. 235–72.

Mishkin, F.S. 1978. 'The Household Balance Sheet and the Great Depression', *Journal of Economic History*, XXXVIII, 4, pp. 918–37.

Mitchell, B.R. 1981. *European Historical Statistics, 1750–1975*, London and Basingstoke.

Mitchell, B.R. and Deane, P. 1962. *Abstract of British Historical Statistics*, Cambridge.

Moggridge, D.E. 1981. 'Financial Crises and Lenders of Last Resort: Policy in the Crises of 1920 and 1929', *Journal of European Economic History*, 10, 1, pp. 47–70.

Morishima, M. 1973. *Marx's Economics*, Oxford.

Nelson, R.R. and Winter, S.G. 1974. 'Neoclassical v. Evolutionary Theories of Economic Growth', *E.J.*, 84, pp. 886–905.

Nicholas, F.J. and Glasspole, J. 1932. 'General Monthly Rainfall over England and Wales 1827 to 1931', *British Rainfall, 1931*, London.

Nicholas, S. 1982. 'Total Factor Productivity Growth and the Revision of Post 1870 British Economic History', *Ec.H.R.*, XXX, 1, pp. 83–98.

Nordhaus, W.D. 1974. 'Oil and Economic Performance in Industrial Countries', *Brookings Papers*, 2, pp. 341–99.

Nulter, W. 1962, *The Growth of Industrial Production in the Soviet Union*, Princeton.

O'jala, E.M. 1952. *Agriculture and Economic Progress*, London.

Olson, M. 1982. *The Rise and Decline of Nations*, Yale.

Parry-Lewis, J. 1965. 'Growth and Inverse Cycles: A Two Country Model', *E.J.*, LXXIV, pp. 109–18.

Passinetti, L.L. 1981. *Structural Change and Economic Growth: A Theoretical Essay on the Dynamics of the Wealth of Nations*, Cambridge.

Phelps-Brown, E.H. and Handfield-Jones, S.J. 1952. 'The Climacteric of the 1890's: A Study in the Expanding Economy', *O.E.P.*, 4, 3, pp. 266–307.

Phelps-Brown, E.H. and Ozga, S.A. 1955. 'Economic Growth and the Price Level', *E.J.*, LXV, 257.

Phelps-Brown, E.H. and Weber, B. 1962. 'Accumulation, Productivity and Distribution in the British Economy, 1870–1938'. In E.M. Carus-Wilson (ed.), *Essays in Economic History*, Vol. III, London.

Pigou, A.C. 1943. 'The Classical Stationary State', *E.J.*, LIII, pp. 343–51.

Pilgrim, J.D. 1974. 'The Upper Turning Point of 1920: A Reappraisal', *Explorations in Economic History*, 11, pp. 271–98.

Platt, D.C.M. 1980. 'British Portfolio Investment Overseas before 1870: Some Doubts', *Ec.H.R.*, XXXIII, 1, pp. 1–16.

Poirier, D.J. 1977. *The Econometrics of Structural Change*, Amsterdam.

Potter, N. and Christy, F.T. 1962. *Trends in Natural Resource Commodities, 1870–1957*, Princeton.

Rasche, R.H. and Tatom, J.A. 1981. 'Energy Price Shocks, Aggregate Supply and Monetary Policy: The Theory and the International Evidence', *Carnegie–Rochester Conference Series on Public Policy*, 14, pp. 9–94.

Ray, G. 1980. 'Innovation in the Long Cycle', *Lloyds Bank Review*, 135.

Richardson, H.W. 1972. 'British Emigration and Overseas Investment, 1870–1914', *Ec.H.R.*, XXV, 1, pp. 99–113.

Robertson, D.H. 1949. *Banking Policy and the Price Level*, London.

Rodda, J.C., Downing, R.A. and Law, F.M. 1976. *Systematic Hydrology*, London.

Romer, C.D. 1985. 'The Instability of The Prewar Economy Reconsidered: A Critical Examination of Historical Macroeconomic Data', Massachusetts Institute of Technology, D.Phil. Thesis.

Romer, C.D. 1986. 'New Estimates of Prewar Gross National Product and Unemployment', *Journal of Economic History*, XLVI, 2, pp. 341–52.

Rosenberg, N. and Frischtak, C.R. 1983. 'Long Waves and Economic Growth: A Critical Appraisal', *A.E.R.*, 73, 2, pp. 146–51.

Rostow, W.W. 1948. *British Economy of the 19th Century*, Oxford.

Rostow, W.W. 1950. 'The Terms of Trade in Theory and Practice', *Ec.H.R.*, III, 1, pp. 1–20.

Rostow, W.W. 1975. 'Kondratieff, Schumpeter, and Kuznets: Trend Periods Revisited', *Journal of Economic History*, XXXV, 4, pp. 719–53.

Rostow, W.W. 1978. *The World Economy*, London.

Rostow, W.W. 1980. *Why the Poor Get Richer and the Rich Slow Down: Essays in the Marshallian Long Period*, London.

Rostow, W.W. and Kennedy, M. 1979. 'A Simple model of the Kondratieff Cycle'. In P. Uselding (ed.), *Research in Economic History*, 4, pp. 1–36.

Rowe, J.W.F. 1965. *Primary Commodities in International Trade*, Cambridge.

Rowthorn, R.E. 1975. 'What Remains of Kaldor's Law', *E.J.*, 85, pp. 10–19.

Sahal, D. 1980. 'The Nature and Significance of Technological Cycles', *International Journal of Systems Science*, 11, 8, pp. 985–1000.

Sargent, J.R. 1979. 'Productivity and Profits in U.K. manufacturing', *Midland Bank Review*, pp. 7–13.

Saul, S.B. 1969. *The Myth of the Great Depression, 1873–1896*, London and Basingstoke.

Saunders, C.T. 1952. 'The Consumption of Raw Materials in the U.K.', *Journal of the Royal Statistical Society*, Ser. A, CXV.

Sayers, R.S. 1933. 'The Question of the Standard in the Eighteen Fifties', *Economic History*, Economic Journal Supplement, III.

Sayers, R.S. 1950. 'The Springs of Technical Progress in Britain, 1919–1939', *E.J.*, LX, pp. 275–94.

Schlote, W. 1952. *British Overseas Trade, 1700–1930*, Oxford.

Schumpeter, J.A. 1911. *The Theory of Economic Development: An Inquiry into Profits, Capital, Credit, Interest and the Business Cycle*, Oxford.

Schumpeter, J.A. 1935. 'The Analysis of Economic Change', *R.E.S.*, XVII, 4, pp. 2–10.

Schumpeter, J.A. 1939. *Business Cycles, I & II: A Theoretical, Historical and Statistical Analysis of the Capitalist Process*, New York.

Schumpeter, J.A. 1950. *Capitalism, Socialism and Democracy*, New York.

Schweitzer, A. 1941.'Speithoff's Theory of the Business Cycle', *University of Wyoming Publications*, VIII, I, pp. 1–30.

Siegel, S. 1956. *Nonparametric Statistics*, Tokyo.

Simon, M. 1968. 'The Pattern of New British Portfolio Foreign Investment, 1865–1914'. In A.R. Hall (ed.), *The Export of Capital From Britain, 1865–1914*, London.

Slutsky, E. 1937. 'The Summation of Random Causes as the Cause of Cyclical Processes', *Econometrica*, V, pp. 105–46.

Solomou, S.N. 1983. 'Long Term Growth Phases: Long Waves, Long Swings and Traverses – A Case Study of Britain, France, Germany and America since 1850', University of Cambridge, Ph.D. Thesis.

Solomou, S.N. 1986a. 'The Impact of Climatic Variations on British Economic Growth, 1856–1913', *Climatic Change*, 8, pp. 53–67.

Solomou, S.N. 1986b. 'Non-Balanced Growth and Kondratieff Waves in The World Economy, 1850–1913', *Journal of Economic History*, XLVI, 1, pp. 165–71.

Solomou, S.N. 1986c. 'Innovation Clusters and Kondratieff Long Waves in Economic Growth', *Cambridge Journal Of Economics*, 10, pp. 101–12.

Solow, R.M. 1957. 'Technical Change and the Aggregate Production Function', *Review of Economics and Statistics*, XXXIX, pp. 312–20.

Solow, R.M. and Samuelson, P.A. 1953. 'Balanced Growth Under Constant Returns to Scale', *Econometrica*, 21, pp. 412–24.

Soper, J.C. 1975. 'Myth and Reality in Economic Time Series: The Long Swing Revisited', *Southern Economic Journal*, 4, 41, pp. 570–9.

Soper, J.C. 1978. *The Long Swing in Historical Perspective*, New York.

Spiethoff, A. 1953. 'Business Cycles', *International Economic Papers*, 3, abridged translation. First published (1925) as 'Krisen', *Handworterbuch der Staatswissenschaften*, Jena.

Spraos, J. 1980. 'The Statistical Debate on the Net Barter Terms of Trade Between Primary Commodities and Manufactures', *E.J.*, 90, pp. 107–28.

Stamp, J.C. 1916. *British Incomes and Property*, London.

Steindl, J. 1976. *Maturity and Stagnation in American Capitalism*, New York and London.

Steindl, J. 1979. 'Stagnation Theory and Stagnation Policy', *Cambridge Journal of Economics*, 3, pp. 1–44.

Steindl, J. 1981. 'Ideas and Concepts of Long Run Growth', *Banca Nazionale Del Lavoro Quarterly Review*, 136, pp. 35–49.

Stone, J.M. 1971. 'Financial Panics: Their Implications for the Mix of Domestic and Foreign Investment of Great Britain, 1880–1913', *Q.J.E.*, 85, pp. 304–26.

Stoneman, P. 1979. 'Kaldor's Law and British Economic Growth-1970', *Warwick Research Paper*, No. 93, also in *Applied Economics*, 11, pp. 309–19.

Svennilson, I. 1952. *Growth and Stagnation in the European Economy*, Geneva.

Sylos-Labini, P. 1962. *Oligopoly and Technical Progress*, Cambridge, Mass.

Temin, P. 1976. *Did Monetary Forces Cause the Great Depression?* New York.

Thomas, B. 1954. *Migration and Economic Growth*, revised edition 1973, Cambridge.

Thomas, B. 1973. *Migration and Urban Development: A Reappraisal of British and American Long Cycles*, London.

Tilly, R.H. 1978. 'Capital Formation in Germany in the Nineteenth Century'. In P. Mathias and M.M. Postan (eds.), *The Cambridge Economic History of Europe* Vol. 7, Cambridge.

Timoshenko, V.P. 1933. *World Agriculture and the Depression*, University of Michigan.

Tinbergen, J. 1981. 'Kondratiev Cycles and so-called Long Waves: The Early Research', *Futures*, 13, 4, pp. 258–63.

Tobin, J. 1975. 'Keynesian Models of Recession and Depression', *A.E.R.*, 65, 2, pp. 195–202.

Tugan-Baranowsky, M. 1894. *Promyshlennye krizisy v sovremennoi Anglii*, Petersburg. A French translation appears as *Les Crises industrielles en Angleterre*, Paris, 1913.

Tyszynski, H. 1951. 'World Trade in Manufactured Commodities, 1899–1950', *Manchester School*, XIX, 3, pp. 272–304.

U.S. Bureau of the Census. 1960. *Historical Statistics of the U.S.*, Washington.

US Department of Commerce, Bureau of Economic Analysis, 1978. *Long Term Economic Growth, 1860–1970*, Washington, D.C.

Usher, A.P. 1971. 'Technical Change and Capital Formation'. In N. Rosenberg (ed.), *The Economics of Technological Change*, London.

Van der Zwan, A. 1980. 'On The Assessment of the Kondratieff Cycle and Related Issues'. In S.K. Kuipers and G.J. Lanjouw, (eds.), *Prospects of Economic Growth*, Amsterdam, Ch. 19.

Van Duijn, J.J. 1977. 'The Long Wave in Economic Life', *De Economist* 125, 4, pp. 544–76.

Van Duijn, J.J. 1980. 'Comment on Van der Zwan's Paper'. In S.K. Kuipers and G.J. Lanjouw (eds.) *Prospects of Economic Growth*, Amsterdam.

Van Duijn, J.J. 1981. 'Fluctuations in Innovations over Time', *Futures*, 13, 4, pp. 264–75.

Van Duijn, J.J. 1983. *The Long Wave in Economic Life*, London.

Van Ewijk, C. 1981. 'The Long Wave – A Real Phenomenon?', *De Economist*, 129, 3, pp. 324–72.

Van Gelderen, J. 1913. 'Springvloed–Beschouwingen over industrieele ontwikkeling en prijsbeweging', *Die Nieuwe Tijd*, XVIII, 4, 5 and 6, April, May and June, pp. 254–77, 370–84, 446–64.

Vilar, P. 1976. *A History of Gold and Money, 1450–1920*, London.

Viner, J. 1924. *Canada's Balance of International Indebtedness, 1900–1913*, Cambridge, Mass.

Wallerstein, I. 1979. 'Kondratieff Up or Kondratieff Down?', *Review*, 11, 4, pp. 663–73.

Weinstock, U. 1964. *Das Problem der Kondratieff-Zyklen*, Berlin and Munich.

Weisskopf, T.E. 1979. 'Marxian Crisis Theory and the Rate of Profit in the Postwar U.S. Economy', *Cambridge Journal of Economics*, 3, pp. 341–78.

Welch, B.L. 1938. 'The Significance of the Differences Between Two Means when the Population Variances are Unequal', *Biometrica*, 29, pp. 350–62.

Wetherill, G.B. 1967. *Elementary Statistical Methods*, London.

White, H.D. 1933. *The French International Accounts, 1880–1913*, Cambridge, Mass.

Wicksell, K. 1898. *Geldzins und Guterpreise*, Jena. An English translation appears as *Interest and Prices: A Study of the Causes Regulating the Value of Money*, New York, 1965.

Wigley, T.M.L. 1983. 'The Role of Statistics in Climate Impact Analysis', *Proc. 2nd International Meeting on Statistical Climatology*, Lisbon.

Wigley, T.M.L. and Atkinson, T.C. 1977. 'Dry Years in South East England Since 1698', *Nature*, 265, pp. 431–4.

Williamson, J.G. 1964. *American Growth and the Balance of Payments, 1820–1913*, University of N. Carolina.

Williamson, J.G. 1984. 'Why Was British Growth So Slow During the Industrial Revolution?', *Journal of Economic History*, XLIV, 3, pp. 687–712.

Zevin, R.B. 1982. 'The Economics of Normalcy', *Journal of Economic History*, XLII, 1, pp. 43–52.

Index

Abramovitz, M., 2, 9, 10, 11, 12, 15, 16, 17, 88, 101, 125, 145, 162
Aftalion, A., 4
Agriculture: climatic influences, 118–20; impact on economic growth, 110–12; shares in aggregate investment, 116
Aldroft, D.H., 27, 152
America; continuity of growth, 54–5; data revisions, 51–2; GDP, 48, 53; industrial production, 49–51; investment, 107; labour productivity, 49, 53; size of primary sector, 151; 1929–33 depression, 149–51
Ames, E., 161
Atlantic economy, 101, 106, 129, 132

Beenstock, M., 77, 178n11
Bieshaar, H., 9, 70, 98, 146
Bird, R.C., 14, 15, 16
Bloomfield, A.I., 136, 137
Bolch, B.W., 158
Bordo, M.D., 82, 124
Bowden, M.J., 122, 123
Box, G.E.P., 24
Britain: climacteric of 1899, 27, 31; compromise estimate of GDP, 28–9, 34, 173n1, 177n5; expenditure estimate, 30–1; impact of war, 34; income estimate of GDP, 29–30; industrial production, 29; investment, 103–6; labour productivity, 31–2; output estimate of GDP, 29; primary sector size, 152; TFP growth, 32–3
Building cycle, see Kuznets swings
Buse, A., 25
Business cycle, see Cycles, Juglar

Cairncross, A.K., 11, 27, 102, 112, 113, 115, 138, 139, 140, 177n3
Cairnes, J.E., 175n4
Cameron, R., 74, 136

Carre, J.J., 46, 47
Chatfield, C., 21
Chatterji, M., 165
Church, R.R., 27
Collins, M., 81, 82
Cornwall, J., 165
Crafts, N.F.R., 27, 80
Credit creation, 6
Cycles: Echo, 6; inter-relatedness of, 13; Juglar, 4, 8, 15, 16, 17, 20, 172n4; Kitchin, 8, 172n8; Kondratieff, see Kondratieff waves; Kuznets, see Kuznets swings; replacement, 6

Dawes plan, 179n4
Denison, E.F., 162
Derksen, J.B.D., 158
Dickey, D.A., 23, 24
Dupriez, L.H., 74

Easterlin, R.A., 10, 12, 101, 145, 158, 176n2
Edelstein, M., 133, 143
Equilibrium, Kondratieff's definition, 4–5, 8
Evans, G.B.A., 23

Falkus, M., 136
Fedder, J., see Van Gelderen, J.
Feinstein, C.H., 27, 28, 29, 110, 120, 121
Financial crises, 128–9, 155–7
Fisher, I., 73, 126, 157
Fleisig, H., 154, 179n4
Ford, A.G., 177n5
Forrester, J.W., 9, 158
France; commodity production, 44; GDP growth, 43, 46; investment, 106; labour productivity, 45, 47; primary sector size, 152; TFP, 45; world depression 1929–32, 151
Freeman, C., 9, 92, 93, 176n15

195